SOUL
MURDER
Revisited

SOUL
MURDER
Revisited

Thoughts about Therapy, Hate, Love, and Memory

LEONARD SHENGOLD, M.D.

YALE UNIVERSITY PRESS

New Haven and London

3951547I

Library of Congress Cataloging-in-Publication Data

Shengold, Leonard.
Soul murder revisited: Thoughts about therapy, hate, love, and
memory / Leonard Shengold
p.   cm.
Includes bibliographical references and index.
ISBN 0-300-07594-4 (alk. paper)
1. Adult child abuse victims—Mental health.
2. Psychoanalysis.   3. Child abuse in literature.   I. Title.
RC569.5.C55S53   1999
616.85'82239—dc21   98-27156
CIP

Printed in the United States of America

A catalogue record for this book is available from the British Library.

The paper in this book meets the guidelines for permanence and durability of
the Committee on Production Guidelines for Book Longevity of the Council on
Library Resources.

10   9   8   7   6   5   4   3   2

To Marc Eric Shengold

Ella Rentheim: I did not know of your terrible crime.

Borkman: What crime? What are you speaking of?

Ella Rentheim: I am speaking of that crime for which there is no forgiveness. . . . You are a murderer! You have committed the one mortal sin! . . . You have killed the love of life in me. Do you understand what that means? The Bible speaks of a mysterious sin for which there is no forgiveness. I have never understood what it could be; but now I understand. The great, unpardonable sin is to murder the love of life in a human soul. . . . You have done that. You deserted the woman you loved! Me, me, me! What you held dearest in the world you were ready to barter away for gain. That is the double murder you have committed! The murder of your own soul and of mine! . . . It is you who have sinned. You have killed all the joy of life in me.

Henrik Ibsen, *John Gabriel Borkman*

CONTENTS

1

Introduction

Belief in the existence of other human beings as such is love.
—*Simone Weil (quoted in* Auden, A Certain World)

The observations in this book are extensions and illustrations of themes involved with child abuse and neglect taken up in my previous books, most specifically *Soul Murder: Child Abuse and Deprivation* (1989), together with some related issues. Time and aging have broadened my perspective, and since I wrote *Soul Murder* child abuse and deprivation have become subject to much more public attention and debate.

Some amount of lack of care and even torment is inevitable in the course of everyone's growing up. *Soul murder* is the term I have used for the apparently willful abuse and neglect of children by adults that are of sufficient intensity and frequency to be traumatic. By that I mean that the children's subsequent emotional development has been profoundly and predominantly negatively affected; what has happened to them has dominated their motivating unconscious fantasies; and they have become subject to the compulsion to repeat the cruelty, violence, neglect, hatred, seduction, and rape of their injurious past.

Although child abuse has become the subject of clamorous attention and serious study in recent years, there is still much that we don't know about its frequency, its causes and effects, and—especially—how to react to it, treat it, and reduce its occurrence. Because mistreatment of children by adults is based on something inherent in human nature—a destructive and sadistic drive—I don't think it can ever disappear.

The dramatic term *soul murder* probably was coined in the nineteenth century;[1] it was used by the great Scandinavian playwrights Henrik Ibsen and August Strindberg. Ibsen defines it as the destruction of the love of life in another human being. In psychiatry, the term was made familiar by the paranoid psychotic patient Schreber, whose *Memoirs* (1903) were the subject of one of Freud's long case histories (1911).

Freud's first ideas on the causation of mental illness were based on the consequences of sexual abuse in childhood, which he at first called "seduction by the father." He initially accepted as historical truth the stories his patients told him of sexual assault in childhood; only later did he realize that many—but not all—of these stories were fantasies.[2] Freud's

1. I had been using the term in my teaching and my papers for twenty-five years before my 1989 book appeared. The first use of the term I was able to find is from a book on the Kaspar Hauser case by a German judge, Anselm von Feuerbach, published in 1832. In 1973, Morton Schatzman published a book titled *Soul Murder: Persecution in the Family.* Since the term was widely used in the nineteenth century and was well known because of Freud's work on the Schreber case, I did not consider priority in book titles an issue, especially because Schatzman's thesis (he feels schizophrenia is the result of bad parenting) and ideas are very different from mine; but I have been reproached in letters for not doing more than mentioning his work in my *Soul Murder.*

2. Blum (1996) puts this well: "Freud came to understand that the reports by his patients of childhood incest were often fantasies, or . . . admixtures of fantasy and reality" (p. 1148).

appreciation of the power of unconscious fantasy led him to the discovery of childhood sexuality and of the Oedipus complex, some of the basic assumptions of his (and subsequent) psychoanalytic thinking. But Freud remained aware of the objective reality of seduction and cruelty suffered by some of his patients.

What appears to be the willful hurting of the helpless and the relatively innocent is a subject full of contradictions and complexities. I have learned how difficult it is to generalize about the former victims of child abuse. My patients have been healthy enough to sustain intensive therapy or psychoanalysis. I have not directly studied those who as children ended up in the law courts, hospitals, or morgues—whose souls, and sometimes bodies, have been fully murdered. My patients did not fit into one diagnostic category but ran a psychopathological range from those who were predominantly neurotic to a very few who might be called psychotic. They also varied greatly in their degree of psychic health (emotional flexibility, ability to love, talents, creativity). Soul murder is a crime, not a diagnosis. Human beings are infinitely complex and varied and cannot be reduced to diagnoses; nor are they made homogenous by having undergone similar traumatic events—only complete murder accomplishes that aim, although concentration camp conditions can approach it.

I have been presenting papers on the consequences of child abuse for more than thirty-five years and feel humbled by how much I do not know about it. My patients were all different, despite certain predictable general similarities. Overstimulation (the result of sexual abuse and perhaps also beatings) evokes traumatic anxiety and rage in the relatively helpless child. With neglect and understimulation, the frustration of basic needs also results in rage and intense sexual craving; this is *reactive* overstimulation. In either instance, overstimulation requires massive defensive efforts by the mind (attempts to deaden emotion and impulse), which usually do not work well or consistently. Furthermore, children who are beside themselves with overexcitement, rage, and anxiety have an imperative need for external help. When the tormentor-seducer is a parent, it is frequently necessary for the child to turn for rescue to the very person who abused—a mind-splitting operation. The other parent is absent or an unconscious (frequently masochistic) abettor or both. If the adult abuser is not a parent, the child's rage is still directed at the parents—generally the mother—for having allowed the abuse to occur.[3] Every child has an urgent need for good parenting, and this makes him or her cling desperately to whatever fragments of realistic benevolent parental functioning exist and to what is frequently the *delusion* of having had a concerned, loving parent.[4] This delusion—which sometimes exists alongside bitter hatred and accusation[5]—arises from the overwhelming need for a caring rescuer. One sees it in George Orwell's *1984*, in Winston Smith's urgent

3. The mother, who is almost always the first to be cast in the intrapsychic role of primal parent (the indispensable one necessary to sustain the infant's life), is usually held primarily responsible for everything (in some level of the mind) and is the chief object of the child's rage. Surprisingly enough (I was surprised but on reflection felt that I should not have been), one finds this in instances when the actual seducer-abuser is another person, even the father. Mother is the original godlike other and therefore should not have allowed such things to be. Subsequently in psychic development this grandiose role is largely or partly shifted onto the father, but in regression it returns to the mother.

4. "At least she always fed me properly," one patient said.

5. This is an instance of what George Orwell, in *1984*, calls "doublethink"; there is a split or compartmentalization of the ego, so contradictions can exist without any resolution.

compulsion to love the Big Brother who has destroyed his soul.

The most destructive effect of child abuse is perhaps the need to hold onto the abusing parent or parent figure by identifying with the abuser; this becomes part of a compulsion to repeat the experiences of abuse—as tormentor (enhancing sadism) and simultaneously as victim (enhancing masochism). The child who is abused quite regularly takes on the guilt of the crime—which the abuser may or may not have felt.[6] This guilt, frequently manifested by a need for punishment, is augmented by the rage involved in the child's identifying with the aggressor and feeling and sometimes acting on sadistic and vengeful impulses. The pathological compulsion to repeat traumatic events results in the passing down of child abuse from one generation to the next—the sins of the parents are visited on the children. So abused children, when they grow up and become parents, tend to abuse their own children, frequently in spite of conscious resolutions not to do so; the impulses at least are there, and frequently the actions too.

Attempts at the soul murder of children commonly have profound distorting and inhibiting effects on the victim's fantasy life and, especially, emotional life (part of Ibsen's definition of soul murder is killing the capacity for joy in another human being). They can cause a suffusion of sado-masochistic feeling and impulses (perverse sexual excitement and murderous wishes) that must be guarded against by massive inhibitory defenses, which do not always function consistently, and brainwashing—effecting many kinds of

6. According to Simone Weil, "Affliction stamps the soul to its very depths with the scorn, the disgust and even the self-hatred and sense of guilt that crime logically should produce but actually does not" (quoted by Auden, 1970, p. 49).

defenses including autohypnosis and a split functioning in the mind that makes possible what Orwell calls "doublethink" and "loving Big Brother." These effects appear in different varieties and combinations.

I have learned to be wary of generalizations about victims of child abuse. There are people who, like some concentration camp victims, appear to have been strengthened by the struggle to survive a terrible past, developing adaptive powers that exist alongside scars and deficiencies (see Rhodes and Rhodes, 1996). Observers have felt that for a number of victims of parental neglect (emotional deprivation) subsequent sexual abuse has resulted in some positive effects because sexual attention is at least some attention. (The child as need-fulfiller can feel central, at least transiently.)

It is always difficult for any adult observer to know exactly what has happened to a child. Legal authorities, obliged to investigate charges of sexual and physical abuse, are familiar with this problem, and so are psychological workers who hear traumatic stories from their patients or who begin to feel that such stories are there for their patients to tell. There is great difficulty in establishing facts about childhood from the vantage point of the psychiatrist who sees adults. Bodily care necessary in early development ensures that fantasies of having been seduced are universally present, at least in the unconscious mind. Conscious memories are unreliable, and any approach to certainty about historical truth can be dauntingly challenging. Even for those who see the purportedly abused child shortly after the alleged trauma, establishing what really happened and "who did it" may be almost impossible, and the attempt to mediate between the accused abuser's version and the child's (especially if legal considerations are involved) is frequently damaging to the child, particularly if the abuser is a parent. There is a universal psychological resistance to the idea of a bad—a depriving or abusing—parent. Unconscious identifications with parents are the cornerstone of our identities and our self-esteem.

So the problem of differentiating fantasy from memory remains formidable for therapist and patient alike. The therapist optimally should be able to suspend disbelief in the possibility of adult and parental seduction and torment; that is, it should be neither assumed nor denied.

This needs to be emphasized. Thirty years ago, denial of the actuality of child abuse flourished ("It's all fantasy!"). Several years ago we seemed long past this predominant denial. But current controversy centers around the prevalence and significant consequences of the abuse of children. When I began to present papers about patients who told me of memories of being seduced or battered as children, usually at the hands of psychotic, addicted, or psychopathic parents, I was frequently told by older analysts that I was naive, that what I had accepted as having happened was the product of the patient's fantasy. Besides, they sometimes added, it doesn't make any difference if child abuse has actually happened since unconscious fantasies of being abused are universal.

It is true that we all have such fantasies and that in clinical endeavors the analyst or therapist works with the fantasies of the patient—but of course some of these are transformed memories. Also, traumatic stories can be used in the service of denial or evasion of personal responsibility for all faults—"Look what they did to me!" The crucial question remains: Does it make a difference if a trauma—say, the Holocaust, or a child's submission to family concentration camp conditions (Jarrell, 1962)—was actually experienced? What we have to deal with in our patients is the effect of traumata on their fantasy life. I maintain my original conviction that having actually lived through overwhelming bad experiences makes for qualitative differences in the developing mental life of any individual victim. We know that in addition to what we are endowed with at birth, environment—what happens to us and around us—also forms our character and affects our fate (one of the themes of Chekhov's great play *Three Sisters*). Freud has shown us the crucial environmental influence of the parents and their predispositions.

Two extreme opposite positions have formed. There are those who feel that child abuse exists chiefly in the minds of therapists and theoreticians, who help create forced memories in their patients. Others assume that abuse of children is almost universal—a belief that certainly can and does foster false memories, especially by way of suggestion from therapist (or even therapeutic institution) to patient. Today in America the pendulum has swung toward what can be called "child abuse cults"; that is, some therapists start by assuming that every pathological manifestation is due to the patient's having been abused as a child. District attorneys and their confederates, presumably with the best of intentions, use suggestive and coercive techniques to extract accusations against adults from children who are assumed to have been abused. Therapists often use the powerfully suggestive technique of hypnosis to encourage patients to recall—or to fabricate—endless repetitive details.

Currently, there are similar therapeutic cults involving multiple personalities and satanic worship. All these may be based on actual pathological entities, but within the cults the possibilities are likely to be stretched to include every comer—assumption, not suspension of disbelief, reigns. The appendix to this book is a revision of a commentary I wrote on a publication by two obviously dedicated clinicians, Jody Messler Davies and Mary Gail Frawley, which seems to me to show the danger of *assuming* that child abuse has taken place, mainly on the basis of patients' use of defensive mechanisms that exist to some extent in almost every human being. Therapeutic efforts can be compromised, patients and parents of patients can be maligned, family ties can be tragically severed by false certainties that are not properly evaluated or that may even have been created in the necessary but delicate, difficult, and sometimes impossible course of trying to establish what has happened in the past. (Davies and Frawley suggest that it is easy to do so!)

At present, in the understandable reaction to the widely publicized "false memory syndrome," there is the danger of a return to the denial of the abuse of children—false certainty in the opposite direction. One sees this in the writings of the brilliant and combative Frederick Crews (see Crews et al., 1996) on false memory, in which certainty is accompanied (and perhaps motivated) by what appears to be an almost monomaniacal hatred of Freud. (Denial of child abuse is tempting because no one wants it to take place; it is one of those events that, to paraphrase Freud, disturbs the peace of the world.)

Sometimes the facts of the abuse are all too obvious, as we know from almost daily newspaper stories, even headlines. The burgeoning public awareness of the existence—the shockingly widespread existence—of child abuse is surely a great step forward from the years of predominant denial of the seduction and torment of children. But there is a price to be paid for the publicity: the danger of further confusing individuals (perhaps especially children) who have trouble differentiating fantasy from reality. I am not thinking primarily of very disturbed neurotic or psychotic people whose ability to make this differentiation is particularly deficient. We are all to some degree neurotic and in some part of our minds are subject to suggestion, distortion from our emotional complexes, and even delusion (more often than we would like to credit; see Shengold, 1995). To put this in another way, we can no longer believe in memory as the simple registration of what has actually happened in the past. It is infinitely more complicated than that. In his recent book *The Island of the Color-blind,* Oliver Sacks says: "Memory, as [Gerald] Edelman reminds us, is never a simple recording or reproduction, but [is] an active process of recategorization— of reconstruction, of imagination, determined by our own values and perspectives" (pp. xi–xii)—and, I would add, by our psychological conflicts and complexes. We would now interpret Freud's statement that hysterics suffer from their reminiscences by assuming that this means suffering from what they have done to—how they have recorded, reacted to, and transformed—their reminiscences.

And yet of course the past has happened; soul murder has occurred; there was a Holocaust, and there have been many holocausts in human history.[7] Pathological doubting is a consequence of child abuse, and sometimes what actually happened simply cannot be determined. Occasionally the memories are clear and there is even external corroboration. In many cases repetition of the past in the course of the treatment (usually in the form of transferences and projections onto the therapist) will make the probability, and even the certainty, of the traumata plain. Sometimes the therapist feels no doubt about the actuality of the abuse, especially if the accused parents are continuing their practices, sometimes

7. In Chapter 6 I make comparisons between the results of concentration camp experiences and what can happen to individual children exposed to soul murder in the "family concentration camps" of childhood. There are of course many very significant differences in addition to the similarities.

as grandparents; it does not necessarily follow that the patient who reports "the facts" is similarly convinced.[8]

The difficulty of establishing what happened is compounded in that, as I have stated, one of the common effects of child abuse is brainwashing—the cultivation of denial of what has occurred and the suppression of what was experienced—in the mind of the child-victim, who has the universal stake in needing good parenting. "This didn't happen" is often explicitly said or in some way forcibly implied to the child by the abuser, who may be motivated by an inner need for denial as well as a wish to evade detection and punishment. This order from without reinforces the child's own need to feel that "this couldn't have happened."

Substantial emotional neglect of children—not caring for them and not caring about them as separate human beings—may have even more devastating effects on psychic development than does physical abuse. Not being cared about means being deprived of the soul's basic nourishment: the accepting and welcoming feelings and smile of the mothering figure.

The American poet Randall Jarrell has written about Rudyard Kipling's terrible experiences as a child. After years of overindulgent parental love in India and of spoiling by Indian servants who obeyed his every whim, Rudyard, age six, was taken to England by his parents. There, he and his sister, age three, were suddenly and without warning left in the care of complete strangers who had made their availabil-

---

8. One patient, G, who "could not accept" what appeared to be a clear "memory" of having been forced as a child to fellate his grandfather, later learned that the older man had been arrested years later for forcing a young cousin to do the same. This did not change G's attitude toward the "memory," which remained for him between mental quotation marks.

ity for the custody of foster children known through a newspaper advertisement. The parents then returned to India and
did not see their children for the next six years. "The House
of Desolation" was Kipling's name for the establishment in
which they were left, ruled by a sadistic, disturbed, capri-
cious, and religiously obsessed woman. Jarrell (1962), who
knew what an unhappy childhood was and was to die a kind
of suicide, calls the place "one of God's concentration camps"
(p. 146).

Kipling was disliked and persecuted by "Auntie Rosa," as
he was forced to call her, and her envious son, who was older
and less bright than Rudyard. (The father in the family was
more accepting, but unfortunately he soon died.) Kipling
wrote that he was "regularly beaten" (1937, p. 6), but his
sister was treated as a kind of favorite by Auntie Rosa, who
attempted to alienate her from her brother. The children
were not starved but were subjected to extreme cold and to
arbitrary and unreasonable discipline. It was the psychological rather than the physical beatings that Rudyard found
hardest to bear, and most of all the fact that their loving
parents had deserted them—without any preparation and
without having said good-bye. (Auntie Rosa would torture
the children by reminding them of this.) The torment,
backed by the accusatory delusional righteousness of Auntie
Rosa, left Kipling with a terrible hatred aimed at his parents,
a hatred that he had to deny but that often lies beneath the
celebration and justification of authority in his writings.
"Kipling's morality," Jarrell writes, "is the one-sided, desperately protective, sometimes vindictive morality of someone
who has been for some time the occupant of one of God's
concentration camps, and has had to spend the rest of his life
justifying or explaining out of existence what he cannot
forget" (1962, p. 146). This description makes it obvious that

Kipling in part identified with the righteous tormentor, Auntie Rosa. The tormenting disciplinarian has to be right. Kipling became an imperialist and a defender of the established order, haunted by hatred that he needed to deny.

One finds a history of child abuse and neglect in the life and works of many other great writers—for example, Charles Dickens, Ivan Turgenev, and Anton Chekhov. I believe that some of their talents may have been adaptively motivated and enhanced—not caused—by the need to master the traumata, the attempts at soul murder, that occurred in their childhood. In Chapter 9 I discuss the English poet Algernon Swinburne, whose life, as deduced from his own writings and those of others about him, shows how difficult it is to be sure of just what happened to him as a child; yet it also seems clear that something "really" happened to determine his being haunted by intense masochistic fantasies that both fed and marred his writings. The environmental contribution that is known was the passion-fueling flagellation practices of the English public schools. I have similar feelings about the contradictory and multiple effects of trauma on creative patients I have treated over the years, whose pertinent case histories I cannot publish for reasons that concern confidentiality.[9] Elizabeth Bishop's life and work, discussed in Chapter 10, offer a clearer case for soul murder, based on her misfortunes in having a psychotic, rejecting mother and in suffering the very early loss of her father.

Part I of this book, "Perspectives on Soul Murder," includes a number of papers, some revised, some new, that

9. These are more convincingly pertinent than those of literary figures because of the direct observation and the glimpses of unconscious revelations that come with psychoanalytic technique. Yet of course the more direct clinical contact still does not necessarily make for certainty about the historical past.

pursue topics connected with child abuse, centrally or periph- erally.

Chapter 2, which describes the mythically and literarily derived "case" of Medea, focuses on a kind of parent fre- quently found in soul murder cases—narcissistic, violent, ruthless. Euripides' *Medea* is perhaps the first convincing portrait of a soul- (and body-) murdering mother in litera- ture. In this chapter I specifically emphasize the importance to the parent of maintaining a symbiotic tie by way of gifts that are aimed at destroying the separate identity of the child. In clinical examples I give a few glimpses of modern Medeas. Chapter 3 uses clinical material from child abuse victims to comment on an aspect of castration anxiety that features the paradoxical combination of heightened aware- ness of and blocking out of potential warning signals (or hypersensitivity and hypnotic evasion; see Shengold, 1989). This is frequently seen in children who have adapted by courting as well as avoiding repetition of past traumata. (This is of course not the only reason for perceptive oversensitivity in people.) The emphasis in this chapter is on the sense of smell.

Chapter 4, "Once Is Never (Or Once Doesn't Count)," is a kind of extended footnote about a specific variety of denial allied with the need for false certainty—a need to which we are all subject but which is especially striking and usually of pathological intensity in soul murder victims.

Chapter 5, which deals with some symbolic meanings of rings, illustrates defensive narcissism based on regression to the centrally important early developmental time of the management of bodily sphincters (whose mental counter- parts function in both the defense [control] and the discharge of impulses; see Shengold, 1988). This is especially obvious where there has been overstimulation in early life. Pathological narcissism involves inhibition of the ability to separate from parents, which makes for a relative inability to care about other people. Soul murder is one way of establishing an excess of pathological narcissism in the child. Chapter 6, which discusses some similarities between concentration camp survivors and soul murder victims, introduces one of the major themes of this book: the need to restore the power to care about others, to love others (in life and in therapy), in order to ameliorate the narcissistically regressive effects of soul murder.

Part II, "The Background of Soul Murder," deals with topics that are essential to the understanding of soul murder but have much more general application to human development and psychopathology. It concerns Freud's controversial theory of instinctual drives (life and death instincts) and his less controversial descriptions of both health (love) and clinical manifestations involving aggression and sexuality (including mixtures such as sadism and masochism). Chapters 7 and 8 are limited glimpses of the complex phenomena involved, not definitive summings-up. Chapter 7 is a study of Proust's and Freud's similar views on love as both men define it—much too narrowly, I feel. Their generalizations are limited to a pathological regressive kind of narcissistic involvement that is a compelling part of everyone's dynamic range of potential for loving others but for many exists in overwhelming proportion. And some of these unfortunates are soul murder victims. The chapter supplies more background for my conviction that the attainment of the power for relatively nonnarcissistic and less compulsive love is the prime essential for recovery from traumatic psychological damage.

Another essential is the acquisition of greater power over rage and aggression, manifest in sadism, masochism, and violence. Chapter 8's discussion of sadomasochism and beating fantasies is illustrated in Chapter 9, which deals with the poet Algernon Swinburne and his preoccupation with flagellation. Chapter 10, on Elizabeth Bishop, tells a soul murder story in which the child, like Swinburne, is able to use adaptive powers (inborn and perhaps enhanced in response to the trauma and deprivation of childhood experiences) that mobilize artistic creativity in an attempt at mastery, with the achievement of at least a partial transcendence of the damage sustained in early life. I stress Bishop's use of the image of the moth as evocative of the murderous-suicidal mixture of aggressive and passive feelings and impulses that can exist in the parent-child relationship.

Part IV returns to the specific question of soul murder: Did it really happen, and does that matter? Chapter 11 describes patients whose clinical picture resembles that of soul murder victims but whose pathology seems to stem chiefly from terror of their own impulses because they have been spoiled by weak, overindulgent parenting. The final chapter places soul murder in the context of human beings who are prone to violent emotions, impulses, and actions (sadistic and masochistic) and a relative failure (some combination of too much and too little) of the defenses against them—whether chiefly because of inherited overendowments and deficiencies, traumatic environmental excesses or deficiencies, or, most likely, an unfortunate combination of both. There are also some suggestions about therapy of the abused and neglected and those whose pathology resembles theirs.

I

Perspectives on Soul Murder

2

Fatal Gifts

Rich gifts wax poor when givers prove unkind.
—William Shakespeare, Hamlet

Customs involving the giving of gifts can reveal much about relationships. In examining some of the phenomena reported and enacted by my patients involving gift giving, I have noted repetitive revivals of experiences and relationships that evoked the myth of Medea and specifically Euripides' dramatic version of it.[1] I am focusing on a certain type of gift, a *poisonous* gift, exemplified by the fatal gifts of Medea and given within the family, especially from a particular sort of bad parent or parent substitute.

This is an expansion and reworking of a 1968 paper originally called "The Fatal Gifts of Medea," co-authored with Shelley Orgel, M.D., who is not to be held responsible for the extensive changes I have made but has generously helped me to revise it, made many valuable suggestions, and authorized its publication in this book.

1. Medea has been discussed before in psychoanalytic literature. Wittels (1933) gave the name of Medea complex to the tendency of the mother whose physical attractiveness is waning to hate and try to restrain her maturing daughter as a potential rival—a specific instance of the parent's envy of the child.

Gifts are usually thought of, and usually are, benevolent. Presents exchanged between any two people can reflect the ambiguities of their relationship and therefore are often full of psychological and moral complexities: good-and-bad or bad-and-good. In contrast, Medea's gifts have the qualities of the primal period of human development so prevalent in cases of soul murder. They have the stark black-or-white differentiation of the mind in infancy, possessing perfervid emotional intensity, either very good (prefiguring bliss) or very bad (prefiguring torment). To put it another way, gifts like the sorceress Medea's are endowed with the promise of good magic or the threat of bad magic. People who characterologically retain these primal contradictory intensities into adult life are regarded as infantile—yet we all, to varied extents, can regress to these qualities of feeling. Often, in such early emotional states, the promise of bliss can conceal murderous intent; this is especially relevant to Euripides' Medea. Her deceptively glittering, irresistible gifts disguise the malignancy of character adhering to the rage, hatred, and misery that are so dangerously present between parent and child in the mind's early development. (Like many followers of Freud and Klein, I believe that these are present in the form of instinctual drives—see Chapter 12.) Of course, the wonderfully intense good feelings of the baby—contentment, joy, even ecstasy—are also present. Freud called these feelings nirvana (for Buddhists, a state of perfect blessedness); for Wordsworth, such feelings were "intimations of immortality."

Exchanges between parent and child can express love, hatred, and all sorts of mixtures of the two. Gifts have their somatic developmental prototypes in bodily parts and the care, or lack of care, extended in relation to them: the mother's breast (which begins, Freud tells us, as part of the self and can be felt as loving or destructive); feces (lovingly presented and received or forced from the child at the parents' insistence and withheld or projected by the child onto the parents with hatred); the phallus (supplying pleasure or pain); the baby (wanted or unwanted). (In this chapter I am not trying to deal definitively with gifts expressive of specific libidinal and aggressive wishes that arise after the stages of early psychic development.)

Gifts can have the adaptive function of what Winnicott calls "transitional objects"—objects from the external world, such as blankets or toys, that carry some of the benevolent power of the maternal bond (and also potentially its malevolent counterpart). The psychically significant transitional object—the pacifier or teddy bear that stands for and transiently takes the place of the parent—is intermediate between the mother's breast (me—not me) and the world outside the child-mother orbit (not me). The presence of a toy or pacifier can facilitate separation from the parental presence by helping to make being without the mother tolerable for gradually increasing lengths of time. Gifts in this sense become associated with junctures in life connoting separation; they mark occasions that can mobilize the need for re-fusion. The great milestones of separation and identity that result in new or enhanced psychic achievements of separateness (the prototype here is birth) have all come to involve gift-giving: birthdays, graduations, confirmations, weddings, funerals. Such occasions always involve ambivalence; they are predominantly painful and full of anxiety for those who in their minds have never sufficiently accepted separation from the parents.

Medea

Euripides was younger than his great contemporaries, Aeschylus and Sophocles. His *Medea* is perhaps the first psychological study of a witch.[2] The creation of her character marks the emergence of the importance of a human woman's powers in Western literature. (Powerful goddesses were depicted earlier.) Clytemnestra, Electra, and Jocasta, all three murderously inclined, precede Medea in the history of drama, but they are merely human and lack magical power. Unlike Medea, they need a man to execute their murderous intentions. One can be revolted by Medea's cruelty, which prevails over her love, but one cannot but admire her force and her fierce sense of who she is. As a witch, she has a magical ability to endow those she loves with a portion of her omnipotence, and her parallel power to destroy those who thwart her will is demonstrated repeatedly long before she invokes the aid of her mentor, the evil goddess Hecate, to hurt her inconstant husband Jason and destroy his new wife and father-in-law.

Euripides' characterization of Medea—passionate, treacherous, ill-used, violently vengeful, prepared to kill anyone who gets in the way of her needs and wishes, unable to allow her children a separate existence—is a psychologically convincing portrait of a parent as soul murderer.

In the myth before the play, Jason and the Argonauts come to Colchis to steal the marvelous golden fleece from the barbarian (non-Greek) King Aetes.[3] Aetes' daughter Medea,

2. If Medea were only a witch, the play would lack much of its power. She also possesses human qualities, ambivalences, and conflicts. Her intense and seemingly limitless emotions (along with her magical powers) make her larger than life—supernatural in ways that reflect what I regard as the psychology of an infant.

3. The fleece was the skin of a magic ram that, on the advice of the Delphic oracle, had been used to rescue Phrixus, a prince of Boeotia, from being sacrificed. The ram, with Phrixus on its back, fled to Colchis, where it was sacrificed and its fleece preserved for its magical properties. When Phrixus died, he was refused burial at Colchis. Jason's uncle Pelias, who had stolen the throne of Iolcos from Jason's

under the spell of the goddess Aphrodite, falls in love with Jason with characteristic overwhelming intensity. She gives Jason the magical gift of a wonderful ointment that makes him and his armor proof against weapons and fire for a day. This enables Jason to fulfill in safety Aetes' perfidious command that he sow a field with dragon's teeth with a team of fire-breathing bronze bulls and to trick the armed soldiers who consequently spring up, the harvest of the teeth, so that they kill one another. Medea helps him steal her father's chief treasure, the golden fleece (which gives its possessor magical powers), by poisoning the sleepless serpent who guards it. She enables Jason and his followers to escape, accompanying him in his ship, the *Argo*, with her abducted younger brother, Apsyrtus. When Aetes follows them in his vessel, she slows his pursuit by killing Apsyrtus and throwing pieces of his dismembered body to the waves, forcing the king to stop to recover them (see Rose, 1959).

So, before Euripides' play begins, Medea is established as a murderess capable of killing and mutilating her own flesh and blood to carry out her wishes. The vengeful tormenting of her father by killing his son is to be duplicated in her "gift" to Jason in Euripides' play. (It is easy to speculate about a fictional character that the revival of her intense hatred of her father for having displaced her with Apsyrtus helps Medea overcome her horror at killing her own sons.)

Jason marries Medea, swearing "by all the gods of Olympus to keep faith with Medea forever" (Graves, 1955,

---

father, Aeson, had been haunted by Phrixus' ghost, demanding the return of the remains of Phrixus to Greece, along with the golden fleece. Pelias felt that he was too old to undertake the mission himself and gladly sent the kingdom's rightful heir, Jason, expecting him to be destroyed in the attempt. The golden fleece in the legend was associated with the magical power of escape from a murderous fate.

p. 238). On the Argonauts' perilous journey back to Greece, Medea performs further magical deeds for Jason—healing wounds and killing the monster Talos after sending him into something like a hypnotic trance (see Graves, 1955, p. 247). She tricks the daughters of King Pelias (Jason's uncle, the treacherous, usurping king of Iolcos) into butchering their father and boiling his remains in a cauldron with the false promise that this will restore his youth. It is after this crime that she and Jason are forced to flee to Corinth, where Euripides' play begins.

Medea appears in the play as the victim of betrayal and abandonment: the ambitious Jason, tired and perhaps frightened of Medea, has left her, despite his vows, and intends to marry the daughter of Creon, king of Corinth. Medea is a barbarian without rights among the alien Greeks, and she cannot go home to Colchis in view of her crimes there. She still loves Jason and is outraged by his ingratitude and inconstancy. She alternates between fury and depression; she has refused to eat and has shut herself up in her house. Her old nurse expresses fear that the violent woman will harm her own two sons by Jason: "Pitiful woman! She has learned at last through all her sufferings how lucky are those who have never lost their native land. She has come to feel a hatred for her children, and no longer wants to see them. Indeed, I fear she may be moving toward some dreadful plan, for her heart is violent" (Prokosch translation, p. 200; all translations are Prokosch unless noted). Medea confirms the danger: "I call destruction upon you, all, all of you, / Sons of a doomed mother, and the father too! / May ruin fall on the entire house!" (p. 202).

She bewails the lot of women as compared to that of men: "I'd rather be sent three times over to the battlefront than give birth to a single child" (p. 206). King Creon enters and says to her: "I am afraid of you . . . I am afraid you will do my daughter some mortal harm" (p. 207). He is determined to banish Medea but yields to her plea for one more day in Corinth to arrange her affairs. (That the wily, realistic Creon, who knows her history, allows her this fateful—and, to him, fatal—concession shows something of the hypnotic force of Medea.)[4] Medea, determined on revenge, invokes the evil witch-goddess Hecate and sends wedding gifts to the Corinthian princess by her two sons: "For I shall send [my sons] with gifts in their little hands, to be offered to the bride to preserve them from banishment: a finely woven dress and a golden diadem. And if she takes these things and wears them on her body, she, and whoever touches her, will die in anguish; for I shall rub these things with deadly poison" (p. 222). Creon's daughter—who, like her father, is aware of Medea's treacherous nature and murderous past—nevertheless is unable to resist the gifts. She puts them on, as Medea had predicted she would. ("'Tis written, gifts persuade the gods in heaven" [Murray translation, p. 480].)

A messenger describes the scene to Medea in details that still stir the senses after almost 2,500 years:

> And before the father and the children had gone far from [the bride's] rooms, [she] took the gorgeous robe and put it on; and she put the golden crown on her curly head, and arranged her hair in the shining mirror, smiling as she saw herself re-

4. The power to induce such hypnotic fascination is an attribute of a universally present figure in unconscious fantasy: the primal parent, the malignant (murderous, cannibalistic, and mendacious) bisexual side of the mental image of the earliest parent, emerging in later psychic development as the murderous, phallic mother and the castrating, raping father (see Fliess, 1956). Medea is one manifestation of the primal parent in myth; another is the Theban Sphinx in the Oedipus story, a disguised depiction of Oedipus's mother-wife Jocasta as primal parent (see Shengold, 1963, 1989).

flected. . . . And after that it was a thing of horror we saw. For suddenly her face changed its color, and she staggered back, and began to tremble as she ran . . . flakes of foam [flowed] from her mouth, her eyeballs rolling, and the blood [fading] from her face. . . . A twofold torment was creeping over her. The golden diadem on her head was sending forth a violent stream of flame, and the finely woven dress which your children gave her was beginning to eat into the poor girl's snowy soft flesh . . . and from the top of her head a mingled stream of blood and fire was pouring. And it was like the drops falling from the bark of a pine tree when the flesh dropped away from her bones, torn loose by the secret fangs of the poison.

The poisonous gifts[5] are cannibalistic; they devour flesh.

The messenger describes the despairing Creon, trying to help his daughter. He holds her and cries out:

"Who has robbed me of you, who am old and close to the grave? O my child, let me die with you!" And he grew silent and tried to rise to his feet again, but found himself fastened to the finely spun dress, like vine clinging to a laurel bough, and there was a fearful struggle. And still he tried to lift his knees, and she writhed and clung to him; and as he tugged, he tore the withered flesh from his bones. . . . So there they are, lying together (p. 234).

Father and daughter are fused in death.[6]

5. *Gift* is the German word for "poison."
6. In Cherubini's opera *Medea*, she herself hears the victims and

Still pursuing her revenge, Medea is determined to kill her sons, "my dearest children." She cannot bear the thought that Jason might keep them or that they could have a life apart from her. Tormented by her ambivalence, she rationalizes that if she does not kill them, other, "more merciless hands" will. The conflict in the mother's mind between love and murder is wonderfully brought out in Euripides' play. Here is Edith Hamilton's version of part of it:

> I will not let them live for strangers to ill-use,
> To die by other hands more merciless than
>> mine,
> No, I who gave them life will give them death.
> Oh, now no cowardice, no thought of how young
>> they are,
> How dear they are, how when they were first
>> born—
> Not that, I will forget they are my sons
> One moment, one short moment—then forever
>> sorrow.
>> (Hamilton, 1940, pp. 129–30)

Medea's fury wins over her love.[7]

the crowd screaming at the murderous result of the gift-giving and intones, "O cries of pain, sweeter to my ears than singing!"

7. This scene, in which loving irresolution becomes the determination to kill, is also tremendously moving. As Rose writes: "To realize the heights to which Euripides rises here it is perhaps necessary to see the play well acted . . . to see, for example, Dame Sybil Thorndyke's performance of [Gilbert] Murray's version is enough to make the spectator realize that a first rate play can overcome not merely the passage of time but the transference to another language and to other stage conventions, if only translator and players have the intelligence and sympathy" (1960, p. 182). A similar effect from a different happy transference is available to today's audience in the recording of the

In the play, after slaying her children, Medea is rescued by a chariot drawn by dragons sent by her ancestor, the sun. The chariot takes her to a prearranged haven with Aegeus, the childless king of Athens, to whom she had promised the gift of offspring. Her rescue by the sun and (in the myth) her eventual reign in the Elysian Fields, possibly (according to Robert Graves) as the wife of Achilles, signify the triumph of the maternal (primal parent) figure. The murders go un-punished; the witch retains her magic.

The compelling effect of the play is largely dependent on the hypnotic fascination of Medea's character (see Kitto, 1957). Everyone—Jason, Creon, Creon's daughter, the Chorus, and the audience—refuses to believe that she will fulfill her potential for violence and evil. Yet from the very beginning her nature and her intentions are obvious, some-times openly stated, sometimes masked by what should strike the listener as transparent lies. The need to deny what she is, to see her as benevolent and loving despite everything she has said and done, is so strong that even the gods forgive her and reward her at the end. The infant has an absolute need for a mother and good mothering. There is consequently universal resistance (which can mask an unconscious attrac-tion) to the idea or the actuality of a bad mother; none of us ever outlives the infant's intense and vital need for mother-ing, which can be regressively renewed in danger situations in even the most secure and mature adults. This largely unconscious but dynamically powerful part of our infantile past is one of the chief obstacles to accepting the fact of child abuse. For many it is unthinkable that any parent, especially

---

scene in Cherubini's Euripides-derived opera, *Medea*, with Maria Callas as the despairing mother who finally resolves that "Love will not triumph" and goes offstage to stab her sons to death.

a mother, would want to harm, seduce, even kill her or his own child. This kind of parenting, unfortunately not always confined to wishes, violates our earliest and most exigent needs.[8]

When infantile needs are initially frustrated, as they inevitably are by even the best of parents, the resultant unpleasant emotions are necessary to help the child accept his or her separateness and form his or her identity. The child needs appropriate no's: spoiling can be as destructive as unempathic chronic rejection (see Chapter 11). But the anxiety and rage that attend the frustration of the impossible demands of our instinctual natures, on one hand, and the exigent compulsions of external reality, on the other, are heavy burdens for the child in even the best of circumstances. And we are all left needing, in individually varying ways and to varying degrees, to cling regressively to the good, protective magic promised by parental care, to the lost paradise of the breast. For the source of Medea's power to seduce and ensnare her victims seems to center on her magical gifts. We all cling to some delusional hope of returning to the original paradisiac expectations. Medea promises triumphant narcissism—omnipotence, eternal youth, the fulfillment of all wishes—a regressive temptation for weak mortals, who have regretfully had to give up much of their need for and belief in magic in their struggle for separation and identity.

Medea's good magical gifts seem to counteract her bad ones: she can use her power both to save and to destroy. Her first gift to Jason is a magic skin that protects him against fire. The gifts to Jason's new bride dissolve the skin and burn into the flesh of those who touch them. The golden fleece, which

8. Freud calls these early needs *narcissistic* and *anaclitic:* the necessity to preserve the self and the other, on whom the infant is dependent.

Medea helps Jason steal, is the skin of the magic ram, which gave its first owner, Phrixus, the magical power to escape, to get away. It is the infant's development of the power of locomotion, to crawl and then to walk away from the mother, that breaks the symbiotic bond. (But it is as if this separation leaves behind indelible magnetic traces of skin-to-skin contact whose pull back toward fusion with the mother is both irresistible and terrible.) The ability of the child to walk away from the mother is the heart of the riddle of the Theban Sphinx in the Oedipus myth (see Shengold, 1963, 1989). The robe and chaplet presented to the Corinthian princess magically prevent escape, fusing parent and child (symbolizing the infant's failure to separate from the mother, or, one might say, regression to infantile skin-to-skin contact).[9] Jason's sowing of the dragon's teeth, performed with Medea's help, causes armed men to spring up—a symbolic representation of impregnation and birth. Its negative counterpart, the replacement of good, procreative power by bad, destructive (infanticidal) force, is enacted in Medea's killing their sons in order to torture their abandoning father. This theme is announced by Medea's bitter remarks at the beginning of the play, so full of ambivalence and envy. I repeat them in the Gilbert Murray translation: "Sooner would I stand / Three times[10] to face their battles, shield in hand, / than bear one child" (1943, p. 457). She would prefer to be a man (or a phallic woman) and kill rather than endure the pain and the

---

9. The emphasis on skin-to-skin contact with the mother's breast and body was suggested to me by Shelley Orgel.

10. Unconsciously this is a phallic wish—at least for those who believe in Freudian symbolism: the number three symbolizes the male genitals. The "shield in hand"—*sword* would suit my thesis better—is, to judge from the absence of the image in other English translations, Murray's addition to keep to iambic pentameter. A psychoanalyst who does not know Greek is condemned to amateur scholarship.

separation of child from mother in childbirth. Childbirth here is felt as the curse of woman and as a castration. (Medea expresses the joy of being a mother later in the play, but joy "does not triumph.")

Separation and abandonment, in active and passive forms, inexorably lead Medea toward murder of her father, in the attenuated form of stealing his possessions and directly expressed in killing and dismembering his son and murdering the father figure Pelias. Her intensely passionate murderous impulses are directed toward Jason, who has tired of her, is about to replace her, and does not protest her exile from Corinth. And, finally, she will kill her sons, whom she cannot bear to leave behind. In response to the threat of abandonment, Medea changes from the giver who would do anything for the one she loves to the destroyer whose gifts and ministrations are aimed at torturing and killing the formerly beloved other. (She is Margaret Mahler's "asymbiotic mother" who feels that the child, if it is not part of her, is nothing.) The turning point of the myth is Jason's breaking his vow never to separate from her.[11] Medea helps Jason steal the magical fleece, which gives its owner the power to get away; yet, ironically, it is that very power that she cannot abide. She represents the omnipotent mother who may give the child the gift of fleeing *with* her but will never permit the child to flee *from* her; the child is to be bound to the mother forever. Medea kills her children not only to punish Jason but to prevent them from walking away from her. She gave them the gift of life; therefore, they are to be hers forever.[12]

11. Ever politic, Jason is aware that in Greece at the time the marriage of a Greek to a barbarian is not legally recognized.

12. A patient felt like "tearing myself to pieces" in what he described as a "guilty rage" when, on every one of his birthdays, his mother would describe, pang by pang, the agonies of birth she had suffered "for you." His guilt turned out to be for daring to separate from

Through Medea's gifts, Creon and his daughter are united in death. The relationship between parent and child regresses to cannibalistic fusion, with the figures of Creon and his child literally eating and melting into one another. This fate has parallels in the psychic interplay between parent and child in latter-day versions of the confrontation between Medea-like ("primal") parents and their children. Fantasies about fatal gifts probably exist in all of us (as do wishes to return to the womb), but they are especially prevalent and powerful in people who have not sufficiently given up, or have regressed to, the symbiotic position toward a parent who has required the bond of mutual narcissism. This is especially common in situations of child abuse, of soul murder, where the child's clinging to the parent (by submission or defiance) and becoming the parent (by identifying with her or him) are compulsive ways of desperately holding onto an endangered but absolutely needed parent.[13] The parent is simultaneously and contradictorily held to be responsible for the injury, insult, or deficiency (overstimulation or deprivation); this fills the child with rage and parenticidal wishes. Clinically, the therapist or analyst finds some version of this paradoxical burden in every patient: wanting to get rid of parents we feel we cannot live without.

With a Medea-like parent, both parent and child assume

---

his mother, violating her wishes to keep him with her forever. No trip away from home was casual for this man. He would experience intense anxiety, anxiety that he was killing his mother or would die when away from her. Another patient reported the same maternal dwelling on birth agonies; he had created the wishful fantasy that he was one of a pair of twins—to share the guilt and to be able to offer his mother a victim in his stead to castrate and devour.

13. This is well illustrated in the movie *Psycho*, based on a story by Robert Bloch.

that the parent has life-and-death power over the child. Medea says: "For die they must in any case: and if they must be slain, it is I, their mother who gave them life, who must slay them!" (p. 234). For the child, out of need and frequently as a delusion, the parent has to be felt as good and giving, and the parental gifts are equated with body parts (breast, phallus, limbs, sensory organs), which the child feels are necessary to complete a body image of narcissistic perfection, with which the mythical timeless bliss of early paradise can be attained once more.

This might be called the gift of narcissistic promise. Defensively the good is called on to distance the dangerous bad. This probably begins with the mental image of the mother's breast, which becomes emotionally charged with ambivalence—conceived of as alternatively providing nourishing milk or deadly poison. An illustration is provided by the fairy tale of Snow White, whose envious witch-step-mother is a model of mirror-gazing narcissism. She offers Snow White the gift of a perfect-appearing but poisoned, trance-inducing apple, and the girl, who ought to know better, accepts it.[14]

In the course of development, the child attempts to get away from the Medea-like mother (the mother as Sphinx; see Shengold, 1963, 1989). This begins with the acquisition of locomotion (the promise of liberation offered by the golden fleece) and continues with attempts to establish nonincestuous relations, in the course of which others beside the parents become emotionally meaningful. Concomitant with this are the development of sublimated activities and inter-

14. The apple is a symbol of the breast, and it evokes the earliest fatal gift, at least according to Genesis: Eve's presentation of the apple to Adam, who eats it, bringing about their expulsion from Eden and the initiation of mortality.

ests and the acquisition of the ability to use reality testing to examine the family matrix of shared delusions—all in the service of an inner need to become a separate individual. The child's healthy attempts to achieve a separate identity may call forth murderous rage and seduction in the Medea-like parent, evoking the child's anxiety, longings, rage, guilt, and regression.

The parent's reactions to the child's individuation are often expressed through gifts and favors or, alternatively, through proscriptions and punishments, administered, according to the parent, "for your own good." Of course, often enough, the child in fantasy constructs out of the inevitable misunderstandings and slights the figure of a Medea-like parent, which exists as a fantasy presence in the mind very different from the real parent. But parents like Medea— capable of true evil, charismatic and even possessing hypnotic power, promising good and bad magic—are not just creatures of fantasy; they actually do exist and, judging from my clinical experience and that of others, are not uncommon.

In psychoanalytic treatment there is always a recapitulation of the individually specific vicissitudes of the patient's early developmental attempts to separate from the mother and acquire individuality. When these efforts encounter soul murder—actual traumatic attacks and abuse by a parent— and, confusingly enough, also sometimes when little or no external traumatization has taken place, it becomes defensively necessary for the child (or former child) to regress to symbiotic psychological merger with the mother. The overwhelming promise of bliss from earliest development is regressively called on in an attempt to contain current overstimulation and rage. Under these conditions, the "fatal" gifts are felt, unconsciously and sometimes also consciously, to be full of promise. Even if there has been childhood experience of frustration and torment, the victim is likely to feel that *the next time, this forthcoming time,* it will be different. Later in life, such people have the unconscious compulsion to repeat the traumatic past, but they insist, consciously or unconsciously, that the parent is good, that torment will be transformed into benevolence; they deny the traumatic memories out of need for the good witch-mother who relieves all tensions and brings sleep.

William Blake, with poetic license, places this traumatic process at birth in his *Songs of Experience:*

> My mother groan'd! my father wept.
> Into the dangerous world I leapt:
> Helpless, naked, piping loud;
> Like a fiend hid in a cloud . . .

This is a depiction of inborn evil and vulnerability to evil. Regression follows the rage:

> Bound and weary, I thought best
> To sulk upon my mother's breast. (1794, p. 42)[15]

The prototype of the gift, as I have stated, is the breast, and gifts from the primal parent figure are accepted in a state of hypnotic surrender. A separate identity is sacrificed for merger; judgment and criticism of the parent (customarily performed by the ego and the superego) are abandoned. The pull toward acceptance of the "fatal," identity-dissolving

---

15. The lines quoted are from "Infant Sorrow," from *Songs of Experience.* The equivalent poem is the 1789 "Infant Joy," from *Songs of Innocence:* " 'I have no name, / I am but two days old.' / 'What shall I call thee?' / 'I happy am, / Joy is my name.' / Sweet joy befall thee!" (1789, p. 36). One of Ibsen's definitions of soul murder is the destruction of *joy* in the life of another human being.

gifts comes from memories (or fantasies) of the magic narcissistic fulfillments of the past (real or delusional), which the parent may repeatedly recall to the child, and from the need to escape from the traumatic anxiety involved in the dangerous release of (sadomasochistic) excitement, longing, and rage in both parent and child in the aftermath of attempts at separation or as a result of traumatic overstimulation or deprivation. The double promise of the gift—to bring good magic and to dissipate bad magic—is made more believable when the parental figure has, like Medea, shown stunning reversals of affect in the past. But even if this has not been true, even with consistent doses of mistreatment from the parent, the need for rescue by a good parent (and the child may simply not have a good parent) can make the promise irresistible.

Clinical Examples

A, a woman in her early thirties, overstimulated and seduced as a child by her mother, was attempting to separate psychologically from her mother in her analysis. The mother had tied the girl to her by continuous, often unsolicited, maternal attentions (including sexual attentions) and gifts. These gifts were lavish and thoughtful; the patient craved them, yet invariably became furious with her mother and with herself after she accepted them. The mother had made the daughter the center of her life. A, who had superficially rebelled and moved out of the parental home even before the analysis, had continued to feel compelled to be fed and clothed by her mother, repeating in attenuation the sexual contacts of the past. The mother had always influenced the daughter's important decisions; she continued, long past A's childhood, to select her daughter's clothes.

After some years in analysis had decreased her dependence on her mother, A for the first time chose and paid for her own rather expensive winter coat. She proudly showed it to her mother, who was obviously upset but said nothing. A few days later the daughter received a package sent from a department store, without any card, containing a much more expensive and more fashionable coat. A became furious and, with difficulty, fought back the impulse to telephone her mother and scream at her. With the help of insight gained from the analysis, she knew that this kind of emotional contact was what her mother wanted. She would have felt guilty, accepted the coat, and been fondled and forgiven by her mother. This would have left her feeling tormented and confused—excited and in a slow-burning rage. In spite of this insight, she felt undone when she looked at her mother's gift and was strongly tempted to keep the coat. All her characteristic dishonesty (in identification with her mendacious mother) appeared in seductive rationalizations: "It's so lovely; I know what I am doing, so it doesn't matter; just this once I can keep it." Like Creon's daughter, she had an overwhelming temptation "just" to try it on, but, she reported, "I knew that if I did, I would have *had* to keep it." She felt that analysis had made it possible for her to refuse the gift.

B, a woman in her mid-twenties, had suffered from megacolon since early childhood. Until she was seventeen, she had bowel movements only with the help of laxatives and enemas administered by her mother. There was considerable evidence that giving these enemas, often with twice the amount prescribed by the doctor and twice as often, satisfied the mother's urges for sadistic power. As an adult, B gave herself enemas and afterwards fantasized that her mother had invaded her body and mind, forcing her to be a bad mother to her own children, to make them sick, neglect them, and beat them. She was tormented by the fantasy that she would destroy them.

B had entered treatment after attempting suicide by taking drugs. To her this had meant killing the "bad" mother within herself and thereby saving her children. Yet, in the suicidal action, B was also carrying out her mother's murderous wishes against her for daring to leave her, marry, and have children. (B felt that, in the event of her death, her children would probably have been given to her mother to raise.)

In treatment, B became aware of the identity-disintegrating effect of her enemas. Yet she reacted with terror when it was pointed out that she could stop them. The enemas represented not only gratification but, more important, a lifeline to her mother, who she expected to curse and abandon her if she gave up the enemas. And B felt that she could not live without her mother. Only when B had worked this over in the transference to the analyst (on whom she had conferred her mother's terrible magic power) and had gradually become less frightened was she able to continue the therapeutic work, come to her sessions regularly, and talk freely. The analyst's gifts, unlike the mother's, were gradually accepted as not threatening, not poisonous.

On the night before her suicide attempt, B had dreamt: "It was Christmas or my birthday—a time to give presents. Mother had given me an enema bag. I felt sick with revulsion against her." The enema bag, which could explode the bowels from below, was equated with the poisonous overdose of medicine she intended to swallow, which would have exploded her bowels from above. The Christmas gift had both oral and anal implications. Her associations included her separation from the mother by having been born—extruded, like feces—and the separation from her children when she gave birth herself. The poisoned gift, the enema bag, was equated with the poisoned dose B actually ingested. Accepting the gift meant reinstating the old sadomasochistic tie to her mother, bringing death as self-punishment for daring to rival her mother and assume her own separate identity as wife and mother. Both murder by the mother and loss of the mother could be avoided by identifying with her—B would become her own Medea and kill herself. Perhaps this would be a way to end the unbearable rage that threatened ego annihilation and the destruction of her mother or her own children. B came to learn in her analysis that she had the unconscious assumption, ineffectually fought against as far as action was concerned, that life without her mother meant no life at all. B held onto her mother by becoming her, turning the impulse to destroy her mother against herself rather than against her children. (This example shows that activities shared with a Medea-like parent can have the same meaning as a poisoned gift.)

Gifts

Gifts can express the variety of good and bad feelings that stem from any level of relationship between two people, from any level of the basic parent-child relationship ranging from fusion to full individuation and mature love: narcissism, need-fulfillment, object-constancy, ambivalence. They also can be the medium of phenomena derived from any developmental stage of sexuality and aggression: oral, anal, phallic, oedipal (see A. Freud, 1965). But the poisonous, fatal gifts of Medea aim at traumatic overwhelming of the recipient's emergent self and lead to the urgent need for regressive return to some early mental state of fusion with the parental figure.

Death as a final and irrevocable object loss is minimized and denied by rites and customs that involve gifts. Gifts and bequests make it possible to hold onto symbolic representations of those who are lost during the time the loss is being worked over and accepted. Gifts can be analogous to the earliest intermediate or transitional objects (favorite toys, pacifiers, pieces of cloth), which make distancing of parents acceptable to the infant.

The loss of a father figure, to be compensated for by gifts, is illustrated by Jean-Jacques Rousseau in an autobiographical story in which the gifts have a predominantly oedipal cast. As a teenager—his mother dead, his father preoccupied with a second family—Rousseau lived for some years with Mme. de Warens, a mother substitute (when they met she was twenty-eight, he sixteen): "From the first day, the most complete intimacy was established between us, which has continued during the rest of her life. 'Little one' was my name; 'Mama' was hers; and we always remained 'Little one' and 'Mama,' even when advancing years had almost obliterated the difference between us" (1781, p. 109). He lived in her house off and on up to his early twenties; she often supported him; finally, she slept with him. It was a ménage à trois, for the kindly woman had a resident lover, her valet, Claude Anet. When Rousseau discovered that Anet was Mama's lover, there was some jealousy, undoubtedly much minimized in his rosy account:

> Notwithstanding, instead of conceiving an aversion to him who had robbed me of her, I actually found that my attachment to her extended itself to him. Before all things I desired her happiness; and, since he was necessary to it, I was content that he should be happy likewise. . . . Without claiming the authority over me to which his position enti-

tled him, he naturally exercised that which his
superior intelligence gave him over mine. I never
ventured to do anything of which he disapproved,
and he only disapproved of what was bad. Thus we
lived in a union which made us all happy and
which could be only dissolved by death. (1781,
p. 184)

Madame de Warens gave Rousseau the gift of relieving
him of his virginity when he was twenty—a gift designed,
according to him, to instruct him and guard him against the
diseases and other unfortunate consequences of the temptations of the world. "Was I happy? No: I tasted pleasure. A
certain unconquerable feeling of melancholy poisoned its
charm; I felt as if I had been guilty of incest" (p. 203). Shortly
after this, Anet died of pleurisy.

Thus I lost the most faithful friend I have had in
my life; an uncommon and estimable man, in
whom Nature took the place of education, who,
in his position as a servant, nourished in his heart
all the virtues of great men, and who, in order to
show himself one of them to all the world, perhaps
wanted nothing except a longer life and a different
position. The next day I was speaking of him to
Mama with the most lively and sincere affliction;
when suddenly, in the midst of our conversation,
the vile and unworthy thought came across my
mind, that I should inherit his wardrobe, particularly a nice black coat, which had caught my
fancy. (p. 212)

Here the oedipally triumphant Jean-Jacques plays the role of
both Medea and the daughter of Creon. He fantasizes giving
himself the poisoned gift of his rival's coat, in an attempt

both to identify with and to hold onto the lost father figure whom he had replaced in Mama's bed. Telling her his "vile" idea, although it killed no one, clearly brought her pain and disapprobation and him regret and guilt. Rousseau manages, not untypically in these confessions, to make almost a virtue of his "vile and unworthy" thoughts and impulses:

> Nothing made her feel more keenly the loss which she had sustained than this contemptible and hateful remark, disinterestedness and nobility of soul being qualities in which the deceased had been pre-eminently distinguished. The poor woman, without answering a word, turned away from me and began to cry. Dear and precious tears! They were understood, and all made their way into my heart, from which they washed away even the last traces of so contemptible and unworthy a thought. Never again, since that time, has a similar thought entered it. (p. 212)[16]

Rousseau presents himself as being able to distance his greed, hatred, and guilt out of love and consideration for Mme. de Warens. This could well have been transiently true or partially true, however impossible it is that a "similar" vile thought (or act) never recurred.

Where the capacity for love, for caring for a separate human being, exists, a gift can amplify the relationship and

16. A likely story! The *Confessions* go on to report how Rousseau (much later in his life) sent his illegitimate children, by a woman other than Mama, to an orphanage to be raised. Here his envy and jealousy showed in what can be seen as his unconscious revenge for the early loss of his actual mother and the indifference of his father. He identified with the aggressor. And he was to be the only orphan entitled to a mama.

add to the sense of identity of recipient and giver alike. Gift-giving of this kind is no longer based principally on expressing or denying primal emotions. Narcissism is, for the time being, transcended; the giver is not only expressing his own drives and feelings in the giving but is (or at least believes that he is) also empathically aware of the drives and feelings of the receiver. The gift is chosen in a benevolent, transient, partial identification with the recipient. Both partners retain and even enhance their self-esteem. A true gift is what the other wants, not what one wants him or her to want or be or become.[17] A true gift involves renunciation of claims for permanent merger with the recipient, signifying the reversal of all but transient fusion, without injury or loss to either party. As in sexual congress of whatever kind, to the extent that it is loving and life-affirming rather than destructive, transient fusion can allow for enhanced and mutual satisfaction and self-regard. We cannot (aside from psychotic aberration) swallow one another, but we can sample one another; we have to settle for less than everything, but we can retain a precious something.[18]

Gifts are concrete manifestations of wish fulfillments shared, sometimes unequally and with differing psychic valence, by giver and recipient. Analysis of the meaning of gifts

17. This is in opposition to the exigent "beneficence" expressed by the kind of mother who reveals her symbiotic intent in, for example, telling the child, "I'm cold, put on a sweater!" In this example there is also the offering of a garment, but of course such mothering can also be transient and certainly need not be murderously intended, as was Medea's. Still, it aims at stifling the separate identity of the child.

18. Rousseau could not control Mama's extravagance as Claude Anet had been able to, and eventually it became necessary for the young man to leave her and find his separate way in the world as an adult. But they did continue to care about each other.

can provide insight into hidden aspects of a patient's relation-ships. Occasions for the exchange of gifts usually imply the surface appearance of mutual agreement that aggression is being controlled. This provides opportunities for instinctual breakthroughs—often displayed at these events by the tell-ing of jokes containing (usually) disguised hostility. Analysis of gift situations suggests the qualities of relationships with important others and the individual's hidden instinctual and defensive predilections. In psychoanalytic jargon, from the study of gifts we can get clues to levels of instinctual and ego fixation and regression, to qualities of the capacity for love and for object relationships, to aspects of emotional sets about the self and important others.

A parental gift evoking narcissistic promise or a poisoned gift can undo or threaten analytic work in the susceptible individual who continues to exist in too much psychic subjec-tion to a parent by bringing on regression to early states of need for and fusion with the parent. This combination of gratification and bondage in a continuing relationship with a parent or parent figure may compromise the transference of such conflict-ridden intensities onto the relationship with the analyst. This should be dealt with in psychoanalytic treat-ment through thorough and repetitive interpretative analysis of the meanings involved in the gift-giving.[19] In some cases, especially if child abuse and a Medea-like parent have been involved, with gifts used as a kind of umbilical cord, I have found it necessary to consider careful application of an absti-nence agreement in relation to the patient's receiving gifts from or giving gifts to parents. (If this step is taken, it must be

19. It is especially necessary to analyze the giving of gifts to the analyst or the wish to do so. Analysts usually but not invariably avert acting out the gift-giving. Much attention has been given to this far-from-simple subject, which will not be explored further here.

preceded and accompanied by a lot of analytic work in order
for the analyst to avoid simply repeating the role of the
exigent and domineering parent.) The analyst must not give
in to the patient's desires for fusion or demands for narcissistic promise (which sometimes take the form of offering overt
or covert gifts) but must interpret them empathically, without hectoring the patient for his or her inevitable resistances
and needs to repeat the past. The analyst can stand for, but
should not try to force, the analysand's individuation. And
often enough, helped by an empathic analyst, even an analysand who has experienced an attempt at soul murder can
eventually renounce submission to the Medea-like parent
and refuse her fatal gifts.

3

The Smell of Semen

"What have we here: A man or a fish? Dead or alive? A fish; he smells like a fish; a very ancient and a fish-like smell"
—William Shakespeare, The Tempest

I have noted in several women patients a preoccupation with the smell of semen. In each there was a predominant aversion as part of a fascinated ambivalence and what appeared to me to be an exaggerated insistence on the olfactory power of seminal fluid. Semen seemed to stink in their nostrils. This led me to wonder why other women did not share this perception, especially in view of the frequent experience of hear-

---

I am indebted to Austin Silber for several suggestions concerning this chapter, which is an expanded version of a paper I originally wrote many years ago as a memorial tribute to our mutually admired teacher, Sidney Tarachow.

Epigraph: Shakespeare here alludes to an intersexual creature—the vagina is still often said to have a fishlike smell. Does this, I wonder, have any phylogenetic significance, as Ferenczi suggests in his speculative essay "Thallassa" (1924)? He sees the fishy smell as an actual or illusionary perceptual remnant that evokes the connection between the amniotic fluid and the birth canal and the sea from which life arose.

ing about vaginal and anal odors from both men and women in analysis and therapy, and why male patients—I puzzled especially over male homosexuals—so seldom insisted on the smell of semen in this or any other seemingly exaggerated way. (I do realize that any individual analyst sees relatively few patients and that men and women are different in many ways, both within and outside gender boundaries.) I realized how ignorant I was about the smell of semen. Does it have a characteristic smell? How much individual variation is there? (There certainly is a great deal in general body odor and in vaginal and fecal odors.) I questioned my colleagues, who seemed equally ignorant and who shared my impression about the comparative rarity of associations concerned with the smell of semen. I was alerted to listen for relevant material, and what I am writing is the result of years of that listening.

Sexual smells are composites of various odors. The composite for any individual is complex. There are external as well as psychic influences, the latter inevitably modifying the former. Objective differences would relate to biological chemical factors (inborn as well as related to diet), to dirt or cleanliness, and to extraneous odors that might accompany sexual ones. Trying to define how something "actually" smells can lead to unsolvable metaphysical problems, but "objective reality" is of course always transformed and distorted by (probably) generally similar but still (undoubtedly) individually varying fantasies that, with maturation and development, effect corresponding changes in perception and apperception. Our fantasies profoundly influence our developmentally important experiences of smell—important phylogenetically as well as ontogenetically. Freud (1909, 1930) speculated that man's assumption of the erect posture in the course of evolution resulted in an involution of the sexual significance of the sense of smell, which seems so much more pronounced in other animals, especially our anthropoid relatives.

Freud said that the ego is "first and foremost" a body ego. Smell is involved with sensual and somatic experiences that are crucial to the development of the mind—experiences of intimacy, of bodily involvements that go into the formation of the ego and the sense of self, of awareness of others, and of the earliest relations with others. The sexual odor of the mother for the infant (at the time, I speculate, when the mother-infant unit comprises the psychic universe, with the mother's odor the odor of the universe) would begin (further speculation) with a mixture of general body odors, in which milk and breast odors would predominate. Past the early nursing stage, in which self and mother are only partially differentiated, the sexual odor of the first other, the mothering person, would consist of the mother's characteristic individual general[1] body smell (itself a composite): odors of sweat and dirt, fecal and urinary odors, odors of menstrual discharge and other vaginal exudates and discharges, and such adventitious and peripheral additions as perfumes, soap, and baking and cooking smells All these odors—even, by contiguity, the vaginal ones—can also emanate from the father. (And of course the vaginal ones can also be displaced onto his mental image by the child.) With the child progressing toward the period in which anality and toilet training predominate (the anal-sadistic stage of libidinal development), the various odors probably acquire a preponderant anal significance. The odors of this stage would involve a confusion or vague equation of vaginal and anal odors: one

1. An oxymoron, but valid.

could call them cloacal odors, powerfully existent in the child's fantasy life. The child's curiosity about bodies and sex would center in part on odors; this seems implicit in the epigraph to this chapter.

There may be a history of traumata that determines the importance of odors for particular people—odors derived from exposure to the primal scene, for example, or from the presence of a primitive or regressed or senile or psychotic household member who may have neglected or repudiated cleanliness or may have been repeatedly incontinent. Such a psychopathic or psychotic adult could have been seductive and exhibitionist, making smell a memorable part of close contact. The sense of smell can be important in soul murder: an abusive adult can have assaulted the child with odors, perhaps directly or as an accompaniment to other things. If the seducer or abuser is a family member, especially a parent or parental figure, this would increase the conflictual and traumatic significance of odors for the child. A focus on the smell of the event could serve as a displacement away from some more traumatic aspect of the experience for the child, usually involving the sense of touch and pain—such as being penetrated. Contrariwise, the smell can retain the potential to bring the whole traumatic event back to life. Proust has made much of the power of sensory perceptions such as smells to evoke what seems to be a kind of isolated yet transiently cosmic reliving—a re-creation of the overwhelming sense of the entire experience of some moments from the past.

A young man, Z, convincingly described himself as the child of two psychotic parents. He had been the victim of sexual abuse by his mother. She was frequently hospitalized. Z reported that his mother as a young woman almost never washed her body or her clothes. She habitually walked about the house partially undressed. She refused to use menstrual pads, simply stuffing wads of toilet paper between her legs, so that during every menstrual period the floor was littered with bundles of dirty, bloody, odiferous matter that she had dropped and left. This was a typical psychotic extension of her characteristic incontinence. Z's father also never washed and hardly ever changed his clothes. He frequently went around with his fly open and in dirty underclothes. Z's parents had effectively restored the primal olfactory conditions that prevailed, to follow Freud's speculations, before man assumed the upright stance. Despite this soul murder background, however, and in contrast to the women patients I am about to describe, Z made no mention of the smell of semen. But, in what I took to be part of his pervasive fear of castration, women for him were modeled on his mother, and he experienced vaginal odor as foul and dangerous as well as exciting. His sexual life was heterosexual but predominantly sadistic, and he proved incapable of forming any lasting loving tie with a woman.

Psychoanalysts are familiar with the fear of and aversion to vaginal odors in both men and women who are in fantasy preoccupied with castration: expecting to be, feeling already, or wishing to be castrated. Especially for heterosexual men and homosexual women, vaginal odors can be, and usually are, preponderantly a source of excitement and idealization. But some people regard the female genitals and their odor as predominantly cloacal: degraded and dirty, mixed with excretory functions and odors. As such the vaginal odor reigns in fantasy as the odor of castration for both sexes. Both the castration and the degradation can still be masochistically or sadistically exciting and pleasurable, but the admixture of the bad and the frightening makes for conflict within the mind. To state this a bit differently, for the relatively conflict-free, the smell of the vagina evokes excitement or pride, being merely a part of a multisensual contact. But with neurotic impairment or perverse narrowing and transformation of sexual enjoyment, there can be a tremendous enhancement of the significance (good or bad) of the odor of the vagina, or the odor attributed to it. One hears repeatedly from both men and women in analysis about the power and pungency of the smell, often characterized as fishlike. It fills the room, the house, even the street, as Mozart indicates in *Don Giovanni:*

> (outdoor scene—Donna Elvira appears)
> *Don Giovanni:* Mi pare sentir odor di femina. (I
>   seem to smell the odor of woman.)
> *Leporello:* Che odorato perfetto! (What a perfect
>   sense of smell!)

What then of the smell of semen? Each of the three women I discuss in this chapter emphasized the penetrating, pervasive, almost overwhelming odor of seminal fluid. I can find no general agreement about the nature or power of the smell of semen. I can only quote what little evidence I have and state my impression that, by and large, the odor doesn't amount to much, although there may be some individual variation. A wise and experienced older colleague wrote to me years ago, when I inquired about his experiences, "We learned in medical school that semen is insipid olfactorily; I recall that the teacher likened it to the paste made of water and flour used at the time by wallpaper-hangers. This seems to be borne out by the great majority of patients (homosexuals included, as you remarked), and seminal smell plays little role in analysis in my experience. But I do remember one woman patient who insisted on the smell of semen with great affect." This is typical of the comments made by of a number of the analysts I asked about the matter.

One patient, bisexually promiscuous and burdened with considerable castration anxiety, once remarked, "Semen has no odor, but the vagina!" The only medical authority I could find writes, not very helpfully, that semen possesses "a characteristic odor" (Mann, 1964, p. 118). That intensely curious, intrepid, and perhaps somewhat masochistic eccentric, the eighteenth-century surgeon John Hunter (the "discoverer" of gonorrhea, who gave himself the disease in order to study its course), smelled and tasted semen and wrote the following description: "The smell of semen is mawkish [that is, insipid] and unpleasant, exactly resembling that of the Spanish chestnut; and to the taste, though at first insipid, it has so much pungency as, after some little time, to stimulate and excite a degree of heat in the mouth" (quoted by Mann, 1964, p. 2). The objectiveness of that opinion is open to question.

Hunter's description leads to another concomitant of body odor: taste. Smelling is part of and a prelude to tasting, and sometimes insistence on smell represents a displacement from taste. This and similar displacements from seeing and feeling the genitals are illustrated in the following clinical material.

Clinical Material

A young woman, Y, one of whose major problems was the hostility toward men involved in her unabashed, consciously avowed penis envy, had been talking about her intense sexual curiosity as a child, a large part of which had been expressed through her nose. The differences between girls and boys, women and men, excited as well as infuriated her, and this had begun in childhood. She told of the sexually arousing compulsion to examine underwear (her own and others') for stains and smells. As a child she had regularly looked at and sniffed her father's discarded pajama bottoms for semen stains and odors. This report was followed by a hostile impulse to fart and force me to smell her emanations, repeating the compulsion from childhood but with Y taking a more active, parental role. In the session, the smell had become anal—anal smells were shared by both male and female; what they did and made on the anal level could be equated, and she herself could take the safer and consciously desired aggressive role. (She did not say so directly during this session, but it followed from many previous sequences of associations that father made smells and father made babies—but so could she.)

Y went on to state that "semen has a very strong, unmistakable odor." This was put forward aggressively with much conviction, as a kind of forceful, provocative gambit; yet, when it met no challenge from me, she expressed great doubt. She was actually not sure how semen smelled—finding this out had been one specific goal of her childhood curiosity. In adolescence she had been told by an older girl of the very strong, pervasive, and disgusting smell of semen. Notwithstanding her subsequent sexual experiences and her habitually extensive olfactory investigations of men's underwear, she still did not allow herself to know what semen smelled like. Yet she had a strong intellectual conviction about its powerful and disgusting smell. (Some sort of mental split and double registration seemed to be operating.)

Y's associations went on to the smell of the vagina, which she described as "cheesy." Her own vaginal odor she found both foul and exciting. With great heat (she seemed again to expect argument—probably, I felt, a continuing unconscious wish for contact) she added that she knew there were "folds" in the penis that could also contain a cheesy discharge like the one that comes with minor vaginal infections; therefore, she announced in a triumphant tone, the penis can smell just the same as the vagina. This, I felt, was the result of fantasies of having been castrated, which required defensive denial and regression to the anal-sadistic fantasy in which differences between the sexes could be undone. This included or featured equation of the odor of semen and vaginal odor—unconsciously conceived as identical cloacal odors (see Chasseguet-Smirgel, 1984)—or a reduction of everything to shit (see Shengold, 1985).

X, another young woman in analysis, declared that she found the odor of semen particularly obnoxious. She quoted with agreement a lesbian in the Ingmar Bergman film *The Silence* who said, "I hate the smell of semen." X, much given to dramatic language, described semen as having a "loathsome pungency that could diffuse the entire room." Her obsessive preoccupation with the smell was used as part of her rationalization for sadistic attempts to keep her lovers from ejaculating. She had developed a repertory of stratagems to accomplish this, but it inevitably alienated all but masochistic men, whom she despised. They were perceived as effeminate, and she hated femininity, including her own. X also equated the smell of semen with her own vaginal odor, which, as the smell of castration, seemed to be the true source for her of the "loathsome pungency." She did, though, consciously endow vaginal odor with destructive power; the equation she made with seminal odor made both smells dangerous. She took active delight in "forcing" cunnilingus on her lovers "to humiliate them" (this seemed to be fantasy—it was obvious that her partners were more than willing). Historically, the danger and obnoxiousness of genital odors seemed to be derived from her mother and especially from a mother figure, her childhood nurse, who had been very seductive in experiences that had a terrible overstimulating and castrative effect. Both seeing and smelling were historically important: the nurse would exhibit her genitals, featuring a mystifying and smelly prolapsed uterus, by enticing and sometimes forcing the girl to stand facing the toilet while the nurse was urinating and defecating. The sight of the difference between male and female genitals was the source of conflict and confusion, compounded by the mystery of the nurse's huge prolapsing protuberance, which appeared to be bigger than her father's penis, yet could be made to disappear.

X's family was given to violent quarreling and to parading in the nude. In the private family setting, castration was very much in the air, with its smell in the child's nostrils. The conflicts and anxieties pertaining to the sight of the genitals were partly added to, but also partly hidden by, a kind of anal olfactory miasma—an insistence on the sameness of bodily smells. These smells had retained a castrative significance into her adulthood. After analytic work, the smell of semen was reduced to a characteristic but minor odor and, apart from some transient regressive return in the terminal phase of the analysis, became a matter of indifference to her.

V, a young woman in analysis, had recently recalled being a frequent witness as a very young child to her father's exhibitionistic masturbation. This seemed to her to be a true memory. Her conviction was enhanced by perceptory details and was sustained during a long period of analytic work during which I did my best to remain neutral. She had shared her parents' bedroom for many years and then had suddenly been relegated to sleeping in a room with an older brother. She was aware of his masturbation when he became adolescent. There was bitter rivalry with this brother, whom V wanted to be, for primacy in the father's favor. Witnessing the father's masturbation, apparently after he had had intercourse with her mother (also witnessed by her), had aroused the wish to suck his penis. She described the odor of his semen as intense and permeating.

V had a dream involving a tight yellow surgical uniform worn by an intern in a hospital setting. She did not mention her then comparatively young analyst but associated first to a green surgical gown she had seen in a recent visit to a friend in the hospital, where the iron bed's barred front and back panels reminded her of her childhood crib in the parental bedroom. She went on to her brother's usually dirty and sometimes stained jockey shorts discarded on the floor of their mutual bedroom. Then she thought of her father's erection as seen through his jockey shorts:

> That detail gives me the cold chills. I always had the feeling, even the wish, that my brother would do something sexual to me, but he would ignore me and get into bed and turn his back on me. The smell of his masturbation is [*sic*] so strong. The smell of his semen is like father's. I couldn't see him stroking his penis, but I could smell it. I have a cold now but it is as if I smell it now. The smell portends the taste of semen to me—the wish to suck it from my father's penis. I have a very acute sense of smell. With my cold and my not being able to smell properly, I feel unguarded here now. Now I recall the smell of a vaporizer—I was sick, that's why my father was home alone with me. Now I really feel chills. I can't stand a vaporizer now—the smell brings terror and excitement. Somehow all this blends into the smell of semen.

V had developed a hyperawareness of sexual odors. Analytic associations showed that this was derived from primal scene experiences as well as from later encounters with her father and brother. (These were at least voyeuristic; the possibility of other incestuous contacts was much debated but was never either established or ruled out satisfactorily.) The olfactory components were derived from anal, urethral, and vaginal sources, from dirt, sweat, and other body odors, as well as from semen. The whole complex was labeled "the smell of semen" and, as with the other two patients, was equated with V's impression of her own vaginal odors: exciting yet frightening, fascinating yet disgusting, penetrating and pervasive. V was habitually on guard for the smell of semen, and having a cold in my presence left her without danger signals (as well as reproducing a memorable sickness from childhood).

As a child she had used her sense of smell as a warning mechanism to alert her to the parental sexual encounters so that she could feign sleep and be a witness. Her wishes to see and to smell led to her wish to fellate her father, to incorporate his penis and have it for her own. In this way she was attempting to undo the great castration fear associated with primal scene exposure (as well as with a traumatic defloration past puberty that had been partially repressed and denied). This sexually experienced woman retained the unconscious fantasy of being a virgin as part of the fantasy of "still having a penis, hidden somewhere." The feelings and wishes associated with the sight (especially of the ejaculation) and the taste (at least in fantasy) of her father's penis were displaced onto her "smell of semen" fantasy. The smell of semen was then equated with "the smell of the vagina."

Comments

In the clinical material the insistence on the smell of semen is important directly as a source of excitement and danger and also in its use to distance other conflict-ridden perceptions: the tastes, sounds, and sights involved with primal scene experiences, sexual abuse in childhood, and other experiences and fantasies that evoke danger situations and especially castration anxiety. All three women had conflicts about exhibitionistic and voyeuristic impulses. The sight of the male ejaculating (the spurting of semen), along with the sight of the penis in erection, is threatening to women with intense penis envy. The spectacular difference between the sexes is especially important to children seduced by adults; in these situations there is also the pronounced difference between the adult's and the child's genitals and sexual functioning. The adult male's orgasm can apparently provide the sexually excited little girl or boy with a tantalizing model for the desperately needed adequate discharge (usually not possible for the relatively nonorgastic child).[2] It can appear to be a sudden, dramatic, and therefore presumably effective release from the painful overstimulation, confusion, and rage with which the child is left. For example, Y would say, when reexperiencing on the couch her sexual feelings from childhood, "If only my clitoris would burst and ejaculate!"

These patients' active and destructive wishes and impulses of oral castration and coprophagia were also expressed

2. I have learned from my patients over the years that some children apparently can have orgasms, or at least some equivalent of orgasm, but the impression I have gained is that these don't provide enough discharge of excitement to deal adequately with the overstimulation attendant on seduction by an adult.

in displacement onto making genital smells—in addition to the more passive sniffing of them. The obfuscating stress on the identity of sexual smells is part of the denial of the differences between the sexes as well as of the differences between adult and child genitals (Chasseguet-Smirgel, 1984). Preoccupation with sexual smells can mask differences in the sight, taste, and functioning of adult genitalia, and the nose and sense of smell can replace other zones and organs of erogeneity.

These women demonstrated phenomena of libidinal regression to the anal-sadistic stage. They were renifleurs—both excited by odors (with unconscious wishes to eat feces)[3] and repelled by them (by way of reaction formation). For them the main sexual dichotomy—to be first "nosed out" and then denied—was not the division into male and female of mature psychic development but the earlier division into those with a penetrating organ who castrate and those with a receptive castrated organ. Here mother and father can play either role, and the predominant unconscious conception of intercourse was that of a hostile struggle for power between two similar partners, the submitting one being orally, anally, or cloacally raped. The victor castrates; the victim is castrated. Simultaneously, though, the castration, and specifically the irreversibility of castration, is denied—the roles are reversible, so that the victim can regain the destructive phallic power and castrate the former victor.

By equating the genital odors of men and women, the patients denied the differences in genitals, so that the fantasy of easy interchange of genitals seemed possible. With the magic powers of primitive fantasy one can identify with both

3. See Tarachow (1966) for a discussion of coprophagia that emphasizes its narcissistic, preoedipal determinants.

undifferentiated parents and become either one: one can have or be everything.[4] Denial is triumphant; the ego distortions that always accompany denial amount to delusions or quasi delusions (see Shengold, 1995) in which there is no permanent difference between the sexes and castration is not irrevocable. Concomitantly, however, by way of an ego split comparable to what one sees in fetishists,[5] these women with intense penis envy had a terrible sense of inferiority based on feeling castrated. In these patients, both castration and its undoing were expressed in terms of sexual smells, the odor of semen equated with vaginal odor so that the man as well as the woman could emit what was for them the evidence of castration. Simultaneously (another ego split here), equating vaginal odor to seminal odor enables both sources to carry the penetrative, potentially castrating odor of phallic power. In this olfactory way (as part of their predominant, regressive, anal-sadistic outlook), they made penis and cloaca interchangeable and castration reversible. It was therefore not surprising that, for all three women, the sexual ideal was their conception of "the" male homosexual,[6] who in their

4. King Lear, in his full madness become a child again, confounds the bearded Gloucester with Goneril in a way that Shakespeare makes clear means that Lear's elder daughters are for him of undifferentiated sex. He says of Goneril: "Go to, they are not men o' their words: they told me I was everything; 'tis a lie, I am not ague-proof" (IV.vi.104–7, my italics).

5. Part of the mind of the fetishist is dominated by a terror of castration; another part actively denies the possibility of castration. The mind is, as it were, divided on this subject into two nonconnecting compartments whose contradictions need not be synthesized or recognized. This kind of mental split is frequently found in soul murder victims but is not confined to them.

6. There is of course no such thing. Homosexuality is a form of sexual behavior, not a character type or a diagnosis that characterizes

similar fantasies represented one sex: phallic and (idealized) cloacal—no (degraded) vagina or vaginal odor; no castration; intersexual creatures who have and can do everything.

There is a specific problem that remains to be understood—the difficult question of choice of pathology. Why is the common condition of penis envy (present in men as well as women) expressed by these patients in relation to odors? I assume that some children are constitutionally more sensitive to odors than others—closer to the phylogenetic, intensely involved and gifted olfactory models about which Freud (1909) speculates. A specific determinant of the importance of odors for these adult patients was the corresponding importance of odors in the traumatic events of their childhood.[7] Patient Y, for example, showed the development of sensitivity to sexual smells based on both the need for a warning signal to ward off primal scene experiences and traumatic seduction and the wish or compulsion to repeat the traumata. For all three women, experiences associated with castration in fantasy had evoked castration anxiety that was associated with a smell connoting castration—for them, the smell of semen.

In males, heterosexual and homosexual alike, there is abundant castration anxiety and a similar possibility of its experiential, early traumatic association with body smells. But in men, at least the ones I have seen as analytic patients, this has usually been expressed by an insistence on the (for

---

individuals. As with heterosexuals, there are many kinds and many spectrums of differences.

7. I have seen olfactory oversensitivity in adult male patients— heterosexual as well as homosexual—with similar childhood traumatic sexual experiences, but without the resultant stress on the odor of semen.

them) predominantly regressively debased and castrating smell of the vagina. A male homosexual, or a heterosexual with a large proportion of unconscious homosexual wishes, may avoid conflict by avoiding the vagina and thereby somewhat obviating the need to displace the degraded vaginal odor onto the smell of semen. In contrast, the women patients required a continuous active mastery of the danger situation and the compelling excitement evoked in them by the smell of semen; the displacement of the odor of the vagina seemed to be a kind of attempt at mastery. A single psychoanalyst cannot see enough patients to be able to form firm conclusions about such observations, and for me a mystery remains about the male's relative absence of insistence on the smell of semen.

Summary

Insistence on the negative importance of genital odors can be a clue to possible child abuse but is clearly not limited to such cases. Such insistence on the power and offensiveness of the smell of semen by three women who suffered from profound penis envy turned out to be the result of their idiosyncratic confusion about and equation of seminal and vaginal odors. Some sort of childhood sexual abuse was involved for all three women, and for at least two of them, this clearly amounted to soul murder (I have not here furnished the details documenting this). The importance of sexual smells—the excitement about smelling and the reaction formation against it—was determined by traumatic experiences in childhood that involved sexual odors. All three showed regression to the anal-sadistic period of psychic development, in which smells are so important and the differences between male and female are not clear. The inter-changeability of sexual odors was used to deny the evidence furnished by all the senses of the differences between the sexes and, apparently above all, to deny the irreversibility of castration.

CHAPTER

Once Is Never
(Or Once Doesn't Count)

Think'st thou I'd make a life of jealousy,
To follow still the changes of the moon
With fresh suspicions? No; to be once in doubt
Is once to be resolved
—William Shakespeare, Othello

I have observed in several patients a need to prove, sometimes repetitively, that an event that occurs only once has no
meaning. In German this attitude has achieved the dignity of
a folk saying: *"Einmal ist keinmal"*—literally, "Once is
never," or "Once doesn't count." When "once is never" is a
principle influencing a person's behavior with compulsive
force, I have found it understandable as an attempt to counteract and deny the frightening notion of irrevocability, of
once and for all. The epigraph to this chapter says the opposite: once is forever. I believe that the two antithetical meanings really resolve into one. Both involve denial and the
possible establishment of false certainty.

The story is told of Voltaire that once as a young man he
agreed to homosexual relations with an Englishman "and

found it far from satisfactory. A few days afterward the latter informed the Sage of Ferney that he had tried it again and provoked the exclamation, 'Once a philosopher; twice a sodomite' " (Burton, 1886, p. 248). For Voltaire, one time—at least his one time—did not count, but (as expressed here with his typical mixture of brevity, cruelty, and wit) more than once meant once and for all.

A very passive, anxious patient of twenty-five, fearful of all his sexual impulses, had been able (with the tolerant cooperation of a friendly young woman) to have intercourse *once*, when he was twenty. He had attained an erection, performed adequately, and even experienced some pleasure. But he was more than content not to try to repeat his achievement. His one time established him as nonvirgin and heterosexual; this was most important in his obfuscating, reassuring rationalizations—but objectively viewed, as a beginning of adult sexual life, it simply didn't count. All his inhibitions and avoidances persisted, and in the rare instances when he tried to fight them, he was no less subject to the terrible castration anxiety that had so strangely lifted for his one bout of lovemaking. It was as if he felt, about fornication, once, a philosopher; twice, Oedipus Rex.

Another patient, whose anal preoccupations were fixed and yet isolated (denied) as part of his predominant obsessive compulsive character structure, had experienced for the first time (after years of analysis) anal and rectal excitement during a session. This persisted, and that night he masturbated using anal stimulation—another first, as far as he remembered. This was reported during the next session. The patient's analysis did not end very successfully. Whenever, subsequent to these sessions, an interpretation of material that seemed to express anal erogeneity was made, the patient would deny the possibility of any such arousal. When reminded of the masturbation, he did not deny that it had occurred but dismissed it as meaningless: "Oh, that! How can that mean anything? It only happened once!"

With both these men, the effective denial of the significance of the one time produced a relatively stable defensive state in which action was inhibited. There are other people for whom "once doesn't count" has become part of a neurotic pattern, paradoxically expressed in a compulsion to repeat a traumatic situation. This surprisingly illogical other form of "once doesn't count" is frequently found in victims of child abuse, of "soul murder."

C, for example, was a young woman whose life seemed to be dominated by the need to prove that once doesn't count by repeatedly violating her own promise to restrict transgressions or limit circumstances to one time. This became obvious in the analysis by her repetitive attempts to be excused or forgiven—both in advance and afterwards—for her frequently missed sessions, "just this once." In these neurotic encounters, this predominantly truthful person would become dedicated to denial and mendacity. (There was similar behavior at her job, where, apparently, only her great talent made her provocations tolerable.) In the analysis she would ask, "What does just one session mean?" and give a variety of pressing, "realistic" reasons for her need to be absent. The analyst's frustrating conduct in not granting permission, absolution, condemnation, or punishment elicited anxiety and rage. The desperation behind her need to prove that these occasions didn't count became apparent. In her life, C had frequently used "just this once" to justify or rationalize giving in to forbidden temptations; at the time she began analysis, this usually meant sexual contact with a sadistic man of bad character who unconsciously represented an incestuous choice. Although she "realized" and could give lip service to the falseness of her "just this once" in a way that showed the contradictory functioning of her ego, C was still compelled to repeat it.

There was a split in her ego functioning here, and the part dedicated to denial triumphed. The unconscious fantasy emerged that, despite her sexual promiscuity, she remained a virgin. She was therefore, in fantasy, being deflowered again and again, each time denying it afterwards. Late in the analysis she convincingly recovered the memory of traumatic events of early childhood. Her father had broken her hymen during sexual "play"—rationalized by the father as teaching the young girl about sex while enjoining her to keep it a secret from her mother. This was the one time that had to be denied—the fateful first time that, as Freud (1918) points out in "The Taboo of Virginity," evokes castration anxiety and is therefore in many cultures avoided by the bridegroom. In those cultures, and in the once-conventional *droit du seigneur* of European civilization, defloration is or was given over, literally or by token, to a parent or a parent figure to perform. C had lived out something of this primitive rite. For her, "one time doesn't count" denied not only the defloration but also the subsequent *many times* of incestuous contact. Alongside the denial was a compulsion to repeat; in her promiscuity she was attempting the wish-fulfilling revival of the sexual games with her father. C was tragically involved in the impossible search for a parent whose seductions would *this time* bring eternal bliss and not the painful defloration, terrible overstimulation, and castration feelings of the past. This instance of "once doesn't count" was part of compulsive repetition phenomena conditioned by actual traumatic experience (soul murder)—here seduction by the father in contrast to the universal fantasy of having been seduced as a child.

D, a young male patient, was also determined to miss "just one" session repeatedly, but he expressed the most anger, righteousness, and insistence about Memorial Day, a working day for me at the beginning of my career. His attempt to get my permission to miss our Memorial Day session the following May would begin in September. Just this once could he not skip just[1] this one session? I did not give in to my assigned role as enforcer of rules but attempted to get D to analyze why this seemed so important to him. This was resisted for many years.

I have observed in more than one patient that the Memorial Day holiday has a special significance that sometimes emerges in dreams, symptoms, and actions. When Memorial Day has this emotional impact, it usually seems to have to do less with the holiday itself than with the injunction to remember what is evoked by it—consciously to remember the dead, unconsciously to remember the past and especially what has been repressed or otherwise excluded from responsible consciousness (which could include emotionally overcharged past experiences, impulses, and wishes—for example, having been abused as a child or wishing someone dead).

This was confirmed in D's case when memories emerged after several years of analysis of his having touched his psychotic mother's genitals when he was a child. Her frequent exhibitions left no doubt in the child's mind about the hollow vaginal cavity, and he experienced and retained rage and severe castration anxiety. He was aware of hating her and of blaming her for his homosexuality, with which he was discontented and for which he had sought treatment. He had been enjoined by his mother, after she had reached orgasm, not to remember what had happened. Basically it was this

1. See Spruiell (1993) on the meanings of *just.*

forbidden incestuous past, filled with unconscious lustful and murderous impulses, that was recalled by Memorial Day. The overstimulation and castration anxiety associated with the sexual contacts evoked intimations of ego dissolution, of ceasing to be (as well as the frightening hatred of his mother, which as a child he had feared would somehow kill her). And D desperately needed to assert, following his mother's injunction, that these things hadn't happened and that all the consequent fantasy wishes and fears "didn't count."

As a defense, "once doesn't count" expresses a range from minimization to denial. Patients who use it compulsively are counteracting the fantasy of something irrevocable—something lost that cannot be regained; some event that cannot be undone; something that can happen only once, like defloration, castration, or death. As Freud (1918) recognized, defloration is an important enough first time, with incestuous and castrative oedipal connotations, to give rise to a universal taboo. Patients whose conflicts center around aggression often need to deny their murderous impulses, murder being an irrevocable act. All irrevocable acts bring out the psychic danger situations outlined by Freud in "The Problem of Anxiety" (1926). They begin with overstimulation in earliest psychic development, which threatens ego dissolution and traumatic anxiety, and continue in developmental sequence with loss of the breast, then loss of the mother as a separate entity, loss of the mother's love, castration anxiety, and loss threatened by one's conscience (loss of the superego's love). The earliest parental figures and irrevocable loss are involved in these situations of psychic danger. All the dangers can be retraversed in regression, and there is always some admixture of the first and worst: overwhelming traumatic anxiety. And these psychological dangers tend to blend together in individual mixtures containing dynamically changeable but usually characteristic proportions.[2] For example, both defloration and death are often apprehended largely in terms of castration, and in an individual's consciousness castration can predominate as *the* irrevocable one time that people vainly try to escape. But castration fear (the apprehension that a vital part of the body is or will be missing or mutilated) threatens both boys and girls with an intensity that evokes the primal fear of overstimulation and ego dissolution.[3]

My patient E felt and stated his predominant mixture of anxieties involving irrevocability (expressing his mixture of danger situations) in terms of castration: "The first time I sleep with a girl it's all right, but after that I don't function. I guess I feel that *this* erection is the last time I will get an erection. The second time I'm afraid, like a tadpole who will lose his tail when he becomes a frog." This inner picture of tadpole ineffectuality was very different from the way he showed himself to others. E was seen by his bachelor friends

2. There is a preoedipal-to-oedipal specific developmental sequence here too, which is both individually different and partly dependent on biological differences that influence development according to gender. "Anatomy is destiny," says Freud, but he sees the universality of bisexuality as part of the biological given; and he says (and we know) that environmental experiences can have crucial impacts on psychic development too. Therefore ranges of difference between and within the sexes exist in any given person in a most complex fashion. It is my opinion that we generally tend to exaggerate the still definite and sometimes crucial differences that our biological (anatomical and physiological) nature imposes on the mind of a given individual and that men and women are not quite so different as it is fashionable to believe. This stated, one can still add "*Vive la différence!*" or, better when thinking of individuals, "*Vive les différences!*"

3. Orgel (1965) points out that the need to deny the irrevocability of castration can motivate someone to become preoccupied with timelessness.

as a sexual tiger—such was his reputation as a successful womanizer. They thought of him as a kind of Don Juan, and rightly so—but they were unaware of the sexual compulsions and inability to sustain a meaningful relationship that make for a Don Juan. E was helped by his initial try at psychoanalysis. His anxieties decreased, and his functioning improved enough so that he could "make it" more than once with the same girl. And so he was able to marry. This made him look good, and at first it felt good. But, sadly, his wife soon became for him a devalued person whom he could not love (although he continued to be able to make love to her), and the compulsion to be a Don Juan in a more successful if not necessarily more satisfying way persisted in a series of affairs, no longer confined to one-night stands. *Einmal* was no longer *keinmal,* but E was not happy, and dissatisfaction motivated him to return to analysis many years after the first attempt.

The patient had projected his psychology to make his metaphor of a tadpole for whom growing up and experiencing adult male sexual functioning meant castration. The adult must eventually confront the inevitability of an end (the once-and-for-all death) as best he or she can, invariably falling back sometimes on the narcissistic delusion of immortality, without a persistent oversimplifying denial. (As Pascal reminds us, being an adult all the time without distraction and delusion is beyond human capacity.) The child reluctantly and only partially (again, each of us to an individually different extent) gives up the narcissistic timelessness of infancy. E was spoiled as a child—that is, he almost immediately countered any prohibition or frustration by his characteristically overindulgent parents, who were afraid of both their own anger and his, with a terrible urgency that they seemed unable to withstand. It was an urgency that he really felt, even though he was aware of how easy it was to use it to blackmail his parents. They were terrified of saying no to him, and he could not acquire from them any tolerable ability to bear frustration; therefore he became terrified of his own desires and impulses. "If I had demanded that they let me kill them, they probably would have considered it," he said bitterly toward the end of his treatment.[4]

As a child, he was almost invariably successful in protesting parental refusals with some variation on: "Please, just this once—what does once matter?" The urgency of this kind of protest, derived from the past and perceptible in his transference to the analyst, was apparent. This kind of urgency may alert the analyst to the possibility that the patient is reacting with desperation to a threatened loss of the omnipotent magical good parent, whose affirmation is badly needed to ward off overwhelming traumatic anxiety. E, in his analysis, had to face and ultimately renounce the magical aura of the good primal parent—a god who promises the abolition of time, loss, castration, and death—for a psychic reality that, in his view, truly contained frightening defects in self, parents, nature, and God. One time means nothing to someone who clings to the narcissistic delusion that he or she is the center of the universe—a universe in which there are no changes brought about by time (see Cohn, 1957; Orgel, 1965), nor any irreversible circumstance, nor any stop or end. All promises can be fulfilled; immortality, omnipotence, omniscience, perpetual youth, renewable virginity—all are possible. I believe that we all cling to what I have called these narcissistic delusions of everyday life (Shengold, 1995) to some extent;

---

4. E was as dependent on, and as terrified of, his murderous hatred of his overindulgent parents as any patient I have had who was cruelly abused as a child by parents (see Chapter 11).

but the people I have been describing possess more than the usual proportion of these powerful remnants of primal mental functioning. However intelligent and sophisticated they may be in other respects, they need to retain infantile promise and defenses to counter infantile terrors.

Denial involves distortion of character. Insofar as we are driven to deny, we tend to be unconscious or conscious liars. Everyone uses denial, but some people are more compulsively involved in it than others. "*Einmal ist keinmal*" is essentially a lie. This was especially marked for E, who lived a life of deception and secrecy centering around his pattern of freely fulfilling his sexual impulses. The price his punitive conscience made him pay for this was to be effectively split off from his "sins." Before coming to analysis he lied freely and consciously to others but was not aware that he was lying mainly to himself.

I have described two kinds of people for whom "once doesn't count" had become a perceptible part of fantasy life and behavior. Some appear to have achieved a kind of stability: one time is enough to establish a subsequent avoidance. Perhaps the one time has created for them a kind of timelessness, one time equaling eternity. But beyond this evocation of the irreversible by the one time, the choice of this stabilizing, limiting, but adapting way of dodging psychological danger is a mystery—one of the innumerable mysteries of pathogenesis. Why is a castration-ridden man allowed pleasurable intercourse for even one time? And if it can be achieved once, why can't it be repeated?

Those involved in the compulsive repetition of "once doesn't count" seem less mysterious. The patients of this sort had suffered various kinds of overwhelmingly charged or frustrating experiences in childhood and seemed to be engaged less in struggling against the general concepts of time and death than in fighting against accepting the significance of the damaging one time (or many times) of the traumatic past that had brought intimations of a stop to time and the horrors of death. They suffered from a compulsion to repeat that past, masked by the idiosyncratic need to assert that the last or the next repetition didn't or wouldn't count. In these soul murder victims, especially if the abuse they have endured has been (or is believed to have been) at the hands of a parent, "this time won't count" can serve to continue the promise that the parent, instead of emerging as bad, will miraculously come out as good with the next repetition. This is a delusion needed in order to hold onto the internal image of a good parent, which every child—but especially the abused child, who desperately requires rescue—feels he or she cannot live without.

For soul murder victims, "this time doesn't count" represents denial of an addiction to the parental abuse;[5] it is a lie, a lie that is enacted. With some, mendaciousness has become a character trait, part of an identification with a parent who somehow, overtly or implicitly, conveyed the message that the abusive or depriving events didn't count or hadn't happened. An event evoking irreversible change can be treated as if it never occurred with the help of the dishonest principle "once doesn't count."

5. The abused child can either repeat the past as victim or choose his or her own victims in identification with the parent. Both roles are always there in fantasy and almost always in enactments.

5

The Ring of the Narcissist

Tubal: *One of them showed me a ring that he had of your daughter for a monkey.*

Shylock: *Out upon her! Thou torturest me, Tubal. It was my turquoise; I had it of Leah when I was a bachelor: I would not have given it for a wilderness of monkeys.*
—*William Shakespeare*, The Merchant of Venice

Rings are precious objects that, as Shylock shows, can be clung to passionately.[1] Rings adorn the body; like clothing, they can be equated with the body unconsciously. In *The Golden Bough* (1890), Frazer describes the magic powers ascribed to rings and knots in various cultures and the taboos adherent to them. There are contradictory meanings; rings promise to protect and preserve as well as to damage and destroy. The ring can serve as a kind of sphincter; it can constrict and it can protect:

1. This chapter does not attempt to deal comprehensively with the psychic significance of rings but only with one narrow aspect that has considerable psychopathological and clinical importance: the meanings of the ring that arise from very early development. These meanings are especially likely to be found in people forced to regress by soul murder, but of course they could turn up in anyone.

A . . . power to bind or hamper spiritual as well as bodily activities is ascribed by some people to rings. . . . [This is then illustrated by prohibitions among the Greek Islanders against corpses' wearing rings.] The ring is conceived to exercise a certain constrictive influence which detains and imprisons the immortal spirit in spite of its effort to escape from the tabernacle of clay. . . . On the other hand the same constriction which hinders the egress of the soul may prevent the entrance of evil spirits; here we find rings used as amulets against demons, witches and ghosts [illustrations follow from Austria, Lapland, India, and Africa]. (Frazer, 1890, p. 186)

My 1988 book about the psychic relevance of the anal sphincter, *Halo in the Sky: Observations on Anality and Defense,* specifically stresses the defensive idealization of the body's sphincteric rings. I took my title from a comment by Edward Glover (1938):

[Idealization] is a common characteristic of the sexual pervert. However devoid of idealization of adult relations he may be, his geese are usually regarded by him as swans. The sexual part-object treated with this combination of sexual overestimation and idealization varies with the individual, but my experience seems to indicate that these reactions are more common in cases of anal and urethral sexuality. . . . Next to this comes those fetishistic idealizations behind which lies a good deal of sadistic intent. *In a typical case the anal ring was phantasied as a kind of halo sus-*

pended in the sky. It was then contemplated, adored and idealized. The qualities attached to it were mystical and the whole attitude of the patient was religious in type. . . . The *primitive idealizations* have in my opinion a specially close relation to anal sadism, a relation which renders them subject to repression. (pp. 294, 296, my italics)

To simplify the quotation: Those with perversions tend to idealize the parts or organs (or fetishes that stand for those parts) that excite them sexually, especially when sadomasochistic feeling is involved. For example, the anal sphincteric ring gets honorifically transposed into a kind of holy ring—a halo that is then worshipped. "Primitive idealizations" stem from early narcissistic development, when idealization includes the promise of magic as well as, to stress the other direction, abrogation of reality considerations.

For example, late in her analysis patient F's insight had partially curbed her compulsion to collect rings—she had come to realize that these rings held a magical power for her. This power of the ring had often been in her conscious thoughts, but it was just now being "owned"—that is, allowed to enter freely and to be retained in *responsible* consciousness. Previously it had been a quasi delusion (see Shengold, 1995) that she somehow made use of in conscious rationalizations justifying her compulsive acquisition of rings.

Here are F's associations, from a session when August and my vacation were approaching:

I realize that when I don't have enough money to pay my bills, I feel I *need* to buy an expensive ring. It's as if that will make everything all right. It sounds crazy, but the desire has always been so close to action, and I feel it as a kind of magic delirium. Now that I am trying to fight the impulse, I'm aware how hard it is to resist. I really have to exercise my will not to buy a ring right now, when I am so behind with my bills. I am not sure I *could* resist it if I weren't coming here. The temptation also comes when you are about to go away. I don't want to pay you when you're leaving me. *Your presence* also promises magic, and you take it away when you leave.

The prospect of the ring's magic was apparently intended to replace the imminent loss of the promise of the analyst's magic. The impulse to withhold her payment to me (retention of money symbolizing the retention of feces) evoked and repeated from the past her provocative rebellion from a toilet training that had featured chronic (and, as it turned out, traumatic) enemas. Buying rings was a characteristic regressive psychic operation that, unconsciously, centered on her anal sphincteric ring.

The oral sphincteric ring, the mouth, can of course also be idealized. Idealization can screen out or allow for concomitant conscious sexualization (the latter combination often seen in excitement about cunnilingus and fellatio). The sexualization can be sublimated (to arrive at a seemingly nonsexual halo). The sublimation need not be religious—for example, the oral orifice can be "worshipped" in the form of the mouth of the diva by the opera addict; consider (to return to Glover and sexual impulse and displaced sexual object) the men, often homosexual, who become obsessed with opera, idealizing and even identifying with prima donnas; they have been derogatively called "opera queens." (Justin Kaplan quotes Walt Whitman from an early edition of *Leaves of*

Grass: " 'I hear the trained soprano . . . she convulses me like the climax of my love-grip.' [Kaplan adds,] 'But for the opera,' [Whitman] was to say, 'I could never have written *Leaves of Grass*' " [Kaplan, 1980, pp. 177–78].)[2]

Sphincteric idealization—anal, urethral, and oral—is always accompanied by (and serves to disguise and deny) its opposite—sphincteric association with devaluation and destructiveness. Idealization denies the subjective "nothingness" of the ring as a hole as well as reversing the reactions of disgust, degradation, and destructiveness manifest in derogatory slang terms such as "cocksucker," "up your ass!," and "fuck you!" (These expressions almost always mean anal or degraded vaginal [cloacal] fucking; they are about destruc-

2. In the poem "Out of the Cradle Endlessly Rocking," an addition, written in 1859, to the 1855 first edition of *Leaves of Grass*, Whitman used a good deal of ring symbolism as I am explicating it. The poem, originally called "A Child's Reminiscence," may have been associated with a real (or a screen) memory associated with the sea and with his mother that Whitman seems to present as a source of his poetic gift. In the elegaic poem, Whitman pictures the poet (himself) as a bard (also as a mockingbird) singing opera ("the aria sinking" [p. 288]) to a boy (also himself) on the edge of the sea. In the later editions the poem is in a section called "Sea-Drift." The aria becomes a narcissistic love trio, full of ambivalence, with the mother (the sea) joining in: "The aria's meaning, the ears, the soul, swiftly depositing, / The strange tears down the cheeks coursing, / The colloquy there, the trio, each uttering, / The undertone, the savage old mother incessantly crying . . . " (p. 288). The poem begins: "Out of the cradle endlessly rocking, / Out of the mock bird's throat, the musical shuttle, / Out of the Ninth month midnight, . . . / Down from the shower'd halo . . . " (p. 283). And later: "O brown halo in the sky near the moon, drooping upon the sea! / O troubled reflection in the sea! / O throat! O throbbing heart! / And I singing uselessly, uselessly all the night" (pp. 287–88). The poem repeatedly uses the images of halo (even "halo in the sky") and cradle (as part of a circle that stands for infinity).

tiveness, not about making love.) Idealization deprives (as it were) the sphincters of the demolishing teeth with which they are regularly endowed in fantasy.[3] When furnished with teeth, the ring, the hole, the sphincter not only can suck and suck in but can bite and bite off. By concealing the teeth of the sphincteric ring, idealization distances awareness of the malignant cannibalistic propensity of the seemingly empty hole. (This is the body ego equivalent of the cosmic "black hole.") The teeth supply frightening destructive magical power to motivating unconscious, and sometimes conscious, fantasies. These anxiety-ridden fantasies evoke the developmentally early, tooth-laden psychological dangers of annihilation, castration, and mutilation.

F had an eroticized physical symptom that involved a ring and seemed to be activated whenever I went away and interrupted the analysis. She suffered intermittently from a perianal inflammation. Once, when this flared up as August approached, she called it her "ring of fire."

That phrase made me recall a young man, N, whom I saw in consultation over a brief period very early in my psychoanalytic career. N had had several years of therapy but reported that, although he could talk glibly "about sex and fears of loss to my therapist, my therapist thinks I didn't feel much about what I was saying, and I guess he's right." The therapy had been discontinued. "He said I didn't put things together, kept everything at a distance," reported N (who indeed tended to talk about himself as if he were a journalist describing someone he had interviewed). His psychotherapist had suggested a trial of psychoanalysis, and N was look-

3. The "endowing with a tooth" fantasy can spread to encompass the receptive organ beyond the sphincter: mouth and throat, cloaca, anus, vagina. For a developmental account see Shengold, 1988.

ing me over with that in mind. He made it clear that I was only one of several prospects.

N made a memorable impression on me even though I saw him only for four or five consultative sessions. In part this was because I was struck by the defenses of emotional isolation and disavowal that his therapist had referred to, by his general stance as observer of his own life; in part because N's communications kept returning to the *leitmotiv* of a ring. Indeed, they started on a Wagnerian note. He introduced the first session by telling me he had just returned from several months in Europe devoted partly to research for his dissertation and partly to attending performances of opera. He had spent a week at Bayreuth where he had seen a new production of "The Ring" (*Der Ring des Nibelungen*), the cycle of four Wagnerian operas he had loved since he had been taken to see them as a boy. Opera was a shared passion in what he called "my rich and cultured family." I was especially attentive to this *Ring*-ridden introduction to N's first consultative session because I had immediately noticed that the vigorous, good-looking, muscular, masculine-appearing young man was wearing five or six large and unusual rings on the fingers of both hands. This manual exhibitionism was an incongruous contrast to his Brooks Brothers gray suit and general sober appearance. Rings aside, he showed no signs of effeminacy, presenting himself as an opera aficionado, not as an opera queen.[4]

He declared, however, that he was considering psychoanalysis rather than going back to his therapist mainly because of "unresolved concerns about my sexual identity." (This was said in an expressionless tone.) He disliked homo-

4. Of course, effeminate men are not necessarily homosexual, nor need male opera enthusiasts be either effeminate or homosexual.

sexuals and homosexuality and would never do anything sexual with another man. Yet in dreams and daydreams he found himself excitedly "engaged in homosexual actions." But of course he would never do anything of the kind. (Here was an instance of "No times doesn't count"!) The therapist had insisted that these fantasies were directed toward him. N had not felt this, although he could see the theoretical relevance of the "transference interpretation." (He had read Freud.) He had "engaged in heterosexual sex" since his early teens but had formed no lasting attachment to a woman. He was bothered about masturbation fantasies that sometimes featured women becoming men and vice versa.

When I asked about his childhood and family, I got the impression, which may or may not have been valid, that the past had not been specifically explored in his therapy. This was despite N's talk about his Oedipus complex (he was referring to incest, not to parricide, and his context was more general and mythical than personal). He described his parents in general and positive terms that did not evoke them as individuals. Outside of the unwelcome sexual thoughts, he said, nothing much was wrong. He came from a happy family. He was doing well in his academic career. His dissertation was proceeding. He had been told that he had brilliant prospects. His health was good, aside from minor skin problems. He added that he did have one homosexual uncle, who had been ostracized from the family.

N was obviously intelligent. He seemed emotionally inhibited. He made little eye contact and showed no warmth. His speech was full of distancing mannerisms, and, perhaps in part because he looked like an actor (a juvenile lead), I thought that he had Hamlet's suppressive "pale cast of thought" without much of Hamlet's passion. I found myself mentally deindividualizing N by diagnosing him, something

I rarely do. Significantly, I placed him in the diagnostic category that puts deindividualization at its core: obsessional character, with its transformation of human complexity in the direction of caricature. I immediately started to add descriptive terms (soothing my conscience)—for example, he was obviously very narcissistic.

Several more exploratory sessions brought out little more. Other people N described did not come to life any more than his parents had. For N, other people seemed to be arranged categorically, classified by their appearance or occupation or relation to him. The categories were further sorted into good or bad according to, as I saw it, his estimation of whether they fulfilled his narcissistic needs; in general, family members were good. Clearly N was chiefly preoccupied with himself, and no signs of caring for others appeared. The word *love* was never mentioned in relation to people; he did say he loved opera, the "shared family passion." As the sessions went on, I felt I was learning little more about this narcissistic, obsessional man.

He continued to wear an array of rings that varied daily. When I remarked on this and asked what the rings meant to him, he showed overt anxiety for the first time in the sessions. The question also produced a change in his communications. Past the anxiety, N began to talk in enthusiastic detail about what he called "ring magic." I thought for the first time (perhaps mistakenly) that he might have the potential to be motivated to explore his psyche. But in relation to me, the more spontaneous communication the magic ring theme evoked turned out to be only an abortive beginning.

N told me that he was a collector of rings. People in his family, knowing this, gave him rings as presents. This had started with his mother's giving him rings as a child—and he still had every one of them. As he talked of these objects and his interest in them he seemed to become a different person. What could only be called passion emerged from this heretofore inhibited and guarded young man. Somehow my question had evoked ardor—such as that he had described in relation to opera. (Was this intensity, I wondered, prohibited in relation to people, yet allowed to flow in relation to things and fictional representations of people?)[5] Certainly individual rings were described in loving detail with a kind of fire that had not been present in his depiction of the human beings in his life. He loved collecting rings; wearing them involved a kind of game, a kind of pretending that they gave him magical powers, as in the Wagner operas. "It's like there is something sexual about rings," he added. And he went on, to my surprise (not so much at the content but at the free flow of the communication), to tell me about thoughts he had had about rings and sexual arousal.

The change from inhibition to free flow reminded me of the following passage from Maxim Gorki. Of his friend Anton Chekhov he says:

> Beautifully simple, he loved all that was simple, genuine, sincere; and he had his own way of making others behave simply.
>
> Once he was visited by three luxuriously dressed ladies; having filled his room with the sound of silk skirts and the smell of strong perfume, they sat down respectfully across from their

5. Tolstoy describes aristocrats weeping over the tragic dramatic representations they were witnessing at the theater and the opera during the terrible Russian winter, with no thought or feeling for their coachmen, freezing in the streets waiting for them. I am grateful to Dr. Milton Horowitz for indicating to me the relevant fact that Tolstoy had an illegitimate brother who was employed by their father as his coachman.

host, pretended politics interested them, and began to "put questions."

"Anton Pavlovich, what do you think? How will the war end?"

Anton Pavlovich coughed a bit, thought for a while and gently answered in a serious and kindly tone:

"Most likely—with peace."

"Yes, well of course. But who will win, the Greeks or the Turks?"

"I think those who are stronger will win."

"And who in your opinion are stronger?" the ladies asked all at once.

"Those who are better fed and more educated."

"Oh how clever that is," exclaimed one.

"And who do you like more?" asked another.

Anton Pavlovich looked at her kindly, and answered with a brief, pleasant smile.

"I love jellied fruit. Do you?"

"Very much," the lady exclaimed animatedly.

"It's so aromatic!" another agreed solidly. And all three excitedly began to speak, revealing on the question of jellied fruit wonderful erudition and subtle knowledge of the subject. It was obvious that they were all pleased not to have to strain their minds and pretend to be seriously interested in the Turks and Greeks, about whom they had never previously thought at all.

Going out, they gaily promised Anton Pavlovich: "We will send you jellied fruit."

"You conversed wonderfully," I noted when they were gone.

> Anton Pavlovich quietly smiled and said, "Ev-
> eryone should speak his own language." (1904,
> p. 9)

I had associated, to put it into psychoanalytic jargon, to Chekhov, a man who was impatient with as-if functioning and knew how to evoke authenticity in others.

With what appeared to be a mixture of shame and excitement, N told me something "it took me years to tell my therapist." Somehow the idea of a ring was connected with his attempts at auto-fellatio. These had started shortly after puberty. Because he had a long penis, and by dint of flexibility increased by exercise, he had become successful at this—and he could still do it but rarely did. This made his body into a "self-sufficient ring." He could service himself and never have to depend on anybody else. He quickly added that he didn't want to, he never would, suck anyone else's penis. Although N had not supplied sexual details about the "homosexual actions" of his fantasies (and I did not ask him for any), I would guess that they included the fellatio he "didn't want"—see his sexual-circle fantasy, below. This contradiction, I suspect, would be the result not of conscious lying but of the presence of a vertical ego split with contradictory wishes that he did not allow to blend—making for something like Orwellian doublethink.

In contacts with girls and women, he did "indulge in the sixty-nine position of mutual oral sex." He told me, eyes averted, of fantasies during masturbation of a sexual circle of people making all sorts of sexual connections—oral, anal, genital, men and women: "It's like a giant sexual ring, with me as the jewel in the center. They are all there to serve me." I thought N became anxious again after telling me this. It was just before the end of this session, and I wondered whether N had the feeling that he had told me too much too soon.

At the next session, which turned out to be the last, he wore only one ring. Massive and bizarre, it not at all resembled a wedding ring, but it was on the finger of his left hand where such rings are traditionally worn. I made no mention of the shift to one ring but asked a different question that seemed to disturb him as he began to elaborate his answer. I asked about his physical health and the skin troubles he had mentioned. His general health was very good. He had been greatly bothered by acne for several years as a teenager. Now what concerned him was a recurrent itching and redness around his groin. This had become chronic. He became visibly annoyed when I asked for details. He described perianal and sometimes perigenital redness and severe itching. The dermatologist had told him that he kept these conditions going by his scratching. He could deal with them and make them go away temporarily with medication. But the itching, especially all around his anus, "burn[ed] like fire." The vividness of this image, stated with a vehemence that had been rare in his discourse up to then, seemed to belie his ensuing insistence that the skin problem was emotionally only "irritating," a *slight* disturbance to his peace of mind. I felt that N was minimizing a symptom that threatened to bring to consciousness the terrible and threatening aspects of the magic promise of the ring—burning is exciting, but it can also be deadly. At the very least, the itching and skin eruption reminded him that something was wrong—a threat to his narcissistic defensiveness that could evoke unconscious catastrophic expectations.

What his burning metaphor made me think of (but not communicate) was the phrase "a ring of fire," which I vaguely remembered as having to do with a confrontation between King Lear and his loving daughter, Cordelia. It was this phrase, used by F, that made me recall N. With N what I thought of was the ring of fire that Wotan summoned up to protect his daughter Brunnhilde in *Die Walküre*. In the final act of that opera, Wotan intends to deprive Brunnhilde of her godhood (the immortality that would keep her forever the virgin servant of her father) in order to punish her for disobeying him by trying vainly to save her half-brother, Siegmund, to whose death Wotan had reluctantly agreed. Wotan loves Brunnhilde despite his rage at her. He realizes that she defied his orders out of love, responding to his unconscious desire to save his son, so he relents and modifies his punishment. Instead of leaving her relatively helpless as a mortal woman who might be taken by the first comer, Wotan surrounds her with a ring of fire. Only a great and fearless hero will be able to get through that barrier. In the next opera in the cycle, *Siegfried*, we learn that this hero proves to be Siegfried, a product of Siegmund's incestuous and adulterous love for his sister Sieglinde, born in the time elapsed between *Die Walküre* and *Siegfried*, while Brunnhilde lay in suspended animation within the circle of flame. Siegfried rescues her and, although he is also her nephew, becomes her husband. The ring of fire here is an inhibitor that both enforces sexual control and, paradoxically, allows for incest. Love (of father and daughter, of wife and husband) is here made possible by the renunciation of godhood, the developmental achievement of giving up the delusional promise of narcissistic immortality.

When I later checked the text of *King Lear*, the phrase I thought I remembered turned out to be "wheel of fire"—with connotations that include an instrument of torture as well as a ring. Toward the end of the play, the poor mad king—who has survived the storm on the heath (the storm without) and the rage and conflict following his older daughters' rejection after he had narcissistically given away his powers to them (the storm within)—speaks to his loving daughter, Cordelia, whom he does not recognize, with the envy of the unloved, abandoned child:

> You do me wrong to take me out o' the grave;
> Thou art a soul in bliss; but I am bound
> Upon a wheel of fire, that my own tears
> Do sear like molten lead

Here is Lear burning with envy and rage, longing and sadness. In the "grave" of emotional deadness he is safe. By so regressing, he no longer feels the "serpent's tooth" of ungrateful children. Cordelia is bringing him back to emotional life, and at first this is torture. Of course, at the end of the play, Lear's tears for the dead Cordelia will mark his return to being a loving adult who is able to put aside the hate-filled regression of narcissistic second-childhood, here too conquered by love.

My *King Lear* association—the "free-floating attention" of the analyst—had connected the patient's symptom and metaphor with unbearable physical and psychic agony and overstimulation. I suspected that these were lurking beneath N's defensive armor (I would describe that as "anal-narcissistic"), which acted like a sphincter to keep the pain and excitement (as well as the ability to feel love for others) from consciousness. (In his own way, was not N—or at least his deepest feelings—in "the grave"?) But N didn't stay long enough to confirm my speculations. I had, Wotan-like, apparently evoked in the consultations a magic ring of fire whose excitement and dangers threatened to be too much for him. He suddenly announced his firm intention to end the sessions with me and "explore" the other names on his list. I recognized the anxiety that underlay his decision. I had the impression that danger had been evoked mainly when I asked him specific questions about his feelings toward his mother. But there were other factors, especially his telling me too much too quickly (transference magic that was turning threatening) and the dwelling on his body and body symptoms, which might have made continuing the consultations with me dangerous for him.

I return to the other ring in the Wagnerian tetralogy—the Nibelung Alberich's ring of power, which gives the operas their collective name. *The* ring, whose magic grants omnipotence, was forged from the Rhine gold that Alberich stole from the Rhine Maidens when he renounced love (substituting or retaining narcissistic greed and hatred). Giving up love was the price of the ability to steal the Rhine gold. The ring of power was in turn stolen from Alberich by the trickery of Wotan, father of the gods. The ring's possessor was then cursed by Alberich. The giants Fafner and Fasolt demanded it from the most reluctant Wotan as payment for their building of Valhalla, home of the gods. The curse leads Fafner to murder his brother over possession of the ring.

The fatal power of Alberich's curse represents the dark (and for the child, terrifying) side of the narcissistic wish for and delusion of omnipotence—one's hostile wishes can kill, and can kill someone who is also loved or at least needed, such as a parent. Later in the opera cycle, the hero Siegfried, who took the ring when he killed Fafner, is in turn killed by Hagen, Alberich's son, in order to steal the ring. Ultimately the ring leads to the twilight and death of the gods (*Götterdämmerung*) when Brunnhilde returns it to the Rhine Maidens to end the curse. Greed for power evolves into the destruction of omnipotence; psychologically this would be the shrinking of the delusion of omnipotence as human psychic development proceeds. In the opera this narcissistic diminishment ushers in the era of human life and restitution of the power to love. As the child's mind develops, the fading (but never the disappearance) of narcissism is necessary for optimal growing up and accepting one's transience and mortality. This acceptance facilitates being able to separate from and to care about and love others, starting with the parents, who initially are seen narcissistically as part of the self.

Narcissists (whether heterosexual or homosexual) are compromised or blocked in their ability to love, and narcissistic regression—to which we are all subject (daily, much more frequently than we are comfortable thinking about, and each in an different way)—continues to deprive us of this precious human quality, to make Alberichs of us, at least transiently. Yet narcissistic regression is a universal defensive need, the mind acting as a psychic counterpart to the developmentally crucial excremental (largely anal) sphincters, to shut down primal aggressive and polymorphous perverse sexual feelings (see Shengold, 1988). In order to reverse this regression in pathologically narcissistic patients we must restore or initiate the ability to love (requiring the ability to tolerate and moderate rage and hatred). This task, sometimes impossible, always difficult, requires the patient to lose or at least diminish the power of the magic that the young child needed and craved—a magic that can be symbolized by a precious ring. This at least partial transformation, when accomplished by therapy, takes endless patience and years of tactful work.

The relevance of this to victims of soul murder seems obvious. They have a special need to deaden their emotions (loving as well as murderous) at a distance, and to help them relax their emotional sphincters to allow for the unbearable feelings of the past is difficult and sometimes impossible. They must permit themselves to love again when the need for love is what led to their desolation and trauma.

I have not attempted a complete exposition of the meaning of rings—which can refer to and symbolize many aspects of relationships with other human beings, from the "transitional objects" of early development (Winnicott) to all sorts of bonds of loyalty, friendship, and love in the life of the child and the adult. I am here stressing the meanings of the ring from the point of view of early narcissistic development— the "body ego" time in which symbolism (in Freud's sense) develops. My examples therefore illustrate the use of rings as magical narcissistic symbols—part subject and part object— derived developmentally from the body ego and ultimately from the body sphincters. Endowed with these regressive primitive meanings, rings are felt to have magical powers that can either preserve or destroy and that can control emotions in the self and in others. In the course of ordinary or pathological narcissistic regressions, rings (consciously associated with many positive feelings and achievements) also partake, insofar as they are Freudian symbols, of qualities associated with developmentally early defensive mechanisms and modes of psychic functioning (projection, introjection; idealization, devaluation). In the cases cited, rings seemed to be specifically associated with (and to symbolize)[6] sphinc-

6. Symbols, again, in the Freudian sense: meaning that they represent something in the external world that stands for an emotion-laden, body-ego-dominated part of the infant's primal psychological world—the universe of the body and its caretakers surrounded by poorly differentiated elements of the surrounding nursery (e.g., ring = anus). The ring as verbal and literary symbol is derived from a later period in psychic development and can of course have all sorts of

teric (largely anal) narcissistic defensiveness—the mind functioning as an emotional sphincteric counterpart primarily deadening and distancing affect but intermittently letting through primitive rage and primal polymorphous perverse sexual impulses. All this is relevant for victims of child abuse and deprivation.

---

meanings arising from those more mature levels, poetically equating any two elements in the real universe, within or without the body, concrete or abstract (e.g., ring = harmonious circle). Either kind of symbol can be felt as good *or* bad, but the verbal symbol can also be good *and* bad.

CHAPTER

6

Child Abuse and the
Concentration Camp

*And though I have the gift of prophecy, and understand all
mysteries, and all knowledge; and though I have all faith, so
that I could remove mountains, and have not the gift of
loving others [caritas], I am nothing.*
—1 Cor. 13:2

In Chapter 1, I quoted Randall Jarrell on abused children
who had grown up in "one of God's concentration camps."
There is an obvious parallel between soul murder and that
paradigm of abuse and destruction of the individual for our
time, the concentration camp. The differences between the
two kinds of experiences are many. I am not an expert on
concentration camps and so am pointing out only some important
similarities, making use of the works of Primo Levi
in relation to an area in which I have no direct contact. The
victim of soul murder is usually in some despot's charge;
every child is so dependent that tyranny and oppression by a

Epigraph: The *New Shorter Oxford English Dictionary* (1993 edition)
defines *charity* (the King James translation of the Latin *caritas*)
as "love of one's fellow men" (p. 375).

sadistic parent are easily possible. Much can be learned from the experiences of those who have survived the concentration camp that is applicable to the child victims of abuse by parents and parent substitutes.[1]

The unforgettability (and even irreversibility) of what can happen to a child raised in a totalitarian household (like the young Rudyard Kipling in the "House of Desolation") has been expressed by the Austrian philosopher Jean Améry, a non-Jew who was tortured by the Gestapo because he took part in the Belgian resistance and who was then sent to Auschwitz: "Anyone who has been tortured remains tortured. . . . Anyone who has suffered torture never again will be able to be at ease in the world, the abomination of the annihilation is never extinguished. Faith in humanity, already cracked by the first slap in the face, then demolished by torture, is never acquired again" (quoted in Levi, 1987, p. 12).[2]

The new inmate at first cannot believe in the sadistic order of the Lager. It is too terrible to be possible. This is like the denial and dissociation of the tortured child, who needs to hold onto some faith in a benevolent world and specifically in the idea of the parent as rescuer and who is then torn by the double bind of having to deny what can never be forgotten.

The acquisition of the need for denial is bad enough; even worse is the child's compulsion, subsequent to the traumatic

1. Both the Holocaust and child abuse are topics that can awaken inner conflicts and resistances. This can result in conflicts in those who have had (as far as their conscious awareness goes) no direct contact with these terrible experiences themselves but who react to what they hear and read with fascination, anxiety, avoidance—and even (in some) denial that resembles that of actual victims: "It's too terrible, it couldn't have happened."

2. Both Améry and (apparently) Levi ended as suicides.

events, to repeat the unforgettable torture, as victim, tormentor, or both. But, as I have stated, what seems to be the most
destructive effect of child abuse is probably the need to hold
onto the abusing parent or parent figure by identifying with
the abuser.

In Primo Levi's *The Drowned and the Saved* (1987), the
last book Levi, a survivor of Auschwitz, completed, he tells of
what were called the "crematorium ravens"—special squads
of prisoners who were allowed to survive for a time because
they were willing to perform the terrible and despicable tasks
involved in the operation of the crematoria. He feels that
conceiving and organizing such groups was "National Socialism's most demonic crime [which] represented an attempt to
shift onto others—specifically the victims—the burden of
guilt [as if to say], 'We, the master race, are your destroyers,
but you are no better than we are: if we so wish, and we do so
wish, we can destroy not only your bodies but your souls, just
as we have destroyed ours'" (1987, p. 37). This was—is—
soul murder. The soul murderer's guilt is assigned and passed
on to the victims, the faceless Jews and other prisoners who in
turn become degraded enough to forget the humanity of the
bodies from which they have to extract gold teeth and hair
and whose ashes they have to dispose of. Since the "ravens"
were witnesses to the crimes of the SS, they were eventually
murdered themselves.

Levi describes an unusual event

> that deserves to be meditated upon. In the gas
> chamber have been jammed together and mur-
> dered the components of a recently arrived convoy
> and the squad is performing its horrendous every-
> day work, sorting out the tangle of corpses, wash-
> ing them with hoses and transporting them to the

crematorium, but on the floor they find a young woman who is still alive. The event is exceptional, unique; perhaps the human bodies formed a barrier around her, sequestered a pocket of air that remained breathable. The men are perplexed; death is their trade at all hours, death is a habit because, precisely, "one either goes crazy the first day or gets accustomed to it," but this woman is alive. They hide her, warm her, bring her beef broth, question her; the girl is sixteen years old, she cannot orient herself in space or time, does not know where she is. [She] has gone through, without understanding it, the sequence of the sealed train, the brutal preliminary selection, the stripping, the entry into the chamber from which no one had ever come out alive. She has not understood, but she has seen; therefore she must die, and the men of the squad know it just as they know that they too must die for the same reason. But these slaves, debased by alcohol and the daily slaughter, are transformed; they no longer have before them the anonymous mass, the flood of frightened, stunned people coming off the boxcars: they have a person. (1987, p. 38)

They revive her and try to save her. Levi comments: "[A] single Anne Frank excites more emotion than the myriads who suffered as she did but whose image has remained in the shadows" (p. 39). A recognizable "person" is part of the human family and therefore hard to kill. ("Belief in the existence of other human beings as such is love": Simone Weil.)

The anecdote shows the temporary and almost miracu-

lous reversal of the defensive dehumanization (ridding oneself of the capacity to care about others) that being mistreated
and tormented imposes on the victims, pushing them toward
taking on the guilt of the tormentors and also toward becoming like them. I tell this story to show something about what
is necessary (and how hard it is) in order for formerly abused
children to be helped in therapy. They must become able
again to *feel* for another human being and for themselves as
human beings when their experience has led them to expect
that opening oneself to feeling leads to feeling *torment.*

One of the terrible lessons Levi learned in the camps
involved ordinary prisoners, not members of a "special
squad." He depicts the general tendency of the victims to
identify with the aggressors, with the need to take on some of
their characteristics in the struggle to survive. Levi describes
the Nazi attitude toward new arrivals at Auschwitz, people
whose souls were still relatively intact despite traumatic sep-
arations, who had not yet experienced the humiliating, dehu-
manizing routine of being treated as nonpersons and whose
bodies had not yet been subjected to beatings and starvation
rations. These people could not help expecting sympathy and
assistance from their fellow prisoners, if not from their cap-
tors. The Nazis viewed their retention of self-esteem as a
threat to the order of the camp and subjected the newcomers
to a

> sinister ritual . . . varying from Lager to Lager,
> but basically similar—which accompanied the ar-
> rival: kicks and punches right away, often in the
> face; an orgy of orders screamed with true or simu-
> lated rage; complete nakedness after being
> stripped; the shaving off of all one's hair; the fit-
> ting out in rags. [But worst of all] the entry ritual,

and the moral collapse which it promoted, was abetted more or less consciously by the other components of the concentration [camp] world: the simple prisoners and the privileged ones. It rarely happened that a newcomer was received, I won't say as a friend but at least as a companion in misfortune.

In the majority of cases, those with seniority (and seniority was acquired in three or four months; the change-over was swift!) showed irritation or even hostility. The "newcomer" . . . was envied because he still seemed to have on him the smell of his home. It was an absurd envy, because in fact one suffered much more during the first days of imprisonment than later on when habituation on the one hand and experience on the other made it possible to build oneself a shelter. He was derided and subject to cruel pranks, as happens in all communities with "conscripts" and "rookies" and in the initiation ceremonies of primitive peoples, and there is no doubt that life in the Lager involved a regression, leading back precisely to primitive behavior. . . . The despised crowd of seniors was prone to recognize in the new arrival a target on which to vent the humiliation, to find compensation at his expense, to build for itself and at his expense a figure of a lower rank on whom to discharge the burden of the offenses received from above. (1987, pp. 22–24)

This attitude is also evoked by sibling arrivals in the already deprived and terrible circumstances of family "concentration camps." It was not true of Kipling, whose six years of good treatment helped him resist a regimen that was, of course, much less destructive than that of the Nazis. It probably helped preserve Kipling's soul that he was able to protect and love his little sister as a "companion in misfortune" despite "Auntie's" attempts to divide the children.

An equally distressing instance of handing down "the offenses received from above" is the tendency of formerly abused children, when they come to parenthood, to abuse their own "newcomer" offspring.

Levi continues: "It is naive, absurd, and historically false to believe that an infernal system such as National Socialism was, sanctifies its victims: on the contrary, it degrades them, it makes them similar to itself, and then all the more when [the victims] are available, blank, and lack a political or moral armature" (1987, pp. 24–25).

Levi makes it clear that not all were corrupted to the same extent. For those who were stronger, who possessed that "moral armature," the soul murder could be partial—as with Kipling and with Levi himself. Levi's goodness and fine character shine through his writings. Although he could never forgive what had been done to him, he refused to indulge in what he called "the bestial vice of hatred." But the self-hatred, some masochistic combination of shame and guilt, broke through when he fell or hurled himself to his death down a stairwell. Romano (1993) points out that Levi had written in an early book (*Survival in Auschwitz*, 1947) that to "come down with diphtheria in a concentration camp would be 'more surely fatal than jumping off a fourth floor.' That book was written in 1947 in Levi's fourth floor flat on Corso Re Umberto" (p. 19).

The guilt involved in what seems to have been suicide[3] is

3. There is still no certainty as to whether it was suicide, but Ro-

documented by Levi's epigraph to *The Drowned and the Saved*, from Coleridge's *The Rime of the Ancient Mariner*:

> Since then, at an uncertain hour,
> That agony returns,
> And till my ghastly tale is told
> This heart within me burns. (II.582–85)

Levi here identifies not with the innocent albatross but with its murderer, the guilty mariner who tells the "ghostly tale." I know too little about Levi's childhood to be able to speculate intelligently about his predisposition to masochism prior to the traumata inflicted on him by the Nazis.

Freud has taught us that traumatic events leave those who suffer them with a compulsion to repeat the circumstances of overwhelming stimulation. This compulsion exists in victims of child abuse, drawing them into sadomasochistic behavior, with individual differences as to the predominance of masochism (as in Primo Levi) or sadism. Part of the compulsion to repeat seems to be the compulsion to establish a reversal of the past that, tragically, can almost never work out: that the next time the victim provokes a traumatic encounter, the parents or parent figures will turn out to have been magically transformed and *this time* will spare, love, and rescue the child. What results is usually an unconscious drive for punishment and the need to be a victim, alongside its opposite, the need to assume the role of the tormenting

---

mano's comments are impressive. When I presented a version of this chapter in Europe, someone in the audience who had known Levi commented that Levi's beloved mother was very ill and deteriorating at the time of his death. In her exhaustive biography, Myriam Anissimov (1997) feels that Levi jumped rather than fell—for multiple reasons, but largely out of taking on guilt for a crime he had not committed.

abuser. This combination makes for an infinite variety of conflict-ridden, contradictory, urgent sadomasochistic wishes, frequently expressed in obligatory traumatic repetitive action: cruelty and perverse sexual acts often directed against children.

Another phenomenon that I have encountered frequently in those who were seduced and abused as children is a terrible reaction to a sudden change in circumstances. Freud has taught us that insofar as we are neurotic (and we all are in some measure), we cannot help seeing the future as a projection of the past. This leaves the abused child with the bad expectations that are the consequence of past torments, along with a compulsion to repeat the torments. He or she then expects a *sudden* change to terrible, painful emotions and sensations such as occurred when the pleasures of seduction suddenly became unbearable overstimulation—or when peacefulness suddenly turned to the agonies of being beaten or the emotional pain of humiliation. The expectation of sudden change leading to attack is part of what Kipling called, in writing about his torment as a child, the need for constant wariness. Sometimes this is conscious, sometimes unconscious and masked by denial and indifference. These contradictory states of mind can be viewed as splits in the ego and are frequently maintained by autohypnosis or similar shifts in states of consciousness. A defensive use of hypnosis, autohypnosis in the service of denial, is depicted in Orwell's *1984* and in the reactions of concentration camp prisoners.

In my "soul murder" patients, I have found that the need to assume that one's parents are benevolent is the chief reason for denying the reality of the abuse. Children feel that they cannot survive without parenting; they need to believe that someone is shielding them from evil and death—that they are living in an ordered universe presided over by a benevolent god. It is hard for a child to maintain any joy or much sense of identity in the face of feeling not cared about, even hated, by mother or father. To defend against the inevitable destructive rage toward the abusing parent, the child usually takes on the guilt for the abuse—a guilt the abusing parent may or may not feel—as Améry and Levi may have taken on the Nazis' guilt in their suicides. Certainly all of my soul murder patients, even the predominantly sadistic ones, suffered from an intense unconscious need for punishment.

The child's craving for denial can triumph completely as far as consciousness is concerned; at the least denial is an ever-present, easy potential. This need to break with past and present realities, for self-brainwashing, is a great obstacle to treatment. The patient is compelled to repeat the past (hoping in vain that it will come out magically different, that "this time Big Brother will love me") rather than to remember and acknowledge with full (but oh so terrible) feeling what was suffered and at whose hands. The most difficult burdens that soul murder victims have had to carry are those of overstimulation and rage—the traumatic intensity of excitement and the rage of helpless frustration. They once had to bear more than is possible for children, and it made them both fear annihilation and want to kill; they were thenceforth in conflict over murderous and cannibalistic impulses. This made it necessary to develop massive defenses against all strong feeling. Some split off their emotions with characterologic obsessional isolation and intellectualization; some needed to function as "hollow men," as one of my patients put it, living "as-if" lives with little spontaneous feeling, becoming emotional zombies. Some, whom I have not seen in my consulting room, cannot contain their impulses and end up as criminals or addicts.

Paradoxically, what many of my patients needed most to distance was loving feeling (with its potential healing power), since it was usually out of love for the parent or parent figure that the naturally seducible and initially trusting child had delivered him- or herself to the original abuser. Love thenceforth is expected to lead to abuse. In therapy, feeling love for the predominantly benevolent therapist-analyst becomes a danger to the formerly abused child. This must be made manifest in the treatment. One patient said to me, "If I let myself love you, I open myself up to torment." Anger and hatred, difficult as they are, are sometimes easier to bear.

A large part of the danger of loving is that it threatens loss—furnishes motivation to give up the dominating unconscious psychic presence of the abusing parent who is "felt"[4] as indispensable and has become part of the victim's identity. Often in the course of growing up these children need to keep away—frequently with parental encouragement—from the saner and more loving households of their acquaintances to avoid raising doubts about what went on at home. When confronted by the contrasts that threaten to lift repression, the abused child will often resort to denial and to splits in awareness—isolating knowledge that would threaten the delusion of benevolent parenthood. Yet the paradox is that only a rehumanization—only love—can restore the soul. (The beginning of this can be seen in the story of the girl and the crematorium ravens.)

Perhaps the quality most needed by the therapist of children who have survived "one of God's concentration camps"

---

4. We speak and write of unconscious feelings; we intuit them in others, infer that they are there, but it is hard to grasp them empathically—especially in ourselves.

is patience. One must tolerate for long periods the patient's rage and masochistic provocation, and one must avoid realizing the sadomasochistic relationship that these patients are compelled to repeat. The inherent benevolence of the therapeutic situation, its predictability and reliability (in contrast to the sudden rages and unexpected crazy attacks in childhood), can in time allow some of these people who have suffered so much and have such bad expectations to trust the therapist enough to own their terrible distrust of themselves and of their abusing parents. (Another soul murder patient: "If you can't trust your mother, whom can you trust?") To help the patient establish the existence and extent of brainwashing is a formidable task. To remember and to feel fully means having to sustain murderous impulses and the expectation of being annihilated. The (usually perverse) sexual impulses associated with child abuse (present either because the child was seduced to start with or because the child needed compensatory sexual contact to try to undo physical, emotional, and narcissistic injury) are full of needed magical promise, and the patient is determined not to give up these gratifications.

The terror of losing the mental image of the caring parent must become conscious. The patient needs to learn in the therapy of his or her terrible dependency and of the other means of holding onto the abusing parental figure—identification. (To be the parent means not to see—and therefore not to be able to use one's will to distance—the parent.) In my experience, the central battle of these long and painful therapies is fought out over the question, "Is there life without mother (or father)?" If transference from the past onto the therapist or analyst is allowed, it is possible to establish what happened and how it affected the patient in a way that can be owned. If the patient can learn to tolerate his or her murderous rage toward the therapist, the need for denial decreases, and a great deal of change can come about. (Simply to be able to think about the abuse in childhood, even with provisional conviction, can help to contain its destructive effects.) This reverses the concentration camp conditions, which make thinking about the conditions of life unbearable. Levi states that the uncultivated generally survived better than the intellectuals because "they adjusted sooner to that act of 'not trying to understand' which was the first wise dictum one had to learn in the Lager. . . . Logic and morality made it impossible to accept an illogical and immoral reality" (1987, p. 115). One had to barbarize oneself to survive. Perhaps therapy can permit some soul murder survivors to attain something like what Levi describes as possible for the philosopher in the Lager: "He could perhaps break down the barrier of common sense that forbade him to accept a too ferocious reality as true; he could finally admit to living in a monstrous world, that monsters do exist, and that alongside Cartesian logic there existed the logic of the SS" (1987, p. 116).

Of course, if one is still "living in a monstrous world" such insight is not necessarily useful. In the camp denial is needed, and this can also be so with children still in the care of an abusing parent. I have the easier task of dealing with adults. The therapy of the formerly abused child must slowly build an inner world of emotion as well as thought that creates some conviction that the tormenting presences from childhood have lost their power. Only loving feeling evoked—not forced—by the therapist is able to do this. The child who was once abused must learn both to remember and to love. To be able to remember helps, but only if—alas, it is a big if—in the course of a long therapy the patient can learn to regard himself "as a person" (as the crematorium ravens regarded the girl who survived) and if some ability to love others can be tolerated, restored, or extended, can soul murder be significantly ameliorated.

II

The Background
of Soul Murder

CHAPTER

7

"That Fixed Obsession Which Is a State of Love"
Where Proust and Freud Can Be Both Wise and Wrong

My love is as a fever, longing still
For that which longer nurseth the disease;
Feeding off that which doth preserve the ill,
Th'uncertain sickly appetite to please.
My reason, the physician to my love,
Angry that his prescriptions are not kept,
Hath left me, and I desperate now approve
Desire is death, which physic did except.
And frantic-mad with evermore unrest;
My thoughts and my discourse as madmen's are,
At random from the truth vainly express'd;
* For I have sworn thee fair and thought thee bright,*
* Who art as black as hell, as dark as night.*
—*William Shakespeare*, Sonnet 147

The destructive effects of child abuse distort and inhibit the emotional life of the child. Soul murder, as I have said, tends to destroy the child's capacity for joy and inhibit the power to care and to love. This inhibition includes love of the self, but it is especially damaging to the capacity for love that can partially transcend narcissism, permitting caring for others.

It should not be necessary to state that there many circumstances besides child abuse and deprivation that give rise to an inability to care about oneself and others. Deficiencies stemming from the environment that interfere with optimal emotional development are always present to some degree, and so are inborn deficiencies, from the slight to the over-whelming—human beings are inevitably neurotic. For example, childhood autism (which also runs a gamut of severity; see Sacks, 1996) is generally considered to be based primarily on an inborn neurological deficiency; it too results in inhibition of the emotions required to relate meaningfully to others. Any such organic deficit of emotional expression is (inevitably, but not necessarily significantly) complicated by a resultant deficiency of parental emotional response. The relevance to victims of soul murder of the capacity to love others as well as oneself lies in the need for this kind of relatively nonnarcissistic love to neutralize the murderous aggression (terrifying in its intensity) that is always enhanced by the traumatization and emotional deprivation thrust on the child victim. Only love can ameliorate, and only being able to develop the capacity for love can make meaningful therapeutic contact possible—in life and in psychological therapy. Yet, especially in cases of sexual abuse by parents or parental substitutes, it was usually the need for love that opened the child up to traumatization in the first place. Therefore, paradoxically, love produces so much anxiety that the child avoids it, resorting to various ways of distancing all feeling. (Massive inhibitory defenses are also often broken through by bursts of feeling and impulsive action.)

The title of this chapter, from Proust, describes a primal, narcissistic quality of being in love. It appears in a description of the feelings of Marcel, the protagonist of *Remembrance of Things Past*, for his early love, Gilberte (see Proust, 1913–27, 3:278). Whether the model from Proust's life for Gilberte was a man or a woman is not really relevant.[1] Narcissistic love, Freud reminds us, is not confined to "inversion," as Proust was wont to call homosexuality, but is frequently predominant in heterosexuality as well. In fact the quotation from Proust in the title of this chapter is remarkably like Freud's description of "the peculiar state of being in love, a state suggestive of a neurotic compulsion" (1914, p. 88). It is unlikely that Proust had read Freud's 1914 paper before making his own almost identical observation—the statements may have been written at about the same time.

Proust was passionately involved in homosexuality, but he demonstrated the general potential for bisexuality by being able, at least occasionally, to make love to a woman.[2]

1. His biographer, Painter, believes it was a woman. It is generally agreed that the narrator's later, more involving beloved, Albertine (female, but a lover of women), was modeled largely on a man.

2. At least with one, Louisa de Mornand (see Painter, 1965, pp. 12–13), and perhaps others. Oscar Wilde, who was married for many years, fathered two children. According to W. B. Yeats, shortly after Wilde's release from Reading Gaol, Ernest Dowson took him to a brothel in France and helped pay for his session with a woman "for the purpose of [enabling him to] acquir[e] 'a more wholesome taste.' . . . The news of the incident quickly became known in the neighborhood and a small crowd began to collect round the entrance to the brothel where Dowson was waiting. Presently Wilde emerged from the building, evidently disappointed by his experience within. 'The first in

Proust's generalizations on love, especially sexual love, seem based predominantly on a projection of his own predilections and capacities. Proustian love is a losing enterprise: "*Les vrai paradis sont les paradis qu'on a perdus*" (The true paradises are those that one has lost—Proust, 1927, p. v; my translation). Compare the masochistic and mysogynistic replay of Tennyson by the lifelong bachelor Samuel Butler: " 'Tis better to have loved and lost, than never to have lost at all" (1903, p. 370). In Freud's "On Narcissism" (1914), love is portrayed as a narcissistic reduction that, as a matter of course, diminishes self-esteem. This of course can be so, but just as often love—especially if it is requited—raises one's self-esteem. The enhanced joy and self-confidence of happy love are scanted by both Proust and Freud (Grinberg and Kernberg point this out in their 1991 discussions of Freud's "On Narcissism").

In Proust's outline of the course of a love affair, after an indifferent or a short, happy beginning—the latter full of the promise that accompanies idealization—a period of boredom ensues that lasts as long as the lover feels himself to be loved. Excitement returns with the idea or actuality of the beloved's secret infidelity. The beloved inevitably turns out to stand for or enact the one who disappoints, rejects, denies, and betrays—the one who, almost by definition, does not desire the lover. This would be true, for example, of the homosexual man who wants only to be loved by "really" heterosexual men who despise and reject homosexuals. This is obviously impossible; that is, it can be accomplished only

ten years,' he said to Dowson in a low voice, 'and it will be the last. It was like cold mutton.' And then, raising his voice so that the crowd could hear, he added, 'But tell it in England, for it will entirely restore my character!' (Hyde, 1975, p. 330). Auden, a lifelong lover of men, had at least one rather long affair with a young woman.

magically, in fantasy. The prospect that can obsessively lead the lover on is held in the form of delusional promise. This inherently unhappy and masochistic love is, according to Proust, not only characteristic of the "invert" but emblematic of all kinds of sexual love. Love is a cruel delusion, but the delusion drives the lover on toward a kind of sexual entrapment that can end only in some combination of masochistic satisfaction and despair: "Loving is like an evil spell in a fairy-story against which one is powerless until the enchantment has passed" (Proust, 1927, p. 13).

Being unloved—betrayed—evokes a need that binds the lover to the beloved in a state of anguished longing. This renews the idealization but not necessarily the sexual pleasure, and often there is what Freud would call a split between the idealized beloved, with whom sex is forbidden or at least not particularly enjoyed, and the degraded, usually emotionally meaningless or at least unloved other, with whom sex and pleasure are allowed. ("A woman whom we love seldom satisfies all our needs and we deceive her with a woman whom we do not love" [Proust, 1927, p. 10].)

Freud, in generalizations that are startlingly similar to Proust's, first approached this kind of split in relation to the object of sexual love in a 1910 paper titled "A Special Type of Choice of Object Made by Men."[3] Freud cites the child's difficulty in connecting the "pure" mother with sexual matters. Both the madonna figure and the prostitute are connected with the original mother as objects of the child's sexual curiosity because of "the unconscious relation between them, since we long ago discovered that what, in the conscious, is found *split* into a pair of opposites often occurs in the unconscious as a unity" (p. 170, my italics). This implies

3. It was in this paper that he first used the term *Oedipus complex*.

that we all, as part of our oedipal fate, derive some splitting of the love object from our earliest attachment, including sexual attachment, to the mother figure who nourishes us.

In this paper Freud describes a specific pathological variation: a type of man who chooses as "love object" and wants to rescue a woman who belongs to someone else and who in some way has or deserves a bad sexual repute. This condition "may be termed rather crudely, 'love for a prostitute'" (p. 166). In Proust's novel, Swann's love for Odette, Marcel's love for Albertine, and the love of the Baron de Charlus for the male violinist Morel, mutatis mutandis, all conform to Freud's "type." And the following words of Freud could have come straight from *Remembrance of Things Past* (there is even some resemblance in the style of writing): "It is only when [such men] are able to be jealous that their passion reaches its height and the woman acquires her full value, and *they never fail to seize on an occasion* that allows them to experience these most powerful emotions" (1910, p. 167, my italics). What Freud is implying here is that heterosexual men of this type (and, we would now add, women, bisexuals, and homosexuals) are driven compulsively to repeat a jealous, triangular love that seems essentially aimed at preserving into adult life the power of a special, transformed, masochistic loser's version of the Oedipus complex.[4] The

4. In men this is frequently called the madonna-whore complex: all women are either saintly and asexual or degraded prostitutes. In women one frequently sees the division of love objects into men who are passive, loving, and asexual and those who are sadistic and sexually exciting. Of course, all sorts of shifting variations exist in individuals who split (and there is probably some such splitting of objects, full of individual qualitative and quantitative variation, in all of us). For homosexuals the "split" sexual objects may be of the same sex, but the qualities they possess or that are transferred to them can correspond to the "madonna-whore" category.

original triangle of mother, father, and child is displaced onto the idealized beloved (and, unconsciously with this type— the other side of the same coin, as it were—the despised prostitute-madonna), her mate, and the subject.

Freud adds an observation that Proust could have made about the effect of the loose-living Odette on Swann. In contrast to what one finds in "normal love," these prostitutelike women "are considered by men of our type to be *love-objects of the highest value*. . . . Their love-relationships with these women are carried on with the highest expenditure of mental energy, to the exclusion of all other interests. . . . These features of the love-relationships which I am describing show their *compulsive* nature very clearly" (pp. 167–68, italics Freud's).

Following the first phases of Proustian love, masochistic submission to the betraying, rejecting beloved begins and becomes an obsessive pursuit, with the concomitant sadism and murderous hatred largely suppressed, turned inward on the self, or displaced elsewhere. Freud would say that the beloved inevitably represents the forbidden incestuous objects: mother, father, and sibling—both from a period of early (preoedipal) dependent development and from a later time of beginning childhood genital sexuality (oedipal development). This developmental derivation of love (occurring in infinite individual variety) is true of everyone, but usually, with maturation, the parental incestuous bind is sufficiently weakened so that, without ever being lost in the psyche, it gets accompanied by the capacity to turn substantially to other people outside the family ("nonincestuous objects") as lovers with a flexibility and relative lack of splitting of the love object not found in Proustian love.[5]

5. In a 1920 paper Freud describes this type of "Proustian" choice in a homosexual woman.

As Proustian love regresses toward predominant masochism, there is, then, a vertical split in the self, with idealized
love taking over in one compartment of the mind, degraded
love in another. The one who betrays is idealized; the one
who gives sexual satisfaction is degraded. It is ultimately the
one the lover feels is unattainable who retains the power to
attract. My descriptions (Proust's are much better) characterize (again) the obsessive sexual love relationships that predominate in *Remembrance of Things Past.*

Proust shows the playboy bachelor, Swann, passing from
initial indifference to Odette de Crecy to obsessive love: "She
had struck Swann not, certainly, as being devoid of beauty,
but as endowed with a kind of beauty which left him indifferent, which aroused in him no desire, which gave him,
indeed, a sort of physical repulsion" (p. 213). Proust general-
izes, describing how a woman, by virtue of the lover's associations of her with former lovers, can become the object of
compulsive monogamy, as Odette does for Swann:

> We come to [Love's] aid, we falsify it by memory
> and by suggestion. Recognizing one of its symp-
> toms, we remember and *recreate* the rest. Since we
> know its song, which is engraved on our hearts in
> its entirety, there is no need for a woman to repeat
> *the opening strains*—filled with admiration which
> beauty inspires—for us to *remember* what follows.
> And if she begins in the middle—where hearts are
> joined and where it sings of our existing, hencefor-
> ward, for one another only—we are well enough
> attuned to that music to be able to take it up and
> follow our partner without hesitation at the appro-
> priate passage. (p. 214, my italics)

Proust's great novel is built symphonically, poly-
phonically; its architecture features the repetition, with vari-

ations, of the equivalent of musical themes. The "opening strains" in the "overture" that begins *Swann's Way* feature the child Marcel's unexpected indulgence supplied by his beloved mother's goodnight kiss, followed by her sharing his bed for the night. Thus, the narrator concludes, began the conflicts that resulted in his neurotic weakness. The incestuous contact becomes the repetitive theme that accompanies his obsessive loves—the deindividualized women coming to represent his first, forbidden love. Swann's love for Odette prefigures Marcel's for Gilberte and Albertine, and the incestuous theme is like the "little phrase" from Vinteuil's sonata (with its connotations of incestuous attachment as part of sexual love) that is the anthem of Swann and Odette's relationship.

Swann is an amateur of art. He (like Proust himself) worships Vermeer, about whom he is writing a never-to-be-finished monograph. Proust shows how Swann's love for Odette is enhanced by his connecting her with women depicted in favorite paintings—unconscious idealized sublimations of the unconscious incestuous attachment to mother:

> [Odette] struck Swann by her resemblance to the figure of Zipporah, Jethro's daughter, which is to be seen in one of the Sistine frescoes. He had always found a peculiar fascination in tracing in the paintings of the old masters . . . the individual features of men and women whom he knew. . . . Perhaps, having always regretted, in his heart, that he had confined his attention to the social side of life, had talked, always, rather than acted, he imagined a sort of indulgence bestowed upon him by those great artists in the fact that they also had regarded with pleasure and had introduced into their works such types of physiognomy as give

those works the strongest possible certificate of
reality and truth of life. . . . Perhaps . . . he felt
the need to find in an old masterpiece some such
anticipatory and *rejuvenating* allusions to personalities of today . . . and perhaps because the abun-
dance of impressions which he had been receiving
for some time past, even though they had come to
him rather through the channel of his appreciation of music [Proust is referring to listening with
Odette to Vinteuil's sonata], had enriched his appetite for painting as well—it was with an unusual intensity of pleasure, a pleasure destined to
have a lasting effect upon him, that Swann remarked Odette's resemblance to the Zipporah of
. . . Botticelli. . . . He no longer based his estimate
of the merit of Odette's face on the doubtful quality of her cheeks and the purely fleshy softness
which he supposed would greet his lips there
should he ever hazard a kiss. . . . The similarity
enhanced her beauty also, and made her more
precious. . . . The words "Florentine painting"
were invaluable to Swann. They enabled him . . .
to introduce the image of Odette into a world of
dreams and fancies which, until then, she had
been debarred from entering, and where she assumed a new and nobler form. . . . He could re-
erect his estimate of her on the sure foundations of
aesthetic principle; while *the kiss*, the physical possession[s] which would have seemed natural and
but moderately attractive had they been granted
him by a creature of somewhat blemished flesh
and sluggish blood, coming, as they now came, to
crown his adoration of a masterpiece in a gallery,

must, it seemed, prove supernaturally delicious. (pp. 243–45, my italics)[6]

The theme of the kiss again sounds here. Proust then evokes Vinteuil's daughter and her lover performing their incestuously contaminated lesbian act in front of her father's portrait:"[Swann] placed on his study table, as if it were a photograph of Odette, a reproduction of Jethro's daughter" (p. 245).

Even more regressively, the beloved comes to stand for indispensable aspects of the self. These Proustian and Freudian generalizations concern what Freud termed "narcissistic object choice" (1914, p. 88) in love, making for a love derived almost exclusively from a projection of part of one's self onto the beloved rather than primarily from the transference of the earliest love object, the parental figure, onto the beloved.[7]

6. Zipporah was the wife of Moses. She is presented in Exodus (4.24–25), in what is called in the edition I am quoting "an obscure passage," as a mother who has circumcised her own son—a castrative woman. This is softened by her doing so "for his own good," as it were, to prevent God from killing either her son (probably) or, and this is part of the obscurity, her husband, Moses (perhaps); it is implied that she is carrying out God's will. She, like Proust's mother, is thus presented as having the best of motives for the castrative effects on the son: "At a night encampment on the way [back to Egypt], the Lord encountered him and sought to kill *him*." (Who this "him" is, is obscure, as is the Lord's motive—it may be that a part of the text has been lost, but the murderous intent or threat seems to me to be aimed at the son rather than Moses.) "So Zipporah took a flint and cut off her son's foreskin, and touched his legs with it, saying, 'You are truly a bridegroom of blood to me!'" (*Torah*, pp. 104–5). The mother would appear to be mutilating the son's penis and making him her incestuous bridegroom. This is clearly, despite the obscurity, an oedipal story, which would have had resonances for Proust.

7. Here too, one would say that not all love is exclusively narcis-

Freud is, in places, less than satisfactory in his otherwise marvelous commentary and conclusions about what he obviously regards as a universal phenomenon—the mixture of more than one kind of narcissistic love. He shows considerable prejudice against both women and homosexuals in his early papers on love, and specifically in the 1914 paper "On Narcissism." Freud makes it clear that narcissism is part of all loving. (Even in 1914, he recognized the role of narcissism in the normal course of development [see Treurniet, 1991], which leads to the obvious fact of healthy alongside pathological narcissism.) Narcissism is certainly part of all living. We never completely outgrow our beginnings, however much these are transformed in subsequent development—but residues of the initial narcissistic attachments and the quality and quantity of their subsequent transformations exist in individually different dynamic mixtures.)[8]

Freud describes two kinds of relations to those we love.

---

sistic, but all love is at least in part narcissistic in the sense that all human phenomena represent some features from the earliest period of psychic development "alongside and beneath"—as Freud put it—later and more mature changes from our primal period of ontogenic existence.

8. This last qualification about myriad individual differences in even universal human qualities applies to all our psychological "laws": for a metaphoric example, which properly brings in body as well as mind, we are all—barring those with genetic physical defects—born with the same general facial features: yet the same combinations of organs result in an infinite variety of differences in our looks. Whatever our resemblances, no two of us—aside from identical twins—look quite the same. This metaphor stands for a truth about the psyche that it is easy to assume we all know, yet it is often brushed aside in the narcissistic heat of generalizing and oversimplifying theoretical tendentiousness.

Both are based on the earliest ties to the parental figures. We begin our love life by "loving" those who fulfill our needs (again, narcissistic needs). But these early godlike parental "objects" of our attachment probably start out registered in our minds as part of ourselves; they have to be separated out as "not-me" in the course of early differentiating ego development. Before acquiring the capacity to register within the mind a representation of mother as a love object—mother as a separate entity, a whole person—the child (as we conceive of him) begins to regard the breast (or the bottle that takes its place) as a part of the external world. This psychic piece of the mother fulfills his need for nourishment and comfort (together with its equivalents, the nursing bottle and comforter, and bodily accessories, the mother's arms and lap). In psychoanalytic jargon, the breast is a part-object. The external world thus starts as that which fulfills our basic needs for nourishment, comfort, and safety. Freud astutely informs us that at the very beginning of the process of separation from the mother (before the mother is realized as a whole person), if the infant were capable of adult thought and speech he might say, "The breast is a part of me, I am the breast" (1941, p. 299). So, in a way, the earliest object of the infant's love is partly—at first mostly—self; this becomes what Freud (1914) calls "narcissistic object choice."[9] In ordinary development this motivation persists, but a large part of it gets

9. The breast as separated-out "part-object" precedes the mother as whole object in the development of the mental registration of the first other and the external world: that which exists external to the registration of the self. First comes the breast as "part of me," then (past the establishment in the mind of boundaries) the separated breast, then the mothering person, and finally the rest of the two worlds initially beyond our conscious awareness: that external to the body and that within the body external to the mind.

transformed into "anaclitic object choice" (p. 87), which is based on the later separated-out mothering figure (though at first it is still predominately narcissistic since it is initially based almost wholly on need fulfillment). Anaclitic attachment, Freud says, means "that a person may love . . . (a) the woman who feeds him; (b) the man who protects him" (p. 90). (More basic, I would say, is the parent who feeds *and* protects him.) In "narcissistic attachment," by contrast, a person may love "(a) what he himself is, . . . (b) what he himself was, (c) what he himself would like to be, (d) someone who was once part of himself" (p. 90). This vista leads to all sorts of combinations and complexities.

Note here how insistent Freud is on exemplifying everyone with "he" and "him," not "she" and "her." Today we would see both men and women loving people based on these models, and we realize how confused, conflict-ridden, and shiftable such narcissistically based motivations are in most people. A minority are truly fixated and seem compulsively (or obsessively, as Proust put it) condemned to repeat the earliest patterns. We also observe how the father can sometimes be viewed as the feeder and the mother as the protector (occasionally or predominantly) by boy and girl alike. We are now more attuned (and it is Freud who has led us to this view) to expect kaleidoscopic complexities in the mind.

Freud, wisely, says:

> We have, however, not concluded that human beings are divided into two sharply differentiated groups, according as their object-choice conforms to the anaclitic or to the narcissistic type; we assume rather that both kinds of object-choice are open to each individual, though he may show a preference for one or the other. We say that a

human being has originally two sexual objects—
himself and the woman who nurses *him*—and in
doing so we are postulating a primary narcissism
in everyone, which may in some cases manifest
itself in a dominating fashion in his object choice.
(p. 88, my italics)

Freud's use of "him" (this was long before the awkward and
unmelodious use of "him or her" for "everyone" became a
politic injunction) perhaps has special significance because,
as I have stated, he is unfair to both women and homosexuals
in the general statements that precede and follow the above
quotation. He describes coming upon "narcissistic object
choice" largely in studying homosexuals (note that he is
writing here of love object choice from a period of development later than infancy):

We have discovered, especially clearly in people
whose libidinal development has suffered some
disturbance [And whose has not? we would ask
today.], such as perverts and homosexuals, that in
their later choice of love-objects they have taken as
a model not their mother but their own selves.
They are plainly seeking *themselves* as a love-ob-
ject, and are exhibiting a type of object-choice
which must be termed "narcissistic." (p. 88,
Freud's italics)

Freud appears to be talking mainly about male homosexuals here. In his time homosexuality was thought of, even by
most homosexuals, as invariably an aberration from ordinary
development. It is only in recent years that most psycholo-
gists have fully realized how complex a phenomenon homosexuality is, how much we do *not* know about it, and how

unsatisfactory it is as a meaningful categorizing designation—that is, how relatively little one can use a person's sexual behavior as a guide to his or her psychic characteristics. Freud, in his compassion and with his firm belief in the universality of human constitutional bisexuality, was far ahead of his contemporaries in seeing the human complexities of "inversion."[10] But Freud went through a period of thinking and feeling before he learned so much from his female students and analysands (and this period included 1914), and he displayed a definite antifeminine prejudice about which he appeared to have had little insight. He felt (with a kind of certainty in an area full of mystery) that women and homosexual men (whom he assumed were more "feminine" than heterosexual men) were more inclined to "narcissistic object choice" than "masculine" men. The following words have understandably offended many contemporary feminists, especially those lacking historical perspective:

> Complete object-love of the attachment type is, properly speaking, characteristic of the male. It displays the marked sexual overvaluation which is doubtless derived from the child's original narcissism and thus corresponds to a transfer of that narcissism to the sexual object. . . . A different course is followed in the type of female most frequently met with, which is probably the purest and truest one. . . . Women, especially if they grow up with good looks, develop a certain self-

10. He clearly saw homosexuality in his own impulses, as documented by the remark he made to Jones about the meaning of his fainting fits: "There is some piece of unruly homosexual feeling at the root of the matter" (Jones, 1953–55, p. 1:317).

contentment which compensates them for *the social restrictions that are imposed on them* in their choice of object. Strictly speaking, it is only themselves that such women love with an intensity comparable to that of the man's love for them. Nor does their need lie in the direction of loving, but of being loved. (pp. 88–89, my italics)

It is not easy to maintain a sense of humor about the implication that most women are incapable of loving. It would be both truer and simpler and even sadder to accept, as I believe one should, that most people—men and women alike—are for much of the time rendered incapable of loving by transient and commonplace narcissistic regressions. It is easy to condescend to Freud as a proper Victorian gentleman and to forget that we know better than he in some ways since we can see farther than he did in large part because we are standing on his shoulders. Note that Freud at least mentions the social restrictions imposed on women. He also says that although "a comparison of the male and female sexes . . . shows that there are fundamental differences between them in respect of their type of object-choice, . . . these differences are *of course* not universal" (p. 88, my italics). And he somewhat grudgingly adds: "I am ready to admit that there are quite a number of women who love according to the masculine type and who also develop the sexual overvaluation proper to that type."

I think someone who understood women better would not think of "sexual overvaluation" of the other in love as characteristically masculine or feminine. Kohut (1971) has helped us to see that such evaluation (clearly a part of falling in love, as Freud states) is inherently narcissistic; "anaclitic" attachment based on the early parent is "overevaluative," as is "narcissistic" attachment based on the self—for both sexes. The human achievement that accomplishes maturation is the *partial* mastery or taming of narcissism (of the residues of early, primal psychic development)—a partial mastery that reduces without eliminating the overevaluation. True loving means caring for the other and the self—with a balanced mixture of idealization and devaluation (a balance that neutralizes and screens out some of the perfervid emotions, the "too-muchness of early narcissistic psychic development). Neither in Freud's 1914 view nor in Proust's near-contemporary one is there a role for mutuality in love (a point made about Freud by Yorke [1991, p. 41]). Both men's views of love also scant the elation, the lift in self-esteem, of happy love. The capacity for true love (what Freud calls "complete object love" [1914, p. 89])—and, it should be added, mutuality and an enhancement of self-regard—seems to me to be at best only intermittently attained by most of us, almost never attained by some, and dependably (or seemingly dependably) present in the relatively rare best of human beings. Yet its intermittent presence is, Freud rightly assures us, necessary for psychic health. And this is what soul murder victims are, for the most part, deprived of.

Freud finds this "complete object love" in women, as does Proust, in the mother's attitude toward her child, especially her son. (Both men are projecting here some part of the idealized mother that has become part of their own self-image.) Freud says: "Even for narcissistic women, whose attitude towards men remains cool, there is a road which leads to complete object-love. In the child which they bear, a part of their own body confronts them like an extraneous object, to which, starting out from their narcissism, they can then give complete object-love" (1914, pp. 89–90). It is true that the child was once part of the mother's body, but it is hard as a father to feel that this inevitably makes a father's love turn out to be less than a mother's. As a psychoanalytic observer (of self and others) I know how much individual variation there is here—which may be based on the fact that both men and women as individuals bear different proportions of identification with both mothers and fathers, and each in individually different combinations of individually different parents.

The reader will have gathered by now that, without discounting anatomical differences and Freud's dictum that "anatomy is destiny," I think that human adaptability in the face of our bisexual instinctual endowment can, for most of us, make for less difference between men and women in our inevitably compromised sexual destiny as individual neurotic human beings than is generally assumed. And whatever is dictated by gender (by anatomy as destiny) wins out in a matrix of ambivalence and discontent, joy and sorrow, love and hatred. In my book *"Father, Don't You See I'm Burning?"* (1991), I describe a not unusual day in my practice when all the women patients want to be men and vice versa, all the heterosexuals want to be homosexuals and vice versa. My conclusion is that we all begin with and to varying extents retain the wish to be and have everything. If this basic assumption is right, it follows that frustration in some degree is our inevitable burden—a discontent imposed not only as a price of civilization but as a product of our biological nature.[11] This is what I think Freud meant by his characteriza-

11. The child's wish for everything, a universal wish we never outgrow completely and one that can return full blast in regression, is marvelously expressed in *King Lear*—that play so full of "nothings" (see Shengold, 1991b)—about the difficulty of renouncing the re-

tion of bisexuality as the biological bedrock of the mind's resistance to change.

Even in what Freud depicts as, potentially, the least ambivalent love of which human beings are capable—that between mother and child—hatred is inevitably also present. For all of us, the Sphinx, the Sphinx as mother (Jocasta),[12] haunts Thebes, and reading her riddle and killing her off are continuing needs. This painful truth can be demonstrated in anyone (although of course we are all slightly different), and therefore it can always be found in the work of writers who specialize in confession, self-demonstration, and self-observation. This is spectacularly observable in both Freud and Proust. Freud's accent on aggression's role in psychic motivation comes after his 1914 paper. Proust shows his awareness of the murderous intensity of aggression, but its oedipal aim in his great novel (or, better, the terrible, cannibalistic pre-

---

newed narcissism that comes with old age and second childhood. The mad Lear, after the terrible storm on the heath, is reproaching malignant or indifferent fate (represented by nature and its thunder, wind, and rain) as embodied in his two elder, formerly sycophantic daughters, who have now exposed him to the terrifying uncontrollable elements: "[It was] when the rain came to wet me, once, and the wind to make me chatter; when the thunder would not peace at my bidding. . . . Go to, they are not men o' their words: they told me I was *everything;* 'tis a lie, I am not ague-proof" (4:6:102–107, my italics). In renouncing his narcissistic claims to omnipotence, the old man turns Goneril and Regan into men; symbolically, the two women stand for the mother; in consciousness, the more dispensable father is easier to hate than the mother.

12. Really the Sphinx as primal parent. The psychic picture of the bisexually conceived-of primal parent (whose malignant propensities are colored by the aggressive preponderance of the drives early on) is usually derived from the internalization of the actual mother or mothering person. But in subsequent development this figure can be chiefly transferred onto the father.

oedipal intensity of its oedipal aim) is more evident in specific incidents in the novel—Mademoiselle Vinteuil's making lesbian love on a sofa in front of a picture of her beloved dead father; the letter by de Charlus revealing that he had the intention of murdering Morel—and in Proust's life, by avoidances and enactments, than in his written generalizations.[13]

Freud and Proust are among the greatest and wisest commentators on psychology, appreciating and extending our knowledge of its infinite variety. Perhaps no other writers except Shakespeare have shown us more of what is so painful to know about human beings—not only about childhood sexuality and incestuous love but about the perhaps even more difficult and developmentally earlier drive to murder—in short, our (in my view, undeniable) instinctual nature.

There are many papers and books about love and even about "that fixed obsession which is a state of love," many of them sounding quite authoritative.[14] This chapter has fea-

---

13. In the novel, Marcel gives "beloved" Aunt Leonie's furniture to a brothel. And according to the author's biographer, "In the dark Paris of the war years Proust frequented a sinister establishment known as the Ballon d'Alsace, a Turkish bath which was also a male brothel, partly furnished, thanks to his generosity, with armchairs and couches which had once been the pride of his dead parents' drawing room" (Painter, 1956, p. 46). This acting out of the fantasy of degrading and avenging himself on his parents (their sofa could have corresponded to that of Mlle. Vinteuil) is part of the dark side of Proust's intense love of both of them, especially his mother. Another example is Proust's hiring men, after his mother's death, to bring rats to his home, where he would watch while the men beat the rodents and stabbed them with a woman's (his mother's?) hatpin (see Painter, 1965, p. 269).

14. There are some recent psychoanalytic books on love (e.g.,

tured two of the best. But of course Freud and Proust can occasionally be limited or wrong as well as wonderfully right. They are wrong to neglect the potential reciprocality of love and mistaken in making love inherently a compulsively absorbing but predominantly unhappy state, in their prejudices against the feminine (alongside wonderful insights), and in their confining of sexual love almost entirely within its narcissistic limitations. The similarity of their views is remarkable.

Love is not a topic that is suited to the dogmatic. I hope I have left the reader with some notion of how much we do not know about it. I want to finish the chapter with praise of the two masters. In the passage in *Swann's Way* in which Proust describes Mlle. Vinteuil and her lesbian friend making love before the picture of her dead father, playing with the idea of spitting on his portrait, he describes Mlle. Vinteuil as displaying "the appearance of evil" (p. 178):

> A sadist of her kind is an artist in evil, which a
> wholly wicked person could not be, for in that case
> the evil would not have been external, it would

---

those by Martin Bergmann and Ethel Person) that are good, but in the vast general literature I will mention only Stendhal's *De L'Amour* (1822), in which the great novelist says of passionate love, "it is madness" (p. xiv) and "it must be spoken of as of a malady" (p. xx). He goes on to describe "real" love, in contrast to more ordinary "sympathy-love . . . sensual love . . . [and] vanity-love" (pp. 4–5), as rare. His concept of "crystallization" is a wonderful description of idealization, resembling the Proustian-Freudian mixture I have outlined in this chapter—especially his "second crystallization" (p. 10), in which he describes love as a kind of obsession (without using the word). For Stendhal too, the obsession condenses around doubts and suspicions about the beloved, but in his formula this follows rather than leads to the idealization of the beloved.

have seemed quite natural to her, and would not even have been distinguishable from herself; and as for virtue, respect for the dead, filial affection, since she would never have practised the cult of these things, she would take no impious delight in profaning them. Sadists of Mlle Vinteuil's sort are creatures so purely sentimental, so naturally virtuous, that even sensual pleasure appears to them as something bad, the prerogative of the wicked, and to make their partners do likewise, in order to gain the momentary illusion of having escaped beyond the control of their own gentle and scrupulous natures into the inhuman world of pleasure. . . . It was not evil that gave her the idea of pleasure, that seemed to her attractive; it was pleasure, rather, that seemed evil. . . . She could delude herself for a moment into believing that she was indeed enjoying the pleasures which, with so perverted an accomplice, a girl might enjoy who really did harbour such barbarous feelings towards her father's memory. Perhaps she would not have thought of evil as a state so rare, so abnormal, so exotic, one in which it was so refreshing to sojourn, had she been able to discern in herself, as in everyone else, that indifference to the sufferings one causes which, whatever other names one gives it, is the most terrible and lasting form of cruelty. (pp. 179–80)

Proust is here mirroring a version of part of his own nature— a split in responsible awareness of the contradictions between the sadistic impulses he has toward the parents and his tender love (*caritas*) for them. The last sentence of the quotation shows Proust as a master psychologist, however much he may be using the generalization to cover up his own disturbing "evil" propensities. Proust recognized the ubiquity of narcissistic indifference to even the most beloved other, a part of human nature that includes but also goes beyond ambivalence. He, like Freud, recognized how difficult and precious it is to care and to love.

8

Comments on Freud's
"A Child Is Being Beaten"

Helena: *I am your spaniel; and Demetrius,*
The more you beat me, I will fawn on you.
Use me but as your spaniel, spurn me, strike me,
Neglect me, lose me; only give me leave
Unworthy as I am to follow you.
What worser place can I beg in your love,—
And yet a place of high respect with me,—
Than to be used as you use your dog?
—*William Shakespeare,* A Midsummer-Night's Dream

This chapter is an expanded version of a paper published in *On Freud's "A Child Is Being Beaten,"* edited by Ethel Spector Person (1997).

Epigraph: Shakespeare, to judge from his use of imagery, hated dogs: "It is quite certain that one of the things which rouses Shakespeare's bitterest and deepest indignation is feigned love and affection assumed for a selfish end. . . . Now whenever the idea, which affects [Shakespeare] emotionally, of false friends or flatterers occurs, we find a curious set of images which play round it. These are a dog or spaniel, fawning and licking. . . . This is so marked in its repetition that it has been noted by others" (Spurgeon, 1935, p. 195).

Soul murder is engendered by, evokes, and flourishes in the climate of sadomasochistic phenomena. Some sadomasochism is present in all of us to varying extents: part of our sexuality, part of our character. It is of course enhanced if there is sexual and violent abuse in one's childhood. But sadomasochistic sexual perversion, a passionate investment in beating or being beaten, arises from many sources. Sadomasochistic sexual perversion (acted out with others or expressed autoerotically in perverse fantasies) is frequently present with compulsive force in adults who have suffered soul murder in childhood.

In a 1919 paper on beating fantasies, Freud presented conclusions and mysteries that follow from his observations of specific sequences of sadomasochistic phenomena in six patients. (He regards sadomasochism as an essential part of human nature.) The sequences center around beating fantasies, which Freud calls "the essence of masochism" (p. 189). Freud's focus in this paper raises questions central to the exploration of soul murder, some of which challenge ordinary assumptions. Why do we want to hurt others, and why do we want to hurt ourselves? Why would anyone want to be beaten? How do such wishes become subject to a compulsion to repeat? How do they get sexualized? How does this become sexual perversion?

Perverse sexual masochistic impulses exist in many varieties of conflictual ambiguity. They tend to involve the promise (in fantasy) of overwhelmingly intense sexual pleasure, which, if enacted, can transiently overcome the usually concomitant, potentially inhibitory "unpleasure"—anxiety, disapproval, and disgust.

When commenting on, reading, and quoting Freud, one needs the perspective in time of a historian of ideas, of Freud's and Freudian ideas. In recent years we have endured a flow of papers and books commenting on and criticizing Freud's case histories. Many of these are without much sense of chronological sequence; they are prone to condemn the Freud of the early 1900s for not anticipating his own later views and even for not following current shifts in psychological trends. Freud wrote "A Child Is Being Beaten" in 1918; it was published in 1919, before many of his major theoretical revisions of instinct theory (1920), his model of the mind (1923), and the theory of anxiety (1926). He had not yet arrived at any systematic view of the psyche in its earliest years—the preoedipal phase of libidinal and ego development—nor had he begun to modify his views on women and the role of the mother (see Young-Bruehl, 1988). And he had something further to say on masochism (1924, 1940, and elsewhere).

In considering the evolution of "Freudian" ideas subsequent to the master's death, I have already used the metaphor of Freud as the giant on whose shoulders later psychological thinkers stand. Some writers seem unaware of this, and others are eager to bite those shoulders. The past few years have seen a great acceleration of attacks on Freud's character and ideas, ranging from the justified and balanced to the biased and murderous. The literary and cultural critic Harold Bloom titled one of his books *The Anxiety of Influence* (1973; see also 1994). The phrase epitomizes his description of tendencies in creative intellectual life to absorb *and* to get rid of the pervasive dominant ideas of the previous generation. This wish to destroy ideas would involve (for psychoanalysts and perhaps for Bloom) deeper unconscious wishes derived from murderous and cannibalistic oedipal and preoedipal impulses. These are sometimes not well sublimated, and primitive, hate-filled passions are revealed, especially in former followers of charismatic intellectual leaders. The emotional road from apostle to apostate has been well traveled in recent decades by one-time adherents of Marx and Freud. Freud-bashing is current intellectual fashion, at least in the United States; Freud has become the child who is being beaten as well as the giant who is being bitten. Looking at his 1919 work may supply some perspective.

The psychologically afflicted who come for help require the therapist's empathy. This is not always easy to supply. The ideal precept for empathy is Terence's "Nothing human is alien to me" (*Heautontimorumenos* I.i.25). The would-be helper attempting to live up to this impossible standard encounters the greatest difficulties when the patient's pathology occupies the psychic realm that Freud locates "beyond the pleasure principle" (1920). In that metaphorical place of illogical and self-destructive mystery exist the murky paths to the understanding of human aggressive phenomena—murder and cannibalism, not only aimed at others (where they can sometimes make defensive and adaptive sense) but also turned inward toward the self, in contradiction to our insistent assumption that we are motivated by instinctual self-preservation.

Aggressive impulses become mixed with sexual ones at some time in the course of early psychic development. The amalgam we call sadism—sexual excitement and even delight in wishing, watching, or causing the suffering of others—is puzzling enough. (Human beings need to cling to the myth of original goodness in paradise.) We experience even more difficulty in following the emotional logic of masochism—an admixture of sexual arousal and aggression turned back on oneself. Sadism and masochism always occur together, as a package, with each human being having an individual, dynamically changeable pattern of confluence. The sadomasochistic impulses are further differentiated (as they are manifested in conscious fantasy and experience) by the countless individual variations of psychic defenses arrayed against them. These infinite varieties produce phenomena formed from the same components, but no two combinations are exactly alike. One of the incidental benefits of doing psychoanalytic work is the excitement of the discovery of fresh composites in the course of exploring these specific idiosyncratic differences.

We know about, yet do not easily accept, the existence of the destructive, evil part of human nature—especially as it operates in ourselves and our parents. (This relates to soul murder.) Can such things really be? Turning away from inexorable reality requires stupidity or delusion and denial. Of course, we are all prone to and even sometimes need such denial (and delusions) and do not easily—and perhaps never completely—give up the promise of Eden, at least in relation to ourselves (see Shengold, 1995). It is perhaps hardest of all to accept aggression as inherent in human biological nature as part of phylogenesis: inherited instinctual drives. This piece of Freudian doctrine (already incipiently present in his 1919 paper but tellingly and pessimistically spelled out in "Beyond the Pleasure Principle" [1920] and "Civilization and Its Discontents" [1930]) has been especially under siege in recent years. It is obviously more reassuring to emphasize the less tragic, invariably present environmental contribution to aggression: to view aggression as a result of inevitable frustration, bad parenting, bad social forces, even—for some—bad supernatural forces.[1] There is more hope that at least amelioration can be achieved when evil comes, or is felt

1. The devil, or an equivalent magically endowed malignant adversary, has been a universally needed figure on which to project and transfer evil. *Satan* (Hebrew for "adversary") does not appear in Genesis but later, in 1 Chronicles and in Job.

as coming, from without rather than from our inherently destructive animal nature.[2] Narcissism pushes us toward belief in some "higher purpose" dedicated to the centrality and improvement of human beings, oneself in particular. But wisdom, *if* present and permitted, does not allow one to count on this.

The darker side of such narcissistic insistence is the developmentally determined human tendency to attribute all evil initially to the outside; this touches on the difficulty of judging accusations of child abuse. God as well as the devil has a psychological origin (I am not commenting on the validity of religious belief) in universal unconscious fantasies centering around good and bad omnipotent, primal parent figures. The influx of evil in these fantasies, which may or may not be based on historical actuality, can be attributed by some to the crime of soul murder—abuse and neglect in childhood at the hands of diabolical parental figures. The inherent inadequacies of parental care during the long period of separation and development inevitably result in the actuality of some neglect and abuse for everyone. Our pathogenic fantasies can, but do not always, lead to traumatic intensities of feelings, depending on inborn and developed vulnerabilities and weaknesses. Emotional intensities can in turn give rise to a compulsion to repeat traumatic situations that are full of sadomasochistic impulses. This is especially likely to happen in those who have suffered traumatization and deprivation in childhood. And the compulsion to repeat does bring about a passing down of soul murder from one generation to another, the former victim identifying with the

2. Lionel Trilling (1955) felt that there may be something hopeful in the possibility of some biological evolutionary manifestation that could change our nature in a way that might reverse the self-destructive direction of our culture.

aggressor and doing to the next generation what was done to him or her (see Shengold, 1989).

Freud's paper begins with a clinical statement that is still valid: "It is surprising how often people who seek analytic treatment . . . confess to having indulged in the phantasy: 'A child is being beaten'" (p. 179). In his practice Freud found that this fantasy (which begins in early childhood) at some point becomes associated with masturbation. As maturation proceeds, the fantasy-action combination tends to acquire a repetitive, compulsive intensity. Freud comments on the probable general prevalence of the fantasy and its consequences, viewing the fantasy-masturbation complex as a transient developmental phenomenon of all children, part of an "infantile perversion" (p. 181) that *sometimes* develops pathological chronicity and intensity.[3]

Beating fantasies, although initiated earlier, become reinforced, Freud says, when the six-year-old goes to school and sees others, generally boys, being beaten (this was 1918): "It was impossible, on account of the one-sidedness of the material, to confirm the first *suspicion* that the relation was an inverse one. [The patients] were very seldom beaten in their childhood, or were at all events not brought up by the help of the rod" (1919, p. 180, my italics).

We need to question Freud's "suspicion" (although not necessarily to reject it). Uneasiness arises especially in view of our current knowledge that Freud's daughter Anna, whom he took into analysis in 1918 (shortly before he started to write "A Child Is Being Beaten"), was a principal supplier of her father's observations on masturbatory beating fantasies (see

3. This idea that beating fantasies are developmentally "normal" when transient but pathological if they persist ("fixation") is also the view expressed by the Novicks in their authoritative 1995 paper.

Young-Bruehl, 1988). I feel that the "suspicion" was based in part on Freud's presumable knowledge that his daughter was not beaten at home; I therefore doubt its general validity.[4] I have seen (or heard about in supervising) adult patients with similar beating fantasies who convincingly report memories of having been beaten in childhood, at home or at school. There are also others in whom no such memories of beating (or other forms of child abuse) emerge in analysis (and may never have existed) but who nonetheless have registered terrifying and exciting *expectations* of being beaten similar to those described in Freud's paper. Individuals from both groups can retain beating fantasies that continue into adult life.

Memoirs, biographies, and fiction of the past few centuries, especially by authors from Russia and England (associated with serfdom and public schools, respectively), have familiarized readers with generations of children who have undergone regular home and school beatings involving the free use of rod, cane, and whip. Notable here are accounts by Dickens, Turgenev, Dostoevsky, Trollope, Samuel Butler, Swinburne, Chekhov, Kipling, and Orwell. Beating and watching beatings are especially associated with slavery (*Uncle Tom's Cabin*, mentioned by Freud) and serfdom (Turgenev, Dostoevsky). Soul murder is a relevant designation for most of these instances from literature and life.

Freud describes the acquisition of the "infantile perversion" (the beating fantasy plus masturbation) as an "event"

4. Freud has been condemned, quite rightly, for taking his own daughter into analysis. That he was a child-beater does not follow; I am not trying to suggest that unlikely role. Physical punishment of children was frequent enough in Freud's time, and probably some was administered to Anna. But the expectation in fantasy would have been enough to lead to her sadomasochistic wishes and fears.

(p. 182).⁵ This seems somewhat ambiguous. Is it the masturbatory action that turns the fantasy into an event? Might not the fantasy itself sometimes be powerful enough to constitute an event? Freud certainly thought so. He brings up the congenital constitutional factor (here, previous premature sadistic development), which always interacts with what has happened or is happening to a child in producing psychic illness. In this book I have insisted that it can be extremely difficult for the therapist to assess "what really happened" in the patient's past. Freud in this paper touched on the sometimes seemingly unsolvable mystery of pathogenesis.

The paper contains one of Freud's most forthright statements about recovering memories: "Strictly considered—and why should this question not be considered with all possible strictness?—analytic work deserves to be recognized as genuine psycho-analysis only when it has succeeded in removing the amnesia which conceals from the adult his knowledge of his childhood from its beginning (that is, from about the second to the fifth year)" (p. 183). I feel that Freud, in idealizing memory recovery, wanted to emphasize the genetic principle, the need to trace psychic pathology to its roots in the first five years of life by "recovering" the past—specifically, by reviving the Oedipus complex in the analysis. In 1918 Freud had a more static idea of memories than we would have today. He did not yet appreciate the importance of working on a variety of resistances and on defenses other than repression, nor did he yet grasp the full implications of the development of the ego and of object relations.

Freud's prescribed strictness would also no longer seem

5. The German word he uses is *Ereignis*, "event, incident, happening"; I believe this has wider connotations than the English *event*—of having lived through something experienced mainly as coming from the outside that is taken in and made into one's own.

appropriate in the light of currently accepted ideas in psychology and neurology about the difficulty of recovering historical truth and the shifting nature of memory. We can retain historical truth as an impossible goal in our impossible profession, but it seems necessary to abandon the concept of fixed memories as well as Freud's related archeological metaphors for memory recovery. We need instead to study the patient's current psychic *registrations* of the earliest years of life (as they exist in memory and fantasy), including their vicissitudes—especially the failures of those registrations.[6] Therapists should always keep in mind the possibility (and with some patients the probability) that something traumatic actually did happen. (I have counseled the suspension of disbelief in the possibility of soul murder as a starting attitude.)

I have found, as have others (see Valenstein, 1973), that patients (whether they are soul murder victims or not) who are repetitively and chronically masochistic are very difficult to treat because it is hard for them to sustain the motivation to give up the current sadistic replacements for internalized sadistic parental figures (and sometimes the original parent or parents). They tenaciously hold onto what can be almost an addiction to painful situations and, as Valenstein empha-

6. The adult mind has "registered" the past in a dynamic state that features (1) patterns compulsively repeated in fantasy, impulses, and actions that are projected and transferred and (2) "memories" (I use the quotation marks to denote unreliability) constantly shifting in relation to contents and conviction about validity and subject to life-long transformations as maturation proceeds. Reconstructions, based on (usually distorted) revivals of the past in transference and projection onto the analyst and other important people in the patient's life, are needed to supplement "memories." I view "memories" as an often indecipherable and invariably distorted mix of historical and psychological truth.

sizes, a negative therapeutic reaction (a tendency to reverse quickly any significant psychic improvement). Murder is turned inward, libidinized, and mental representations of parent and early self are preserved.

Freud presents the developmental "transformations of beating fantasies" (p. 184). The presentation can at times give the unfortunate impression that these are *the* transformations, scanting the countless potential individual variations to be found.

My patient J was an intelligent and capable man driven to psychoanalysis by anxiety, work inhibition, intermittent low self-esteem, and distress about masochistic sexual impulses (generally not acted out). When he was about six, his parents were in a motor accident that hospitalized and disabled them for a long time. J and his slightly older sister were unable to be cared for at home. His sister was taken in by relatives, but J was sent to a private boarding school, where he was younger than the other boys in his class. It was a kind of military academy with a good reputation for scholarship; the school was upper-class, eastern, Protestant. Although seemingly almost chauvinistically American, it was vaguely based on the British public school model, featuring the study of classical languages. The boys were caned for misconduct as a matter of course. This appears to have been due to the tastes and training of the headmaster, who kept a collection of well-used birches in his office. There were daily line-ups of boys waiting to be beaten.[7] (J subsequently heard that the school

7. Kipling says of the masters "set in office o'er us": "And they beat on us with rods / Faithfully with many rods—/ Daily beat on us with rods, / For the love they bore us" (1899, p. xv). In the poem this leads to the preparation of the glorious leaders of the empire being "to serve the lands they rule, / Serve and love the lands they rule" (p. xvi).

had dropped the beating policy right after the headmaster had retired.)

J's descriptions evoked the sadistic atmosphere of the British public school at the beginning of the twentieth century so vividly and bitterly recalled by Orwell (1947) and idealized by Kipling (1899). The headmaster had declared more than once, as do so many parents, "This hurts me much more than it does you," and J remembered feeling guilty. Despite the man's stern and unchanging facial expression, J had the impression of the headmaster's fierce (later J concluded it had been impassioned) involvement with the beatings, administered to the boy's bare buttocks. J remembered that after being beaten he wanted the headmaster to comfort him. But this did not occur. "Nothing overtly sexual happened," J added. In the course of telling me about all this, he expressed another unsolicited, negative assertion: he had never been beaten at home by his parents.

J reported having felt confused, despairing, and guilty toward his parents for sending him away, but his rage was suppressed. Later in the session he amended the disclaimer about parental beatings. He was not sure why he had said it—he had believed it while he was saying it, but in fact his mother had often threatened to beat him with a leather belt. Although this never occurred, J was left with fantasies of being belt-whipped and fetishistic excitement about leather. And occasionally, when his usually "nice" mother had lost her temper, J had been spanked by her or by his father, but "they never made me take my pants down" (in contrast to his headmaster). His parents were obviously reluctant to spank and were upset afterwards; the spankings were rather gentle but humiliating; they made him very angry. It was easier to be angry with his father than with his mother. J found the idea that his mother had allowed him to be sent away to school so painful as to be almost unbearable.

The school experiences, so imbued with the danger of separation and of rage at his parents as well as with sado-masochistic excitement, had clearly scarred J and influenced his fantasy life.[8] He suffered afterwards from a need to be punished, and he remembered that in adolescence he began to have occasional obscure daydreams and dreams of being beaten by anonymous men or of administering beatings, usu-ally to younger boys. These dreams still occurred.

In one session, on my return from vacation, he reported a dream: "I am punishing a boy but I seem to be only lightly touching him with a familiar cane. The boy is crying. I feel loving toward him and want to comfort him." The "familiar cane," J said, was a peculiar heavy one his headmaster carried but did not use for beating. J repeated his wish for "tender-ness" from the headmaster after being beaten. In the dream he had cast himself as a tender version of the headmaster and as the boy who was rather tenderly treated. J said there were no sexual feelings in the dream, just some generalized loving emotion toward the boy. He had, however, awakened with an erection.

This seemingly predominantly heterosexual man had strong homosexual longings that he did not act out. His sexuality was marred by inhibitions, and, aside from sporadic casual contacts with prostitutes and other women on whom he looked down, J had lived what he called a "Spartan and measured" sexual life. He had avoided lengthy attachments.

---

8. The confluence of pathogenic factors I outline here, simplified as it is, still shows how cautious one must be in trying to evaluate child abuse and especially in blaming the patient's parents.

He had suppressed wishes to beat and be beaten during sexual contacts. His mildly erotic feelings toward men featured the craving for tenderness displayed in his dream. The dream seemed to me to express wishes to be loved by the father, the phallic mother, and now by the analyst—apparently a predominantly negative oedipal phenomenon, regressively expressed in mildly sadomasochistic terms. (All this was also evident in fantasies of being punished, often direct or disguised beating fantasies, sometimes accompanied by masturbation.)

In general, J was subject to an idealization of sadomasochistic excitement (occasionally homosexually tinged in fantasy) that seemed especially to screen out penetration, destruction, and hatred. Instead of wanting to kill or even aggressively to "fuck" the female or male headmasters of this world or to submit to their aggression (the other side of the predominantly anal coin), he had tried to avoid the destructiveness involved by equating punishment with love in masturbatory fantasy. This confirms one of Freud's general conclusions.[9]

J's frequently provocative masochism seemed partly designed to hold onto the mental images of parental objects whom he expected to lose—especially to preserve them from the destructive rage associated with such expectations. Novick and Novick (1995) convincingly present a view of pathological masochism as mainly an attempt to counter the danger of loss of the mental image of parents, defending them from the child's sadism. Patient P illustrates this clinically.

P, returning after my August vacation (which had

9. I am trying to show the clinical usefulness of Freud's generalizations in this 1919 paper, whatever modifications or qualifications one might want to add to them, and even when one finds that there are variations from the specific details Freud describes.

evoked the same threat of object loss in him as in J), was additionally distressed when I needed to cancel another session at the end of my first week back because of a minor illness. In the next session P said he "thought" he was angry when I canceled on the previous Friday, although he had noticed that I was coughing the day before and "hadn't been all that surprised."[10] He had the thought, "I'll pay you back"—meaning that he would further postpone paying July's overdue bill. His not paying me involved, I felt, an unconscious holding onto the parent as represented by the analyst—the link in unconscious fantasy was that the money owed stood for the analyst's fecal phallus in P's anus. I did not interpret this. The resolution to withhold payment seemed to P to be irrationally provocative, and he started to laugh as he told me about it. I remarked that he had said he "thought" he was angry and wondered if he had felt the anger. "It goes away when I see you," P said. "I must be afraid of it." (It was typical of this bright man that he could permit himself intellectual insight if he used it unconsciously to ward off concomitant threateningly intense feelings from consciousness.)

On the Friday that I had canceled P was home alone and, after the transient anger, had felt lonely and anxious. "I did what I do so often when I feel that; I resorted to the beating fantasies." He had talked about these fantasies from the beginning of his analysis, but only in recent months had he begun to reveal their details. The fantasies usually consisted of being beaten by an anonymous woman, "handsome," large, and tough. With great pleasure he submitted to her commands and to her beating him on his bared backside.

10. P hated surprises. He was one of those patients who overreacts to sudden changes: this sometimes is, and in P's case was, a residue of abuse in childhood (soul murder) in which the child's contact with the other suddenly changed to overstimulation and pain.

Sometimes the roles were reversed and he did the beating—another common variation from Freud's formula. Friday's had been his more typical masturbatory fantasy, in which he was beaten by a "dyke-ish" woman. He "thought" that maybe she stood for me, but actually she had reminded him of a much-admired camp counselor from boyhood about whom he had recently dreamt. This young man had been "tall and handsome," with a reputation for seducing the pretty female counselors. In the dream, P was a boy watching the counselor; it wasn't clear if the latter was a man or a woman. "But," P asserted, "there was *no* beating and *no* submission in the dream!" (I regarded his emphasis as an expression of *negation*, in Freud's sense.) He had felt little about the dream, but it had remained in his mind for some time and had not been previously mentioned in the analysis.

During his early camp years P had admired this young man greatly and had vague "romantic feelings about him—*not* sexual!" (compare J's declaratory negations). "I was a kind of favorite of his. But once he did yell at me and swatted me on the behind, and then I hated him so I wanted to kill him. I had beating fantasies then too, but it was a woman who beat me, and if I pictured a real person I felt rage at her. I guess I felt rage at you. You aren't young and you aren't handsome, but you are large." The analysis took place many years ago. I was younger than P and believe that I looked it, but he had the insistent, multidetermined belief that I was of an older generation. "My counselor stood for you [pause], I guess."

P had been physically punished regularly as a child, hit on the buttocks with a hairbrush by his "generally cold and disapproving" mother. He remembered the experience as pleasurable at first; at least it showed that she cared. But eventually it became obvious to P, as his suppressed rage at her (and at his father for allowing the beatings) emerged, how terrifying these would become. There had not been much pain, but his excitement had become overstimulation, helplessness, rage, and, perhaps most of all, terror, terror of his rage. "The beatings would go on too long," he had said earlier in the analysis. As a child, he had felt the rage, but he tried to focus it away from his mother onto the hairbrush. How he had hated that hairbrush!

P found later in the analysis that he was terrified of anger so intense that it made him want to kill the mother he felt he couldn't live without. The intensity of the feeling itself seemed to have magical murderous power. During the session I am quoting, P was able to say that he had been afraid of losing me, especially when he had briefly felt—as he finally acknowledged—"murderous" toward me. That had occurred at home, before the masturbatory fantasy; the submission and "anal" contact in the fantasy preserved me and the relation to me. Punishment temporarily became "love," or at least a preservation of the hope and need for love. Genetically, both parents seemed involved in the transference onto me. Freud speaks of the "regressive debasement of the genital organization itself to a lower level. 'My father loves me' was meant in a genital sense; owing to the regression it is turned into 'my father is beating me.' . . . This being beaten is now a convergence of the sense of guilt and sexual love. [The beating] is not only the punishment for the forbidden genital relation, but also the regressive substitute for that relation" (p. 189). But with P and with J—contrary to what Freud says elsewhere in his paper, "*in both [boys and girls], the beating phantasy has its origin in an incestuous attachment to the father*" (p. 198, italics Freud's)—the mother seemed more imbricated than the father in unconscious and conscious fantasies with forbidden genital *as well as* regressive

anal sexual and aggressive content. And both sets of parents—phallic mother and active father as well as, in reversal,
passive mother and passive father—became transferable in
all these versions onto the analyst, who began to appear in
both P's and J's beating fantasies.

For my patients, for Freud's, and for patients in general,
regressive retreat from oedipal conflict even more profound
than the anal libidinal conflict can be involved in beating
fantasies. Toward the end of this Monday hour, P said: "If I
had a beating fantasy about you, in my fantasy you and I
would be in it together; I wouldn't be alone. I hate to get up
off the couch and walk out the door at the end of my hour. It
means showing you my ass. I hate you while I'm telling you
this. I feel so ashamed. And yet hate comes with separation. I
guess I would hold onto you with the shame and excitement
if I let myself put you in the fantasies. I want it, but, you
know,[11] that being together also threatens to make me lose
my identity, as if I'll become part of you. This is not just about
sex. There is pleasure in my fantasies, but this is the terrifying part."

It was one of the terrifying parts. On the anal developmental level are sadistic impulses with their terrifying dan-

11. I was not surprised by what the patient said, but of course I
did not know. The "you know" sounded here as if it were involuntary.
I feel that this kind of "you know" was a projection, as it often is.
Something that P himself would not or could not know was emerging
in the second person, in projection onto the analyst: "I know" becoming "you know." This everyday kind of projection does involve a transient and tiny loss of identity, a giving away of "I"—marking in this
example with P the ego's momentary retreat from an emerging insight, a miniature shift in the long backward and forward (dynamic intrapsychic) struggle involved in the analysis. This kind of "you know"
means that what the person is saying is not "owned" (see Shengold,
1995).

ger of loss of the parental Other—which the concomitant anal passivity and masochistic submission (also full of danger) are meant to counteract. The terror of losing identity comes with the wish for oral merging. This danger stems from a time of development, earlier than the anal, when the mother is felt as the indispensable "only" Other who starts out (we know today) as part of the self.[12] What is dangerous is also desired—the trap of narcissistic regressive defense (see Shengold, 1988).

This was one of those sessions that fits Ernst Kris's description of "good" (1956, p. 255) in which the analysand is able to accomplish emotional integration on the road to insight. But the insight P had come to here took many years to work through emotionally so that he could safely *own* it and use it to liberate himself enough to attenuate the sadomasochistic burden he had carried since he was a child.

The erotization of beating and being beaten features a fixation on and regression to what seem to be predominantly anal feelings and impulses (involving anal erogeneity [body feeling] and sadomasochistic libido [energy]; see Fliess,

12. The contact and merging on both the anal and the oral level are both gratifying and terrifying, representing the ubiquitous psychic compromise between impulse and defense stressed by Brenner. A current developmental view is that the earliest mental representative of the parent starts out, as I have said, "The breast is part of me; I am the breast" (Freud, 1941, p. 299); in the course of development, the mothering figure gradually is separated out as a whole person. The father becomes important later on, at first in displacement from the mother and then in his own right. But the earliest mental impressions are never erased, and the mothering figure as primal parent retains a basic importance for both men and women. (Dying people tend to call for Mother or for God, unconsciously perceived as the primal parent.) This view grants a complex perspective that modifies Freud's insistence on the father as primary in beating fantasies.

1956). Freud stresses regression from oedipal impulses—from passively submitting to the father (or, we would now add, phallic mother). In her 1922 paper "Beating Fantasies in Daydreams," Anna Freud presents a case history according to the "stages" outlined in her father's paper (undoubtedly her own story) and restates his insight that the beating fits are regressive "substitutes for an incestuous love scene" (p. 152).

This is illustrated in the enthralled lifelong preoccupation with being beaten evident in the letters, poems, and novels of the Victorian poet Algernon Charles Swinburne. Edmund Wilson (1962), generally praising the novels, remarks:

> One's enjoyment of the splendor and wit of these novels is . . . likely to be somewhat disturbed by an element which seems bizarre and repellent, and this element appears in [Swinburne's] correspondence in an even more repellent form. As a result of his experience as a boy at Eton, Swinburne had made a cult of the traditional British practice of flogging, and this had become for him inseparable from his capacity for sexual gratification, which seems to have been exclusively masochistic. The pleasure and importance of being flogged are made to figure in . . . these family fictions. . . . In *Lesbia Brandon* Swinburne pulls out all the stops, and howls of pain become cries of ecstasy. (pp. 28–29)

Wilson cites Edmund Gosse's postscript to his memoir about his close friend: "He says that Swinburne [in his twenties] found a brothel in London which specialized in flagellation [by strong women]" (p. 29). (I will deal with Swinburne at length in the next chapter.)

Freud was thinking about masochists such as Swinburne when he maintained that such men *always* have fantasies of being beaten by women. Freud at this time was still insisting on the father as the object of such men, unconsciously hidden beneath the female beater. Today we would see a much greater variety of multilayerings involving both father and mother in complex individual ways that need to be elucidated in analysis.

In regard to fantasies of being beaten, Freud views the girls as wanting to be boys and the boys as wanting to be girls. Today we recognize that anal-sadomasochistic phenomena can aim at denial of the differences between the sexes and the generations (see Chasseguet-Smirgel, 1978, 1983). Beating fantasies, regarded by Freud as almost universal, at least in their transient forms, are for me another confirmation of the assumption that in relation to sex we all basically want to be and to have everything—mother *and* father, girls *and* boys, women *and* men.

Freud felt that the ubiquity of beating fantasies establishes that "the perversion is no longer an isolated fact in the child's sexual experience, but finds its place among the typical, not to say normal processes of development which are familiar to us." He saw (p. 192) the generic childhood perversion as incestuously founded in relation to the "child's incestuous love-*object*" (it should be object*s;* Freud is still thinking too much of father *or* mother). The parents are inevitably the first others and so become the objects of the drives as they develop. This is, we would now say, the preoedipal road to the Oedipus complex: preoedipal incestuous objects become incestuous oedipal objects. Along with this, continuing with the travel metaphor, one can also accept Freud's tracing "the origin of infantile perversions [to] the Oedipus complex" (p. 192) if we take this to mean that defensive regression from the complex largely or partly traverses the road back toward established and never completely abandoned preoedipal perverse positions.

In this paper Freud tends to contradict himself in an uncharacteristically clumsy way. On one hand he outlines rather fixed general rules, formulas, and sequences for beating fantasy formation and for the causation of perversion; on the other he makes it clear that many of his conclusions are based on limited observation and are speculative and indefinite and that much is unknown. (We now believe that sadomasochistic tendencies are multidetermined and can follow a variety of paths and form a variety of patterns.) A hard-to-attain *balance* between what is known and unknown, certain and uncertain, is necessary for psychoanalytic clinical and theoretical work. This is another impossible part of our profession that cannot be avoided in the psychic realm. One needs a mind like Freud's, capable of containing contradictions. But in this paper the balance seems off; the contradictions jar. The paper features a comparatively rare unqualified (that is, not modified or negative) use by Freud of the words *always* and *never* as expressions of too much certainty in his generalizations.[13] Most of the words and phrases expressing invariability pertain to the beating fantasies of girls, which are central to Freud's clinical material. The paper also con-

13. The *Concordance* lists 1,053 instances of the use of *always*, but most of these either do not express invariable generalizations or are *almost always*. *Never* is usually *almost never*. There are also alternative ways of saying these absolutist words. In this paper Freud uses "certainly," "invariably," "cannot fail to," "almost invariable," "precisely the same," "no less a necessity," "as a rule," and other phrases to the same purpose. (Strangely enough, a listing of the *nevers* is omitted from the *Concordance*, which skips from *neutra* to *nevertheless*—an unexplainable "slip" of the editors or printers.)

tains many instances of Freud's more characteristic and happier balance of uncertainty with assertion;[14] he says that, in contrast to what he declares about girls, "I have not been able to get so far in my knowledge of beating fantasies in boys" (p. 196).

Freud's paper is based on an analytic study of six patients—four women and two men. He mentions the diagnosis of five (four obsessional, one hysterical), but the sixth is neither diagnosed nor further mentioned. I wonder (with Young-Bruehl) if this sixth is his daughter Anna, Freud's "Antigone," whose analysis was a major impetus for this paper. Six cases are an inadequate base for a theory of masochism or perversion, but Freud brings his prior experience to bear on his generalizations (most of which follow from his 1905 "Three Essays on the Theory of Sexuality," which he continued to change and add to). Jones calls the 1919 paper "a purely clinical study" (1955, p. 305), but it contains notable contributions to Freud's changing theoretical views, especially those on instinct theory, sadomasochism, and perversion.

Mahony points out "Freud's extensive use of the present tense [in this paper]" (1987, p. 140). This, he says, is a characteristic (although intermittently used) feature of Freud's style, one that provides immediate "impact" (p. 140) and conveys dramatic and emotional intensity—especially obvious when Freud writes about dreams and clinical narratives. Freud's use of the present tense gives a sense of "imminence" (p. 128).[15] If there is unusual emotional intensity in

14. There are many phrases stressing how much is not known: "impossible to say," "perhaps," "most probably," "doubt remains," "seems to be," "not uncommon."

15. Mahony points out that the present-tense instances in Freud's German are not always so translated by Strachey in the *Collected*

this paper, it could be (speculatively) attributed to the centrality of Anna Freud's contribution to it as her father's patient. (She also wrote her first paper in 1922 based on what Young-Bruehl characterizes convincingly as disguised beating fantasies of herself from ages eight to ten.)[16]

So some of Freud's failings in this important paper can be ascribed to his involvement in the oedipal and preoedipal family complexes that affect us all—*revenants* from his infantile and phylogenetic past that came alive when, to use his metaphor, he drank blood, like the ghosts in the *Odyssey*. Freud's strength is that, despite his awareness of inevitable failings, he tried and demanded that his followers try to fight denial and take account of the drives toward cannibalism, murder, and incest. The guilt that is part of the human condition does not lessen Freud's individual deficiencies, but he reminds us of the inexorability of our own and our parents' burdens of evil and relative helplessness—we all have to face in our own way what Hamlet and Oedipus faced. This is too much for some of Freud's critics.

Freud reminds us of the burden of these complexes at the end of his paper. In my comments, I have stressed the conflicted and inhibitory consequences of their sometimes neglected reversed form: impulses directed from the parent toward the child. I underline my modernizing modifications: "Infantile sexuality [*and aggression*], which [*are*] held under repression, [*act*] as the chief motive force[*s*] in the formation

---

Works, but he specifically cites the beating fantasies paper as an example of the retention of the first person in its English translation.

16. "Anna Freud several times protected her privacy by declaring that the clinical material for 'Beating Fantasies and Daydreams' came from her own analytic practice. But the paper was actually written some six months before Anna Freud saw her first patient" (Young-Bruehl, 1988, p. 103).

of symptoms; and the essential part of [*their*] content, the Oedipus complex [together with its preoedipal antecedents,[17] transformed but not eliminated by it], is the nuclear complex of neurosis" (p. 204).

I have added "aggression." The Oedipus complex and "its preoedipal antecedents" of course involve murder as well as sex. Accepting our individual immersion in cannibalism, murder, and incest is both a narcissistic blow and a source of terror, but it is all too easy to demonstrate the universality of this dark side of human nature. Our need for denial, another necessary part of our humanity that is hard to transcend for long, makes it inevitable that Freud's role as a disturber of the peace of the world (maintained in the Freudian analyst's role as a mirror of the patient's mind and impulses in every analysis) will continue to foster anxiety and hostility toward Freud and psychoanalysis.

I want to connect patient J, a child who was being beaten, and Anna Freud as Freud's patient; the link is that both had dreams that featured tenderness.

Anna Freud wrote in her notes in 1942, three years after her father's death:

> About Losing and Being Lost/Concerning last night's dream: I dream, as I have often done, that he is here again. All of these recent dreams have the same character: the main role is played not by my longing for him but rather by his longing for

17. One of Freud's statements in this paper is relevant: "The emphasis which is laid here upon the importance of the earliest experiences does not imply any underestimation of the influences of later ones" (p. 183). The statement could also be repeated with "earliest" and "later" reversed.

me. The main scene in the dreams is always of his tenderness to me, which always takes the form of my own, earlier tenderness. In reality he never showed [tenderness] with the exception of one or two times, which always remained in my memory. The reversal can be simply the fulfillment of my wish [for tenderness], but it is probably also something else. In the first dream of this kind he openly said: "I have always longed for you so." The main feeling in yesterday's dream is that he is wandering about (on top of mountains, hills) while I am doing other things. . . . [I] feel that I should stop whatever I am doing and go walking with him. Eventually he calls me to him and demands this himself. I am very relieved and lean myself against him, crying in a way that is very familiar to both of us. Tenderness. My thoughts are troubled; he should not have called me, it is as if a renunciation or a form of progress had been undone because he called. (1942, pp. 296–97).

This is very moving, not least because of the obvious but gentle reproaches toward her father. The reproaches are not only for the rarity of his expressions of tenderness. They also refer to his demands for a damaging or at least inhibiting too-closeness. And muted but not directly spelled out is, I feel, a complaint against her father for having "called" her to be his analysand.

The notes finish with a retreat from anger and reproach toward longing, love, guilt, and denial: "Sympathy and bad conscience. Associations: The poem by Albrecht Schaeffer, 'You strong and dear wayfarer . . . I was with you at each step of the way—/ there was no victory I did not also win—/ no sorrow I did not suffer beside you, / you strong and you dear wanderer' " (p. 297).

These dreams of Anna Freud's bring her dead father back to life. I feel they demonstrate the masochistic child's need to suppress hostility toward the parent and direct it toward the self, to avert or try to undo the loss of the parent. To suffer ill treatment is to keep a connection with the parent, without whom the child feels that life is not possible. This need is then sexualized. There is a compulsive craving for the beating, emotional or physical, to turn to tenderness and love.

In her note, Anna Freud is predominantly the adult, able to face with dignity much of the weakness and badness in herself and in her father. I am not trying to denounce or reduce Freud in providing this glimpse of him as partial soul murderer. Before judging individuals, we must try to see them in all their contradictory complexity. With our human weaknesses and failures, and because of the conditions of our existence, we are all condemned, at least to some extent, to be victims and perpetrators of soul murder. When we dare to judge and condemn, we should try to consider whether we can answer with any certainty what Freud might have called questions of psychic economics: how much do the facts and circumstances feature narcissistic selfishness, evil, neglect, and hatred; and, alongside this, how much can we see of caring, goodness, nurturance, and love? Such judgments are often very difficult to make, for analyst and patient alike.

III

Literary Examples

9

Algernon Swinburne
A Child Who Wanted to Be Beaten

Each of Redgie's floggings was a small drama to [his sister Helen]. She followed with excitement each cut of the birch on her brother's skin, and tasted a nervous pleasure when every stroke drew blood. . . . It is certain that Helen felt real and acute enjoyment at the sight of her brother horsed and writhing under the rod.
—Swinburne, "Reginald Harewood" ("Kirklowes fragment")

The English poet Algernon Swinburne, in his life and writings, provides an example of a child who grew up with beatings and as an adult retained fantasies of being beaten that amounted to obsessions.[1] The beatings that he idealized

Epigraph: "Kirklowes fragment" is a try-out that Swinburne wrote in 1861 for the novel *A Year's Letters* (1863). The novel was not published under his own name until 1905, when its title was changed to *Love's Cross Currents*. The hero, Reginald Harewood, is often flogged by his father with a birch. Redgie and his sister, Helen, are very close. ("Kirklowes" is the name of the family farm.)

1. Swinburne's preoccupation with masochism is obvious in his poetry; flagellation is implicit in some of the poems but explicit to the degree of monomania in his letters and novels.

were the ones administered to him as a student at Eton at the hands of a "stunning tutor" (Swinburne, 1854–69, p. 78).[2] In a letter written as an adult, he says of Eton, "I should like to see two things there again, the river—and the flogging block" (quoted in Fuller, 1968, p. 25). Here he linked two of his obsessive preoccupations—swimming and flagellation. Fuller adds: "Flagellation was to haunt his poetry, his novels and his letters; all his life he was to be drawn back to it, as it were, longingly" (p. 25). She quotes from a manuscript of Swinburne's called "Algernon's Flogging," part of a collection titled "The Flogging Block":

> Every fresh cut well laid on
> The bare breech of Algernon
> Makes the swelled flesh rise in ridges
> Thick as summer swarms of midges;
> Every stroke the Master deals,
> Every strike the schoolboy feels,
> Marks his breech with fresh red weals;
> How he blubbers, how he bellows!

2. "Let it be said that he not only liked to be whipped, but he experienced an ecstatic pleasure in letting his mind rest on flagellation, and in conjuring up scenes of it. He said that the taste for this punishment had come to him at Eton, and he wrote, in 1863, 'Once before giving me a swishing that I had the marks of for more than a month, [the tutor] let me saturate my face with eau-de-cologne. He meant to stimulate and excite the senses by that preliminary pleasure so as to inflict the acuter pain afterwards on their awakened and intensified susceptibility'" (Gosse, [1920?], p. 244).

In the same letter, Swinburne says of the "stunning tutor . . . I have known him [to] prepare the flogging-room with burnt scents; or choose a *sweet* place out of doors with the smell of firwood. *This* I call real delicate torment" (Swinburne, 1854–69, p. 78, italics Swinburne's). In the poet's flagellation fictions the boy protagonists are "swished" either by their father or by a tutor.

On those broad red nether cheeks
That their own blood scores and streaks,
That the red rod streaks and dapples
Like two great red round streaked apples . . .
(p. 25)

On the basis of his posthumously published novel *Lesbia Brandon*, one would judge that Swinburne had little insight into the unusualness of his perverse preoccupation. Almost every character in the book, women as well as men, refers in public, in salacious innuendo, to schoolboys' being beaten, as if the topic and the associated, partially concealed excitement were a universal, mundane, but lively interest that is obviously expected to be shared and so regarded by the reader. No doubt the flogging block, as well as the playing fields, of Eton influenced the character, ambitions, and sexuality of generations of young men of the English upper classes, but surely most were less affected than Swinburne, who, in many ways, never grew up.

Algernon Swinburne was born in 1837, the oldest child of a doting mother and an idolized father who was a high officer in the Royal Navy and often away from home. His family background was aristocratic on both sides. Four sisters followed and then a brother, born too late to be a playmate to Swinburne as a child.

The Swinburne family home was on the Isle of Wight, which was also the home of Swinburne's mother's sister, Lady Mary Gordon, and her husband (who was a cousin of Swinburne's father). Swinburne was very close to his cousin, their daughter, also named Mary Gordon. (Near-incestuous relationships in interconnected family settings were to appear in his novels and in some of his plays.) There is much speculation that the younger Mary Gordon was the love of

Swinburne's life and the original of the seductive, dominating, sometimes cruel, athletic heroines of his poems and novels: Dolores, Faustine, Atalanta, Lesbia.[3] (This is the chief thesis of Fuller's 1968 study of Swinburne.)

Too little is known of the poet's childhood to make a convincing case for soul murder beginning at home (although there are hints that the boy Algernon was beaten by his father [see Fuller, 1968, p. 30]). The protagonist of his first novel, *Love's Cross Currents,* and its preliminary sketch, "Kirklowes Fragment," the boy Redgie is flogged regularly by his father; in the slightly later second novel, *Lesbia Brandon,* the boy's tutor is the one who wields the birch. In the earlier novel, Reginald, an older schoolboy, tells the as yet unflogged Frank: "I was swished twice [this] morning. . . . My father is the most awful Turk. He likes to swish me—he does really" (1863, p. 61). It seems clear that Swinburne at least fantasized having been "swished" by his father; actual beatings would have contributed further to his overwhelming and lasting perverse reaction to the floggings at Eton.

In two of these three fictions, there is a sister who looks on and enjoys the beatings. (In *Lesbia Brandon,* all the young lovers and would-be lovers, including the tutor, Denham, turn out to be siblings.) The sister character was probably drawn from his cousin Mary, who was in some relevant ways closer to him in his childhood and adolescence than his sisters were. (Mary Gordon might well have been represented as the

3. In "Dolores" (1865), Swinburne is ostensibly describing the effect of Dolores on the boy god Love, who plays the poet's characteristic passive role: "Thou shalt touch and make redder his roses / With juice not of fruit nor of bud; / When the sense in the spirit reposes / Thou shall quicken the soul through the blood. / Thine, thine the one grace we implore is / Who would live and not languish or feign, / O sleepless and deadly Dolores, / Our Lady of Pain" (p. 51).

"sister" Helen watching the child being beaten in the quotation I have used as the epigraph to this chapter.)[4] He had told Mary of the beatings at Eton (see Swinburne, 1854–69, p. 110, letter 65) and perhaps of some even before that, and their correspondence reveals her enthusiastic interest in the details. (According to Thomas, "In childhood and in adult life, they indulged their enthusiasm for the birch and for girls who played the part of boys. Much of this at least took the form of literary fantasy" [1979, p. 16].) Swinburne showed Mary the manuscript of *Lesbia Brandon* as he was writing it in the 1860s—before she married a much older man. With Swinburne's help, Mary wrote and published (in 1864) a novel, *The Children of the Chapel*, whose "sexual preoccupations . . . are with flagellation and transvestitism" (Thomas, 1979, p. 98). Schoolboy floggings were still being gleefully referred to in Mary's letters to Swinburne in the 1890s, when they were both in their fifties (see Fuller, 1968, p. 272).

In the Isle of Wight, and in his grandfather's house in

4. In *Lesbia Brandon*, Bertie at thirteen is obsessed with Helen of Troy, whom he obviously identifies with his older sister. When grown he is in submissive love with his cousin, Lesbia (of whom her father says, "The truth is she wanted all her life to be a boy, as everybody thought she would till she was born, and must have a boy's training and do a boy's lessons; minus the rod afterwards, you know [1864, p. 240]). Lesbia is described as being and looking like a young version of her grandmother, Lady Midhurst, "the venomous old beauty" (p. 230) who has a lively interest in verbal and literal flagellation: "Cruel she certainly was on occasion, cruelty amused her and she liked to make her cuts tell" (p. 246). She calls herself a "Madame de Merteuil" (the sadistic beauty from Laclos's *Les Liaisons Dangereuses*). Her first name is Helena; Fliess (1973, p. 82) makes much of the derivations of that name from those of the Greek moon goddess (Helen, Helle, or Selene), but he leaves out the moon's anal connotations, e.g., buttocks as moons and "mooning" (for anal exhibitionism).

Northumberland, which Swinburne often visited as a boy, he
was surrounded by the sea. It became an object of passion in
his life and in his work. He was an ardent swimmer, encour-
aged by his father. As an adolescent he frequently swam in
dangerous waters. Panter-Downes (1971) reports that Swinburne would plunge into the sea in all weathers. Once, in his
thirties, he swam far out in the ocean and was swept away by
the current. He probably would have drowned if he had not
been picked up by a boat whose crew luckily spotted him. His
letters confirm explicitly that Swinburne's love of swimming,
besides providing exciting ordeals that confirmed his bravery, also afforded him masochistic gratification. He liked to
be pounded and slapped about by the inexorable "great sweet
mother" (Swinburne, 1862, p. 34).[5] Panter-Downes says:

> Even his descriptions of nature are frequently of a
> force, a mightier Amazon, who is most beautiful
> when she sends mortals spinning, penetrates
> them, like ecstatic pagan Saint Sebastians, with
> her keen silver arrows of rain and wind, and strikes

5. In Swinburne's "The Triumph of Time" the rejected lover (see
footnote 13 below) vows: "I will go back to the *great sweet mother*, /
Mother and lover of men, the sea. / I will go down to her, I and none
other, / Close with her, kiss her and mix her with me. . . ." And this
mother is a powerful, cruel, and imperious woman: "O fair green-
girdled mother of mine, / Sea that art clothed with the sun and the
rain, / Thy sweet hard kisses are strong like wine, / Thy large embraces are keen like pain" (1862, pp. 15–16). Swinburne was influenced here by his early enthusiasm for Walt Whitman, especially the
American poet's "Out of the Cradle Endlessly Rocking," with its imagery of the poet and the mother-sea. Whitman's biographer says: "Algernon Swinburne read this major new poem in the 1860 *Leaves of Grass*
and called it 'the most lovely and wonderful thing I have read for
years and years . . . such beautiful skill and subtle power.' (His own
'Triumph of Time,' evoking the 'great sweet Mother and lover of men,
the sea,' bore the impress of Whitman's elegy)" (Kaplan, 1980, p. 240).

them senseless to the ground. . . . In his second
novel *Lesbia Brandon,* the rough sea scourges the
boy, Herbert Seyton, who gives himself up rap-
turously to its stinging embraces as young Algernon Swinburne used to do, throwing him back on
the beach "whipped . . . into a single blush of the
whole skin." (1971, pp. 18–19)

The ocean was connected in his mind, both symbolically
and experientially, with his parents. In a poem, "The Garden
of Cymodyce" (1896), he addresses the sea as mother, one
who has meant more to him than lovers or his poems:

Sea, and bright wind, and heaven of ardent air,
More dear than all things earth-born; O to me
Mother more dear than love's own longing, sea,
More than love's eyes are, fair,
Be with my spirit of song as wings to bear,
As fire to feel and breathe and brighten; be
A spirit of sense more deep of deity,
A light of love, if love may be, more strong
In me than very song.
For song I have loved with second love, but
　　thee,
Thee first, thee, mother. (p. 318)

The sea is described as feminine and murderous in an
exchange from *Lesbia Brandon* (1864) between the hero,
Bertie, and the sadistic tutor, Denham, who beats him and
bathes in the sea with him. Bertie, prompted by Denham,
who is excited by sadistic women, is talking about women
from Greek mythology:

The boy flushed and flinched as Denham patted
him. "I think they were right to put a lot of women
in the sea: it's like a woman itself: the right place

for the sirens to come out of, and sing and kill
people. Look there, what a jolly wave for one to
come riding in upon."

"They stay on shore now mostly," said Denham: "but I don't know that they do the less harm
for that." (p. 211)

Swinburne's father, an admiral, was often away at sea. In
1875, Swinburne wrote about his childhood to an American
admirer:

As for the sea, its salt must have been in my blood
before I was born. I can remember no earlier enjoyment than being held up naked in my father's
arms and *brandished between his hands,* then shot
like a stone from a sling through the air, shouting
and laughing with delight, *head foremost into the
coming wave*—which could only have been the
pleasure of a very little fellow. I remember being
afraid of other things but never of the sea. But this
is enough of infancy: only it shows the truth of my
endless passionate returns to the sea in all my
verse. (1875–77, p. 12, my italics)

Being cast naked into the wave by his father behind him
clearly was a sensual delight for the child. One wonders
whether this memory is not one of the nodal points of his
obsession with being beaten—reinforced by the actual experiences of school beatings at Eton—and also whether it is a
memory screening beatings by ("brandished between" the
hands of) his father that occurred before Eton.

In *Lesbia Brandon* there is a link between the boy's being
flogged by a tutor and being whipped in the waves of the sea.
Two protagonists, Bertie and (again) Redgie, are obvious

stand-ins for the author.[6] (Redgie, the more masculine and aggressive of the two, is a devotee of flagellation.) When Bertie is twelve and is about to go to Eton, he is repeatedly flogged by his tutor, Denham. This is rationalized as preparing the youth for the flogging customs of the public schools. Denham is described as becoming increasingly excited by these contacts: "[Denham's] heart beat as hard as [Bertie's] when they entered the library . . . the cuts stung like fire . . . ; [Bertie] chewed the flesh of his hands rather than cry out, till Denham glittered with passion" (1864, pp. 218–19). Both the tutor and his charge are passionately involved in their sadomasochistic struggles, and "every flogging became a duel without seconds between the man and the boy" (p. 205). Interspersed with the floggings is a description of Bertie and Denham together bathing in the sea, which seems simply to be a continuation of the sadomasochistic delight and challenge of the beatings:

> [Bertie] panted and shouted with pleasure among breakers where he could not stand two minutes; the blow of a roller that beat him off his feet made him laugh and cry out in ecstasy; he rioted in the roaring water like a young sea-beast, sprang at the throat of waves that threw him flat, pressed up against their soft fierce bosoms and fought for their sharp embraces; grappled with them as lover with lover, flung himself upon them with limbs that yielded deliciously, till the scourging of the surf made him red from the shoulders to the knees,

6. Swinburne frequently used the name "Redgie" in both his fiction and his plays, and he often signed himself "Redgie" in letters to friends who were aware of or shared his interests in beating and being beaten.

and sent him on shore whipped by the sea into a
single blush of the whole skin, breathless and un-
tired. (pp. 205–6)

Many of Swinburne's letters are missing, even though
there are about two thousand letters in the six volumes collected by Cecil Lang.[7] Mary Gordon printed some expur-
gated family letters from Swinburne in her memoir of the
poet, but she burned most of his early letters to members of
his family. And many others, presumably because of their
sexual content, were destroyed or bowdlerized by relations of
recipients from outside the Swinburne family circle.

In the few early family letters that have survived one
learns that he called his father "Pino." (All members of the
family had nicknames; Swinburne's was "Hadji," his
mother's, "Mimmie.") In his first extant letter, written at
seventeen, he addresses his father, congratulating him on his
birthday, as "My darling Pino" (1854–69, p. 1). (This has an
infantile phallic clang, and its familiarity is a puzzling contrast to the emotional and physical distance that seems to
have been characteristic of the seemingly predominantly benevolent father-son relationship.)

"Mimmie" was apparently a hovering presence in childhood. At first Swinburne was taught by his mother, to whom
he owed his early mastery of French and Italian. When he
was eight he was sent across the Isle of Wight (a pony ride
away from his cousin Mary's family) to be taught by the vicar
at a preparatory school, Brooke Rectory, where he may well
have been beaten. There is a facetious, somewhat cryptic

7. Swinburne's letters are not great letters, like those of Keats, By-
ron, or Flaubert. But, as Edmund Wilson points out, they are of great
psychological interest and very lively. Lang (1959) calls them full of
"wonderful trivia" (p. xxxiii).

allusion to this in a letter written to Swinburne in 1893 by Mary Gordon, when they were both in their fifties. Early in the letter Mary says that she had been to Brooke Rectory and seen again the room in which he had slept as a schoolboy (she had visited Swinburne there as a child with her mother). Then, after mentioning the floggings at Eton, she remarks, in relation to Brooke Rectory, "the verie Worthie the Vicar had *old fashioned* ideas of discipline" (quoted in Fuller, 1968, p. 272, her italics).

Going to Eton was a turning point in Swinburne's life. (He was subject to the fateful combination of abandonment by being sent away to school and being beaten there that was present for my patient J, described in the previous chapter.) In his letters Swinburne continued intermittently to assume the persona of an Etonian schoolboy—specifically in relation to his interests, his courage, and his masochistic preoccupations.[8] Wilson writes:

8. Swinburne's cousin Lord Redesdale, who was with him at Eton, wrote: "He carried with him one charm—he was absolutely courageous. He did not know what fear meant" (quoted by Gosse, 1917, p. 322). After he left Eton at seventeen, Swinburne wanted to become a soldier (the Crimean War was still on) and was crushed when his father refused to allow him to go. This humiliation (he felt that his father doubted his physical capability) was probably reinforced in retrospect when Mary Gordon, his beloved cousin, married a soldier in 1865. In an 1875 letter to her he called being forbidden to join the army instead of going on to Oxford "the great disappointment of his life," speaking of himself (strangely but significantly) at first in the third person—the humiliation must have been still too much to bear: "He wanted to go into the Army. Didn't he, poor chap. . . . I'm sure you won't deride it because he was but a little, slightly built chap. My mother was not altogether against it, and told me that they must take three days to think the matter over. . . . At the end of the three days they told me it could not be; my father had made up his mind" (Swinburne, 1890–1909, p. 251). Swinburne then describes how, in reaction,

It was at Eton that Swinburne discovered the Elizabethan dramatists, familiarized himself with them more thoroughly than many boys of that age can have done, and conceived the enthusiasm for them that was to last all the rest of his life; he was still writing about them at the time of his death. It was at Eton that he first also read Hugo and Landor, who were to remain for him supreme heroes, his attitude toward whom was quite abject. . . . It was at Eton that he received the floggings which were to remain, also, one of his obsessions and which seem to have conditioned a crippling of the whole of his emotional life. (1962, p. 7)[9]

For the rest of his life Swinburne was given, in his correspondence, especially with friends who shared or tolerated his fascination with flagellation, to break into what Wilson calls

his childish impersonation of a schoolboy who wants to be flogged. He cannot leave the subject alone. . . . He thanks [his friend] Powell for sending him a birch rod and "desires a sight of the swishing room;" the view of "a fine rapid river winding under fir-woods between banks clothed with broom and wild roses" makes him reflect that

---

he had resolved to climb up the sheer wall of nearby Culver Cliff, a feat that no one had ever done. He nearly fell and could easily have been killed, but he persevered and conquered the cliff.

9. See Thomas (1979, pp. 23–24) on the difficulties of ascertaining whether or how much Swinburne's talk of being beaten by his tutor, James Joynes, was memory or just fantasy. Thomas leaves no doubt about the general prevalence both of sadistic beatings and of homosexuality at Eton during the years when Swinburne was a pupil.

there is "birch enough to hand for the bottoms of
all Eton." "How could you be at Eton," he is still
writing Powell in this vein at the age of thirty-
seven, "and not remember to invest for me in at
the least two of the large photographs of the flog-
ging-block when you know how I wanted them
and was shy of writing to order them?" (1962,
pp. 30–31)

As a child he was weak and slight and not expected to live
long. He grew up to be five feet four and a half inches high,
"afflicted with a nervous system so highly strung that his
short arms and legs jerked as though manipulated by strings"
(Panter-Downes, 1971, p. 17). The little man had a huge
dome of a head, a receding chin, and a great mop of flaming
red hair, which gradually evolved toward baldness. He could
become wildly excited and speak in a high-pitched screech.
More than one witness has compared him to an awkward,
exotic bird.

From earliest childhood he had the trick, whenever he grew the least excited, of stiffly drawing
down his arms from his shoulders and giving quick
vibrating jerks with his hands. . . . If he happened
to be seated at a moment of excitement, he would
jerk his legs and twist his feet also, though with
less violence. At such times his face would grow
radiant with a rapt expression. . . . His mother . . .
applied to a specialist for advice. After a close ex-
amination the physician's report was that these
motions resulted from "an excess of electric vital-
ity," and that any attempt to stop them would be
harmful. (Gosse, 1917, p. 26)

The painter and poet Dante Gabriel Rossetti (with whom Swinburne and other friends had shared quarters for several years) once told Edmund Gosse, "Algernon used to drive me crazy by dancing all over the studio like a wild cat" (Gosse, 1917, p. 106).[10] He was also subject to epileptiform fits in which he would suddenly fall and lose consciousness, awakening, often with bruises, but with no memory of what had occurred.[11]

Swinburne was a true genius, with a prodigious memory;

10. I wonder whether Swinburne suffered from Tourette's syndrome. Here are two suggestive descriptions:

Georgina Burne-Jones (wife of the painter and Rudyard Kipling's aunt) was very friendly with Swinburne from the time she was married; he addressed her in letters as "Dear Georgie" (1875–77, p. 69). She wrote of the twenty-three-year-old poet: "He was restless beyond words, hopping about the room unceasingly, seeming to keep time by a swift movement of the hands at the wrists, and sometimes of the feet also, with some inner rhythm of excitement" (quoted by Gosse, 1917, p. 66). And here is Gosse's depiction of Swinburne at their first meeting: "As he talked to me, he stood, perfectly rigid, with his arms shivering at his sides, and his little feet tight against each other, close to a low settee in the middle of the studio. Every now and then, without breaking off talking or bending his body, he hopped on to this sofa, and presently hopped down again, so that I was reminded of some orange-crested bird—a hoopoe, perhaps—hopping from perch to perch in a cage. The contrast between these sudden movements and the enthusiasm of his rich and flute-like voice was very strange" (1917, pp. 200–201).

11. Gosse says: "There was always, I believe, a difference of opinion among the doctors as to the actual nature of this disease, which was, however, epileptiform. It took the shape of a convulsive fit, in which, generally after a period of very great cerebral excitement, he would suddenly fall unconscious. These fits were excessively distressing to witness, and produced a shock of alarm, all the more acute because of the deathlike appearance of the patient. Oddly enough, however, the person who seemed to suffer from them least was Swinburne himself" (1917, pp. 98–99).

he seemed to have read everything and remembered and could quote it all. The poetry of his early manhood was probably his best work, and it was very popular but always controversial. He had wit but not always humor; he was a superb parodist. Lang (1959) calls him, "quite simply (to use his own kind of phrase), the greatest parodist who ever lived" (p. xv). He has been called the most erudite English poet since Milton. The quality of his poems declined in middle age, however; by then his idiosyncratic wildness had been domesticated, apparently by the relationship with Theodore Watts (later Watts-Dunton; see below). After the death of the (proper and respectable) Victorian poet laureate Tennyson, Swinburne was considered, even by Queen Victoria, to be England's foremost living poet. But he was not appointed poet laureate—probably because of his open atheism, his reputation as a debauchee, and his support for antiroyalist revolutionary causes in Europe.

Throughout his life, Swinburne seemed completely incapable of tending to the ordinary business of life and was looked after by his mother and sisters (when he would allow it) and later by his friend and companion Watts-Dunton, as if he were a privileged, precious, and fragile creature.

Swinburne never married. His attachment to his cousin and sister surrogate Mary Gordon seems to have had an incestuous intensity. (Preoccupation with brother-sister incest is abundant in his writings.)[12] In 1865 she married

12. In *Lesbia Brandon*, Bertie, who had been asking his tutor about Electra, says he thinks she must have been like her aunt, Helen of Troy, rather than like her mother, Clytemnestra. He adds: "I should have liked to be Orestes; not when he grew up, you know. I think [Electra] was like [Helen]. Because if she had been like her own mother instead, [Orestes] couldn't have killed [Clytemnestra]" (1864, p. 210). But Orestes does grow up and, spurred on by his older sister, Electra, does kill his mother. Here is an exchange between Bertie and his sister, whom he loves passionately, sensually, and masochistically:

Colonel Gordon Leith, a professional soldier old enough to be her father. (It is probably because it meant too much to him that Mary's marriage is not even mentioned in Swinburne's copious correspondence that year.) It may be that Mary Gor-

---

" 'I say, let your hair go,' said Herbert, pressing his arms under hers: she loosened the fastenings, and it rushed downwards, a tempest and torrent of sudden tresses, heavy and tawny and riotous and radiant, over shoulders and arms and bosom; and under cover of the massive and luminous locks she drew up his face against her own and kissed him time after time with all her strength. 'Now go to bed and sleep well,' she said, putting him back. His whole spirit was moved with the passionate motion of his senses; he clung to her for a minute, and rose up throbbing from head to foot with violent love. . . . 'I wish you would kill me some day; it would be jolly to feel you killing me. Not like it? Shouldn't I! You just hurt me, and see' " (1864, p. 265). In the fragment that begins *Lesbia Brandon* (parts of it are still missing), Herbert and his older sister are described like twins; they have essentially the same face: "While yet a boy her brother was so like her that [her] description may serve for him. . . . There was a strong feminine element in Bertie Seyton; he ought to have been a pretty and rather boyish girl. . . . He looked at times so like a small replica of his sister, *breeched and cropped*" (p. 216, my italics). Bertie emerges as the masochistic partner to his sister's Dolores, Our Lady of Pain. But essentially Swinburne, who as a youth also had a lovely, girlish face (Rossetti used him as a model for an angel), is portraying himself in two guises: as the passive boy and as the aggressive, cruel, phallic woman. (This split identification, similar but also different, can be found in the homosexual but more aggressive and not [sexually] overtly sadomasochistic Lytton Strachey, who has been described as presenting himself, in his Freud-influenced fictionalized biography *Elizabeth and Essex*, both as the infatuated, older, indeterminately sexed, and castrative queen and—what he wanted to be—the young and beautiful Essex, whom she ultimately sends to his death. Maynard Keynes wrote to Strachey shortly after the book was published, "You seem, on the whole, to imagine yourself as Elizabeth, but I see from the pictures that it is Essex whom you have got up as yourself" [see Holroyd, 1994, p. 612].)

don rejected Swinburne's advances years previously, when he presented himself as a serious suitor.[13] It appears that her engagement to Colonel Leith sometime in the early 1860s was another ominous turning point in the poet's emotional life; afterwards, Swinburne began to drink so heavily that not only his creativity but his survival was threatened. During these years of chronic alcoholism, he also began to go to be beaten by female prostitutes. Gosse [1920?], in "Confidential Paper on Swinburne's Moral Irregularities," a long-unpublished manuscript he deposited in the British Museum, wrote that Swinburne then frequented "a mysterious house in St. John's Wood where two golden-haired and rouge-cheeked ladies received, in luxuriously furnished rooms, gentlemen whom they consented to chastise for large sums" (p. 245).

Swinburne's overprotective mother (his father by this time had died), torn between denial and concern, was in despair about what she knew and what she feared of her son's dissipations, which she felt unable to control. He gave up the visits to the brothels after five or six years, when his mother finally tried to curb his habits by withholding funds. But the drinking continued.[14]

In 1879 Theodore Watts (he added his mother's maiden name, Dunton, after her death in the 1890s)—a lawyer and

13. Swinburne's poem "The Triumph of Time" (1862) charts a reaction to a rejection by a woman. Wilson, Fuller, and others believe that the woman was his cousin, Mary Gordon.

14. A witness described having seen the great explorer Richard Francis Burton (a boon companion after meeting the poet in 1861) "walk downstairs carrying [the drunken] Swinburne under his arm; after putting him down on the pavement he called a hansom. Swinburne could not find the step and complained that 'hansoms were getting their steps higher and higher each year'" (quoted in Swinburne, 1854–69, p. 223 n.).

writer, five years older than his friend—rescued the forty-two-year-old Swinburne, who was by then living alone in a state of almost complete physical collapse. In his letters the poet ascribed his condition to physical illnesses. Despite outbreaks of delirium tremens, Swinburne denied having a drinking problem, apparently in part because he had little memory of his uncouth and destructive behavior after he had downed a few glasses of wine. Watts-Dunton made a home for the poet in The Pines, a villa in suburban Putney, which was bought with Swinburne family money; the move had the family's enthusiastic backing. Watts-Dunton became a kind of custodian, weaning the poet from alcohol: he was allowed a pint of beer a day. Swinburne, to everyone's surprise, was able to live in happy subjection to his older friend's Spartan regimen (with occasional minor rebellions);[15] in turn Watts-Dunton for the most part humored and honored his whims and wishes. They lived together for thirty years, until Swinburne's death at seventy-two. (Swinburne called Watts-Dunton "major" and himself "minor," which not only was a reversion to the jargon of Eton but also gave himself a lesser significance; it may have been an unconscious claim to be Watts-Dunton's child.)

Swinburne gave Watts-Dunton the only copy of the manuscript of *Lesbia Brandon* to read, and "major" refused to return several chapters of it, thus preventing its publication in the author's lifetime. (It was not published until

15. Despite the obvious positive effect of Watts's care, Swinburne's mother continued to worry about his backsliding and treated him as if he could not be trusted to look after himself. "Even in 1892, when her son was fifty-five years old and had been watched and warded by Watts for thirteen years, the question whether Swinburne could be trusted to travel ninety minutes alone [by train] was a matter for anxious conspiracy" between her and Watts (Lang, 1959, p. xliv).

1962). His letters to Watts-Dunton often show the poet openly adopting the role of a schoolboy, with frequent allusions to deserving or craving birching. It is not known what, if anything, was acted out between the two men in this regard, but most commentators agree that there probably was no overt sexual contact. Panter-Downes says of the pair, when Swinburne was forty-seven and Watts-Dunton fifty-two: "[Watts-Dunton] and Swinburne had now lived together for five years, and their joint household resembled, in all particulars but sex, a steady and successful homosexual union. Swinburne was the docile stay-at-home "wife," Watts was the "husband" who managed all their business affairs, dictated the decisions, and doled out the pin-money" (1971, p. 68).

It is remarkable that in late middle age Swinburne reversed so many of his youthful rebellious attitudes and antiestablishment views, becoming almost as enthusiastic a supporter of imperialist England as his despised fellow poet Kipling. Swinburne never would, or perhaps never could, acknowledge his political inconsistencies. According to Gosse, Swinburne's political views were reversed under "the pressure" (1917, p. 292) of Watts-Dunton.[16] There was perhaps some brainwashing going on that brought on a confor-

16. For example, in an 1883 letter to his mother, Swinburne wrote of "those noble and heroic patriots who have made the very name of Irishman as loathsome in the American republic as in the English kingdom. [I will send you] the numbers of the Pall Mall Gazette containing the very curious . . . history of the extermination of a league of Irish murderers by the united action of private citizens in America. I think you will—as Watts does—agree with me that there is some danger of these wretches being the means of introducing into England the spirit of the Lynch law—which is perhaps better than none at all" (1883–90, p. 14).

mity with the views of "major." Swinburne also had Watts-Dunton—influenced turnabouts in his early enthusiasm for two people his protector hated, the painter Whistler (whom Swinburne had characteristically addressed in his letters as "*mon père*") and Walt Whitman. In 1859, at twenty-two, Swinburne, in a letter to a friend, had called the author of *Leaves of Grass* "the immortal Whitman" (1854–69, p. 28), and in 1871 he had written an admiring article. But in middle age, he described the American poet's Muse as "a drunken apple-woman, indecently sprawling in the slush and garbage of the gutter amid the rotten refuse of her overturned fruit stall."[17] Gosse calls this remark "an interesting example of the slow tyranny exercised on Swinburne's judgment by the will of Watts, who . . . hated [Whitman] most heartily" (1917, p. 267). Watts similarly urged Swinburne to turn against another homosexual, Swinburne's former friend the painter Simeon Solomon (see below). There is more than a whiff of soul murder here.

Identification with the aggressor is strikingly exemplified by a letter written in 1877 (Watts was by then a heavy moral presence) to the editor of the periodical *The Athenaeum*. Here Swinburne fulminates, at excruciatingly excessive length, against the "moral abomination . . . a gross and hideous outrage on the simplest and deepest instincts of human decency" (1877–82, p. 6) of Emile Zola's novel *L'Assommoir*; in the same (to use a favorite Swinburnian adjec-

---

17. In 1871 Swinburne had written the poem "To Walt Whitman in America": "O strong-winged soul with prophetic / Lips hot with the bloodbeats of song, / With tremor of heartstrings magnetic, / With thoughts as thunders in throng, / With consonant ardours of chords / That pierce men's souls as with swords" (p. 730). The "prophetic lips" were no longer so hot by 1887, when he wrote an essay harshly critical of Whitman.

tive) stercoraceous and self-righteous manner in which he himself had repeatedly been criticized (for example, by Thomas Carlyle—see below). I quote a small portion of the letter in which the poet, after pages of denunciation, suddenly addresses a hypothetical reader who might feel that he, Swinburne, is obliquely pushing the novel while appearing to criticize it. (This superficially strange notion is a projected identification if ever there was one.) Swinburne says:

> I can desire no heavier punishment for any one whose mind could give entrance to such a shameful and insulting thought than that he should act on it, and read "L'Assommoir" from the first page to the last, a thing that I confess I most certainly have not done, and most assuredly could not do. If he does not find this perusal a most heavy and most loathsome form of judicial retribution, a chastisement comparable to none in Dante's hell but that inflicted on the damned whose scalps were so densely overlaid with something I cannot mention (as M. Zola would) by name—to borrow a bold phrase from Mrs. Browning, so "immortally immerded"—that Dante could not see whether the crown were shorn or unshorn—if he feel otherwise than this, he is not one for whose possible opinion or imputation I could ever care. (pp. 8–9)

Here is anal masochism partly transformed into oral sadism, anal fascination turned into condemnation by projection and identification with the active partner. Words and feces are used as destructive weapons; it is striking but not unusual that the anally obsessed Swinburne cannot allow himself to directly use a word, much less a four-letter word, for excrement but resorts to "immerded"—and does not even own

this unfamiliar word. Somehow, idiosyncratically and myste-
riously, Swinburne cannot use the word *shit*—and he characteristically hates writers such as Zola who can blithely throw
it around.

It is astonishing (and one would think it would have been
for Swinburne too—which may be underestimating his capacity for denial) that Watts-Dunton, at age seventy-three,
after twenty-five years of living with Swinburne, married a
twenty-nine-year-old-woman, who later wrote that she had
wanted to marry him since she began working as his literary
assistant when she was seventeen. Swinburne, with the cooperation of the strange couple, lived on with them and continued to be served as before. He seemed at times to be uncertain
of who the young woman was. He, heretofore so characteristically hostile to the marriages of his friends, was able—
swathed in denial, his nebulousness enhanced by almost
complete deafness—to live as if nothing had changed.

Gosse clearly feels that, aside from his interest in flagellation, no sexual activity was meaningful to Swinburne. Here
Gosse is describing Swinburne's young manhood, past the
time of Mary Gordon's rejection in the early 1860s:

> I believe that the generative instinct was very fee-
> bly developed in Swinburne. When I walked
> about London with him by day or night, I was
> struck by the fact that he never seemed to observe
> the faces or figures of people whom we met, or to
> receive from them any of those electric shocks
> which are the torment and ecstasy of youth. He
> was fond of the society of women, but without
> what could be called fatuity, and he was never
> known, so far as I have seen or heard, to indulge in
> the least flirtation. He occasionally remarked on

the form of a woman, or her colouring, but always
as he would speak of a work of art, and generally in
relation to some painter. . . . His manner with
women was very courteous, . . . never in any degree suggesting the amorous, or as though love
entered his mind. I have seen advances made to
him, but he neither accepted nor repulsed them;
he simply seemed not to perceive them. He was
rather like a child, who witnesses the embrace-
ment of grown-up people [a Freudian would insert
"seemingly" here] without interest and without
perturbation. ([1920?], p. 243, interpolation mine)

Some of Swinburne's friends, attempting to wean him
away from the flagellation brothel in the late 1860s, tried to
arrange for him to be seduced by Adah Menken, an American
theatrical performer. Menken was an amateur poet who admired Swinburne's poems. The two were very close and may
even have lived together for several weeks, but she "apologetically observed to [Dante Gabriel Rossetti that] she didn't
know how it was, but she hadn't been able to get him 'up to
the scratch,' and so felt she must leave him. . . . She naively
remarked to Rossetti, 'I can't make him understand that
biting's no use!' " (Gosse, [1920?], p. 246). Swinburne remained fond of Adah, and, according to Gosse, "never hinted
at any impediment" (p. 246) to their sexual satisfaction.

Those who have written about Swinburne disagree about
whether he had homosexual experiences when he was a
young man. His letters to certain friends are full of comic
homosexual innuendo, overtly making fun but clearly also
expressing fascination.[18] For example, he asked Charles Au-

18. An example: Swinburne wrote to Theodore Watts-Dunton on
September 1, 1894, about Berkeley Castle, where the homosexual king

gustus Howell, one of the usual epistolary sharers of his
beating fantasies, in a letter of 1865, to "Write—and communicate to the ink *une odeur melangée de sang et de sperme*
(1854–69, pp. 122–23). This to me indicates at least a tendency toward mutual masturbation inspired by shared flagellation fantasies. (There are also similarly coy, oblique, and
sometimes smirking references to the Marquis de Sade in his
letters to Howell and to many others.) Lang, an expert on
Swinburne and the editor of the six volumes of his letters,
writes, "Whether he was overtly homosexual, as a persistent
oral tradition maintains, I do not know" (1959, xlix). Swinburne, prompted in part by Watts-Dunton, certainly condemned homosexuality after his close friend, the openly ho-

---

Edward II, following his deposition, was murdered in 1327. Edward
had lost the throne in large part because of public outrage against the
honors and power he granted to his male lover, Gaveston: "I have been
to Berkeley Castle. The sight of that infernal oubliette actually gave
me a bad night. Even if the poor wretch *was* given to what Heywood
(in his English History from Brute to Charles I) calls sodomitry (is not
that an elegant form of the word Platonism?), I must say I could not
have found it in my heart to consign the late Mr. Soddington Symonds
himself to such a fate as that" (1890–1909, p. 74). John Addington
Symonds had died earlier in the year. Although married and a father,
he was, notoriously, a "secret" homosexual.

The popular novelist and historian Thomas Costain comments on
the much-believed rumors about the details of Edward II's death:
"One circumstantial account, contained in a chronicle prepared some
thirty years after the event, seemed to fit the known facts and was
generally believed. . . . The three assassins waited until their victim
was sound asleep and then flung a table over him, which was held
down by two of them to prevent him from moving. The third man
then proceeded to burn out his inside organs with a red-hot bar of
iron. As it was inserted through a horn, no marks of violence were
made on the surface of the body" (Costain, 1958, p. 226). Costain apparently cannot bring himself to mention the anal penetration directly.

mosexual artist Simeon Solomon (with whom he may have
had sexual contact, at least in connection with flagellation, as
a young man), was convicted of what was then regarded as
criminal sexual behavior. (Thomas, speaking of the household Swinburne shared with the Rossetti brothers and others
in 1862, writes: "With a new acquaintance, Simeon Solomon,
he romped naked about the house, sliding down the banisters
and shrilly waking the echoes" [1979, p. 76].)

Panter-Downes comments on the subsequent condemnation:

> The gifted Jewish artist, Simeon Solomon, . . .
> whose wonderful bright morning had ended
> abruptly, . . . had run into trouble and a gaol sen-
> tence in 1873. His dog-like devotion to Swinburne
> had made him only too eager to turn out the draw-
> ings of flogging blocks and victims suggested by
> the author of "Atalanta." . . . After the scandal,
> Swinburne hastily dropped him; his references to
> homosexuality, made to Watts and other friends,
> are always uncompromisingly hostile. They may
> have been part of his constant preoccupation with
> proving to himself his own virility, by accepting
> the challenge of the unclimbed cliff, the stormiest
> sea, the most testing physical pain. (1917, pp. 60–
> 61)

The references to homosexuality in his letters are not,
contra Panter-Downes, always uncompromisingly hostile.
During the Franco-Prussian War Swinburne commented on
a newspaper report:

> "That poor [George Augustus] Sala has been 'sub-
> jected to terrible and painful outrages' by the mob

at Paris as a Prussian spy." *Can* this imply that his personal charms were too much for some country-man of the Citizen Sade (ci-devant Marquis) who exclaimed to an ardent and erect band of his fellows—*"Foutons, foutons ce cul divin, qui nous promet mille fois plus de plaisir qu'un con"* ["Let's fuck this divine ass, which promises us more pleasure than a cunt"]? (1869–75, p. 127, my translation)

This doesn't sound very hostile to me.

There are references to homosexuality in Simeon Solomon's letters to Swinburne that seem to anticipate a friendly reception.[19] (Swinburne's letters to Solomon, which the im-

---

19. Solomon's letters to Swinburne are preserved in the British Museum. Fuller found with them a letter from Gosse: "The enclosed letters from Simeon Solomon contain direct reference to his notorious vices, and an implication that [Swinburne] was quite aware of their nature. I therefore suggest . . . that they should be destroyed at once" (quoted in Fuller, 1968, p. 181). The following are some brief excepts from Solomon's letters to Swinburne: "I cannot tell you what pleasure it will give me to see something by you on me (that sounds rather improper) and in print" (p. 184); "I will write again and tell you more of Cecil, who is without exception one of the naughtiest boys I ever knew; could you guess what he did the other day? but no, I will not create fresh prejudices against him" (p. 185).

In 1875, after Solomon had gotten into trouble with the law, Swinburne wrote in a letter to Watts that he had advised a mutual friend, Powell, "not to be led away by any kindly and generous feeling towards an unfortunate man whom he has been used to regard as a friend . . . a person who has deliberately chosen to do what makes a man and all who associate with him infamous in the eyes of the world. . . . I do not think I need fear to be accused of lukewarmness in friendship . . . only in such a case as this I do think a man is bound to consider the consequence to all his friends and to every one who cares for him in the world of allowing his name to be mixed up with that of a————let us say a Platonist" (1869–75, p. 261).

poverished painter later sold, have vanished.) What is perhaps most morally damning is the intimation in Solomon's
letters that the subject of being whipped as a source of sexual
excitement was introduced to him by Swinburne. In an 1869
letter Solomon describes a pornographic illustration from a
pamphlet on flagellation. It is a picture of a young girl un-
dressing, about to be beaten by an old man holding a rod;
dildos are visible on the floor. Solomon had shown the pamphlet to a man named Nesfield, a collector of pornography
whom Solomon describes as "genuinely fond, I deeply grieve
to say, of women" (quoted in Swinburne, 1869–75, p. 32).
The painter offers to introduce this man to Swinburne; he
states that Nesfield, although he was beaten at Eton, is not
excited by the rod: "I should unhesitatingly pronounce him
to be not at all of a sensual temperament in your and my
conception of the term" (pp. 32–33). Solomon then mentions
having shown the pamphlet to a fellow painter, Albert
Moore: "When [Moore] read it he asked me with open mouth
and eyes what it meant; he was entirely ignorant of [the]
whole subject, and I sighed to think how I was in his happy,
innocent condition before I knew a certain poet whom I will
forbear to mention, but, I warrant you, I quickly enlightened
him" (p. 33).

It is possible that Swinburne's homosexuality was largely
unconscious and was channeled into fantasies and reenact-
ments of being beaten by the "stunning tutor" and his suc-
cessors (male as well as female), but there is no way of being
sure. And does it matter?[20] There can be no doubt that, in

20. *Homosexuality* is a descriptive term that refers to sexual behavior and fantasies of such behavior between those of the same sex.
People are called homosexuals if such sexual behavior is compulsive or
habitual. But homosexuality is not a diagnostic entity. In my observation of patients, people who are homosexual in action show a spectrum
of psychic health (including the capacity for love and relating to

Swinburne's fantasy, being beaten by a man involved excitement for both parties. He wrote about this obsessively in his erotica about flagellation and in his novels. Fuller (1968) quotes from a never-published manuscript called "Eton: Another Ode" (Swinburne had written the formal "Eton: An Ode" for his school's 450th anniversary); the protagonist is obviously the male adult tutor, who addresses Swinburne:

> Tell me, S_____, does shame within burn as
>   hot (Swish! Swish!) as your stripes, my lad,
> Burn outside, have I tamed your pride? I'm glad
>   to see how it hurts you—glad—
> Swish! (p. 27)

Gosse considered Swinburne to have "been cured of his mania about flagellation" after his removal by Watts-Dunton to The Pines. It is true that the subject only occasionally turns up in the letters of his later years. But in 1920 Gosse discovered two long pieces in verse about flogging that seem to have been written in 1893, featuring two names that often appear in the flagellation writings: Reginald, always Swinburne himself, and Frank, the name of the other masochistic alter ego in *Love's Cross Currents*. Gosse destroyed these writings, calling them "ridiculous and repulsive 'poems' which had nothing sexual or strictly indecent in them, but merely gloated over the endurance of physical pain in one particular form" ([1920?], p. 234).

Swinburne's *The Sisters*—a play set in the nineteenth century, done in blank verse—was written at about the same

---

others) and pathology (including pathological narcissism) that does not differ much from those of my patients whose predominant sexual activities and fantasies are heterosexual. My basic, always surprising perception is how different individuals can be, whatever their sexual preferences.

time (1892). At the end of this melodrama—featuring Redgie and his cousin Mabel—three of four young protagonists, all cousins (and all steeped in romanticism, as if in a play by Victor Hugo), die of poisoning. Before this incredible and somewhat ridiculous dénouement, an old man delivers a speech about flagellation that shows the old obsession, although in dramatic terms it is entirely a non sequitur. It comes after Redgie praises the beauties of the Northumbrian countryside, familiar to "Algie" from the many summers he and his cousin Mary spent visiting his grandfather as children and adolescents. Another of Redgie's cousins, Sir Alfred, old enough—he says—to be Redgie's and Mabel's father, suddenly launches into a startlingly irrelevant rhapsody. (It has perhaps been evoked by Redgie's previous mention of "the Eton playing-fields" in his disquisition on landscape):

> Woodlands too we have,
> Have we not, Mabel? beech, oak, aspen, pine,
> And Redgie's old familiar friend, the birch,
> With all its blithe lithe bounty of buds and
>   sprays
> For hapless boys to wince at, and grow red,
> And feel a tingling memory prick their skins—
> Sting till their burning blood seems all one
>   blush—
> Eh? (1892, p. 290)

At fifty-five, a child being beaten still makes the child Algie within the middle-aged poet burn. The landscapes of his childhood are imbued with flagellation.

Mabel, the character modeled on Mary Gordon, affirms her nature as a partly sadistic, partly loving Amazon, saying apologetically:

Well, you always were the best to me;
The brightest, bravest, kindest boy you were
That ever let a girl *misuse him*—make
His loving sense of honour, courage, faith,
Devotion, *rods to whip him*—*literally,*
You know—and never by one word or look
Protested. (1892, p. 273, my italics)

One wonders at the "literally." There can be no doubt that, for Swinburne, being beaten was equated with being loved.

Writing biography is a risky business that requires much tact, self-knowledge, and humility on the part of the author. Psychobiography is perhaps an even greater challenge. Lytton Strachey, who dabbled in both and set the tone of biographies for decades after the publication of his first "bestseller," *Eminent Victorians*, wrote in the preface to that book:

> [The historian] will row out over that great ocean of material and lower down into it, here and there, a little bucket, which will bring up to the light of day some characteristic specimen, from those far depths, to be examined with a careful curiosity. . . . My choice of subjects has been determined by no desire to construct a system or to prove a theory. . . . I have sought to examine and elucidate certain fragments of the truth which took my fancy and lay to my hand. (quoted in Holroyd, 1994, p. 41)

The psychoanalyst at least has direct access to the patient's attempt to tell his story by way of free association. The material available for applied psychoanalysis is second-hand and inferential. An artist's text is a product worked over by conscious awareness of shaping form and content; like all human psychic manifestations, artistic work contains obvious as well as cryptic unconscious communication as well. But the psychoanalyst has no privileged access to it; he or she may be an expert in picking up certain unconscious tendencies—but this can be an advantage or a disadvantage, depending on the tact of the observer, who still must base his observations on speculation, on educated guesses. Along with "a careful curiosity," humility in relation to recovering historical truth is especially needed. Both the literary artist and the psychoanalyst should be aware, as they attempt to interpret the life of a human being from his writings (and for the psychoanalyst, to a lesser extent, from his patient's associations), of the subtle implications of George Gissing's statement, "The only true biography is to be found in novels" (quoted by Holroyd, 1994, p. 606).

Bearing this in mind, I would like to speculate about Swinburne as an illustration of Freud's ideas in "A Child Is Being Beaten." At some point in early childhood, the young Algie, perhaps born with an instinctual endowment loaded with a preponderance of masochism, tried to hold onto the internalized image of a parent by fantasizing himself as being beaten by that parent. The parental role could have shifted back and forth from mother (primal parent) to father. It would appear that he was overindulged by his mother and had to deal with a father who was absent a good part of the time. In Victorian times, servants were very important in the actual raising of a child, and, we know very little about their part in the Swinburne household. Swinburne appears to have been a spoiled darling, surrounded by women, girls, and servants. There may have been some physical punishment as well. He was sent away to a boarding school (preparatory for Eton) at eight, and there was tutored and perhaps flogged—

as was common in those times. Whatever the impact of such experiences on his fantasies, there was an early establishment of masochistic fantasy life in which rage and murderous impulses were idealistically transformed into being loved, and all was covered by a sexualization that gave the promise of satisfaction. Swinburne clearly felt this sexual satisfaction at Eton, where it seems to have been both shared and transmitted by at least one of his tutors. Enduring the pain also became a challenge that could prove his courage and endurance. All this, after the Eton experiences, became obsession and perversion. But, paradoxically, even the passivity cultivated by the flagellation practices at Eton was justified and rationalized (and not only by Swinburne) as inculcating bravery and manhood (see Thomas, 1979, p. 18).

He had an overlarge head and had some sort of neurological condition that set him apart as a small child. As an adolescent he was determined to overcompensate for his physical inferiority by daring and dangerous feats of swimming and climbing and also by suffering and even provoking physical punishment. It was a tremendous blow to Swinburne's self-esteem when he realized from his father's reaction to his wish to become a soldier that the admiral considered him physically unfit.

Swinburne was twelve or thirteen when he started at Eton (the age of Frank in *Love's Cross Currents* and of Bertie in *Lesbia Brandon*), and by then masturbation could have provided some relieving discharge of his sexual excitement. Whatever progress Swinburne might have made in the direction of activity and heterosexuality was suppressed following the humiliating rejection of his (actual or wished-for) sexual advances toward a girl (probably his cousin Mary Gordon) as a teenager. His feminine ideal at this time, to judge from his poems and novels, was an active, sadistic, and powerful Amazon figure. Mary Gordon was an enthusiastic and fearless horse rider—as is Mabel in *The Sisters;* the hero of *Love's Cross Currents* has an "ecstatic ride with his cousin [that] seems exactly to correspond with [Mary Gordon] Leith's account of her reckless country rides with Algernon, in the course of which, as in the novel, they carried on the most animated conversations" (Wilson, 1962, p. 15). The rejection increased Swinburne's masochistic turn away from genital toward anal excitement and erogeneity, away from activity toward passivity, away from sadism toward masochism. Flagellation was further idealized, and he soon sought out female prostitutes (degraded women with rods) who would beat him. The ambiguously sexed beater could have evoked either father or phallic mother (a figure that held for him a Medea-like destructive fascination).[21] There may also have been some homosexual enactment—at least of the beating fantasies—perhaps with Simeon Solomon. Aggression turned inward was expressed most destructively through Swinburne's uncontrollable alcoholism, which became almost suicidal in its manifestations. The alcoholism was dealt with by denial. (It is fascinating that he apparently neither drank excessively

21. Swinburne loved a painting of Medea as a witch preparing the threads for the magic garment that was to destroy her rival Glauce that one of his pre-Raphaelite painter friends, Frederick Sandys, painted from 1866 to 1868. (It is now in the Birmingham Museum and Art Gallery.) Swinburne wrote that it showed "beauty distorted by passion and made ghastly by despair. . . . Pale as from poison, with the blood drawn back from her very lips, agonized in face and limbs with the labour and the fierce contentions of old love with new, . . . the fatal figure of Medea pauses on the funereal verge of the wood of death" (Swinburne, 1868, quoted by Wilton and Upstone, 1997, p. 161). He goes on to "catalogue with the utmost relish [the painting's] sinister elements" (1997, p. 161). Medea was, for Swinburne, another fascinating lady of pain.

nor had his epileptiform fits when he was with his family on the Isle of Wight during those years.) After Swinburne's death, Mary Gordon Leith was furious with Edmund Gosse's much bowdlerized 1917 biography of her cousin and insisted that "he was never intoxicated in all his life" (quoted by Gosse, [1920?], p. 237). Perhaps she really believed this, but she also declared that, contra Gosse, Swinburne was not irreligious; she must have known that this was not true.[22]

The drives toward cannibalism, murder, and incest are clearly evident in *Lesbia Brandon* and especially in much of Swinburne's invective.[23] In his letters we see Swinburne's

22. According to Gosse [1920?], Mrs. Leith was "infuriated at what I had said about Swinburne's relation with Adah Isaacs Menken. She had the naiveté to say . . . 'Algernon was far too well-bred a gentleman ever to *speak* to a woman of that class!' " (p. 237).

23. In *Lesbia Brandon*, Bertie's tutor, Denham, is in love with both the boy and his sister, but it is a love filled with murderous cruelty, suppressed toward the woman, expressed in the flagellation of the thirteen-year-old boy. Denham is looking at them: "Standing with her hand over Bertie's shoulder, the woman waited half smiling. The glory and the terror of her beauty held down desire and absorbed despair. Rage rose in him again like a returning sea. . . . He would have given his life for leave to touch her, his soul for a chance of dying crushed down under her feet: an emotion of extreme tenderness, lashed to fierce insanity by the circumstances, frothed over into a passion of vehement cruelty. Deeply he desired to die by her, if that could be; and more deeply, if this could be, to destroy her: scourge her into swooning and *absorb the blood with kisses; caress and lacerate her loveliness,* alleviate and heighten her pains; to feel her foot upon his throat, *and wound her own with his teeth;* submit his body and soul for a little to her lightest will, and satiate upon hers the desperate caprice of his immeasurable desire; to inflict careful torture on limbs too tender to embrace, suck the tears off her laden eyelids, *bite through her sweet and shuddering lips.* . . . Two creatures more beautiful never stood together. . . . If mere infliction of pain had so subdued the boy's face to perfect beauty that it was now identical with hers in expression also,

violent hatred toward many authority figures, popes, and statesmen such as Gladstone—whom he once wished would be "sent by a genuinely reformed government to the guillotine—whither God may speed him! and may I be there to see him [breathe his last] in a bag à la Marat" (1877–82, pp. 45–46)—and Napoleon III—"I never wrote anything in prose on the late unlamented Louis Iscariot, otherwise known to infamy as Judas Buonaparte" (1877–82, p. 57).[24] This kind of rage was not reserved for authorities. He wrote with true paranoid intensity about poor Simeon Solomon, a broken-down wreck after his arrest for homosexuality, reduced to

what final transformation to some delicious excess of excellence would suffering not work upon hers?" (1864, p. 225, my italics). Note the alternations between masochism and sadism and the intimations of cannibalism. (Compare Swinburne's poem "Anoractia" [a translation of Sappho] from *Poems and Ballads* [1866], with its cannibalistic evocation of lesbian love.)

24. From a letter: "[Gladstone is] the venerable apostate-apostle of reaction and disunion" (1890–1909, p. 26). Gosse (1917) quotes from lines Swinburne wrote in a lady's album: "Choose, England: here the paths before thee part. / Wouldst thou have honour? Be as now thou art; / Wouldst thou have shame? Take Gladstone to thy heart" (p. 292).

Swinburne described Napoleon III as "the most infamous of all public criminals" (1869–75, p. 244) and wrote in 1870 of Italy after France's defeat by Bismarck's Germany: "If that satellite of a dead dog [Napoleon III is the dead dog] Victor Emmanuel goes to Rome I shall be furious, and would kiss the toes of a priest who would poison him in a wafer" (1869–75, p. 125).

Because the critic J. M. Ludlow dared to print an article praising Tennyson while disparaging Swinburne's idol, Victor Hugo, Swinburne wrote: "Ludlow—who writes by some such fate as mocks / An eunuch with hereditary pox, / Whose style of internecine English-French / Like burnt-out tallow, sputters into stench—/ Crawls here and sucks and nibbles. Give him food: / Give him your dung: he does not want your blood" (1854–69, p. 33).

selling Swinburne's letters to him to stay alive, as "now a thing unmentionable alike by men and women, as equally abhorrent to either—nay, to the very beasts" (1877–82, p. 107). (The other side of this primitive devaluation was his idealization of good authority figures such as Victor Hugo, Walter Savage Landor, and Giuseppe Mazzini. One also sees from the poet's letters that the Marquis de Sade was— with excruciating repetitiveness—intermittently, although mostly humorously, idealized, but without the desexualization that shielded the others; he was crowned with the "halo in the sky" [Glover, 1938, p. 294; see Shengold, 1988] that so often covers perverse anal and sadomasochistic phenomena. Sade was, for Swinburne, a kind of "stunning tutor" from the distant past.)

Thomas paraphrases a letter in which Swinburne "confessed, during his affair with Adah Menken, that the rear view of a callipygean Venus was the sure means of erecting any man. It offered, after all, the means for most of the important Sadean pleasures" (1979, p. 105). Swinburne's anal preoccupations, idealized in relation to the buttocks in his excited fascination with flagellation, also included a seemingly contradictory and certainly nonidealized, violently antipathetic reaction to feces. Hence his uncontrolled loathing of Emile Zola's and Jonathan Swift's obsession with dung. For example, Swinburne had read an interview with Emerson by an anonymous author stating that Emerson had "condemned Swinburne severely as a perfect leper and a mere sodomite, which criticism recalls Carlyle's scathing description of that poet—as a man standing up to his neck in a cesspool and adding to its contents" (1869–75, p. 274). Swinburne, who already hated Carlyle, reacted with magnified mirroring invective against Emerson in a letter to a friend:

A foul mouth is so ill matched with a white beard
that I would gladly believe the newspaper scribes
alone responsible for the *bestial utterances* which
they declare to have dropped from a teacher whom
such disciples as these exhibit to our disgust and
compassion as performing on their obscene plat-
form the last *tricks of tongue* now possible to a *gap-
toothed* and hoary-headed ape, carried at first into
notice on the *shoulder* of Carlyle [any wish to
exonerate Emerson has by now been swept away
by passionate crescendo of hatred that he had already felt toward Carlyle], and who now in his
dotage *spits and chatters* from a dirtier perch of his
own finding and fouling; Coryphaeus or choragus
of his Bulgarian tribe of *autocoprophagous* baboons
who make the filth they *feed on.* (1869–75, p. 274,
my italics)

In 1883, Swinburne wrote of Carlyle, who had recently died:
"The filthy and virulent old Arch-Quack of Chelsea must, I
do hope, have carried down his influence with himself into
'the Eternal Cesspools' [of hell] whereon his fancy loved to
play—a noisome and noisy dung-fly—while *his breath* still
infected the upper air" (1883–90, p. 21, my italics). Carlyle's
undeniable and Emerson's purported anal vituperation kin-
dled the anally obsessed Swinburne's fascinated, hostile over-
reactions. The exchanges confirm Freud's linkage of aggression and anality (and orality) in his conceptions of sadism and
masochism. (I have emphasized in the two above quotations
the concomitant orality that is of cannibalistic intensity; I
have written elsewhere about the cannibalistic significance
of the shoulder: see Shengold, 1991b.)

We know nothing about Swinburne's masturbation or his

masturbatory fantasies—but we know enough from his letters to be able to speculate that the latter probably involved
sadomasochism and, specifically, flagellation—similar to the
fantasies of my patient P, described in the previous chapter.

Can Swinburne be seen as a victim of soul murder? We
cannot know for sure. He was certainly a victim of conflicts
over impulses related to cruelty and the wishes to be beaten
and to beat, fostered in a susceptible child and adolescent by
an institutionalized method of educating young boys of the
upper classes. A letter from Freud to Strachey emphasizes
how much those who do analysis—and especially how much
those who attempt to apply analysis to figures from the past
known only from their writings and from hearsay—do *not*
know. Freud was writing to Strachey in 1928, after reading
the biographer's recently published *Elizabeth and Essex:*

> I am acquainted with all your earlier publications,
> and have read them with great enjoyment. But the
> enjoyment was essentially an aesthetic one. This
> time you have moved me deeply, for you yourself
> have reached greater depths. You are aware of
> what other historians so easily overlook—that it is
> impossible to understand the past with certainty,
> because we cannot divine men's motives and the
> essence of their minds and so cannot interpret
> their actions. Our psychological analysis does not
> suffice even with those who are near us in space
> and time, unless we can make them the object of
> years of the closest investigation, and even then it
> breaks down before the incompleteness of our
> knowledge and the clumsiness of our synthesis. So
> that in regard to the people of past times we are in
> the same position as with dreams to which we

have been given no associations—and only a layman could expect us to interpret such dreams as those. As a historian, then, you show that you are steeped in the spirit of psychoanalysis. And, with reservations such as these, you have approached one of the most remarkable figures in your country's history, you have known how to trace back her character to the impressions of her childhood, you have touched upon her most hidden motives with equal boldness and discretion, and it is very possible that you have succeeded in making a correct reconstruction of what actually occurred. (quoted in Holroyd, 1994, p. 615)

10

The Moth and the Mother
Elizabeth Bishop

The caterpillar on the leaf
repeats to thee thy mother's grief.
Kill not the moth nor butterfly
For the Last Judgment draweth nigh
—William Blake, 1803

This chapter deals with the use of the image of moths to depict the destructive and the vulnerable: destructive and vulnerable parents (mainly, but not exclusively, mothers) and children who are drawn to and have identified with them. A thesis—that the moth can serve as an allusion to, and perhaps be an unconscious symbol of, the mother—is illustrated by a clinical example and by the life and writings of the great American poet Elizabeth Bishop. The story I have to tell is one that is imbricated with soul murder; it illustrates the complicated consequences for pathology and for creativity of early parental loss and rejection.

R, a young woman with strong masculine strivings, had attended a screening of Laurence Olivier's (Freud-and Jones-influenced) movie version of *Hamlet*. She commented on

Olivier's striking use of black and white, darkness and light. She had been upset and yet moved by the closet scene (she referred to it as the scene at night in the mother's bedroom). R remarked that the actress playing Gertrude (Eileen Herlie) did not look much older than her "son" Hamlet (Herlie was actually younger than Olivier) and that she felt vaguely angry toward her. During her analytic session she compared Gertrude with her own mother.

That night she "dreamt of being attacked by two huge dark moths. It was a terrifying dream. The moths seemed like spiders, all hairy and disgusting. I felt I was going to be bitten and killed. They were as much like pterodactyls as moths—like the one in *King Kong* who attacked Fay Wray."

Her associations went on to another movie—one of Ingmar Bergman's, in which God appears in a hallucination as a huge, black, hairy spider. She had seen *King Kong* (another film in black and white) as a child on television and it (especially the hairy monster and the pterodactyls) had frightened her when she was alone in her room at night. She had felt disgusted with the hapless heroine-victim and had identified with the young man who rescued her. (As a child, the patient had wanted to be a boy and was very envious of her older brother.) Then she referred again to the closet scene in *Hamlet*, noting that Hamlet had seemed to be sexually involved with his own mother. She had been frightened by Hamlet's sudden action—the impulsive stabbing of Polonius, hidden behind the arras, spying on Gertrude and Hamlet.

This was early in the analysis, and R had brought in, mostly intellectually up to this point, a good deal about "the Oedipus complex," applying it to sexual "feelings" toward both parents. As far as I could judge, these were at this time not really, certainly not fully, felt, and there was no mention of murderous feelings. There had been some recent primal-scene material in which she, as a child, was the spy, like Polonius; this also, I felt, echoed the emphasis on night and darkness (the moth is a nocturnal creature) and on hair (*King Kong*) in the associations. R's mother had been exhibitionistically seductive toward her in childhood, and she clearly remembered views of her mother's pubic hair. ("Spider," I thought to myself, when I reflected on this after the session.)[1] R had visited her parents the night before the dream and had again felt that her mother was, characteristically, overattentive to her and her brother while neglectful of her father. This made R angry, as she had often been as a child and a teenager on the basis of similar feelings. (The mother had always been too curious about the girl's dates and would try to elicit details about her sex life.) In the initial session to be centered around the moth dream, despite the seemingly unerring aim of her associations, the patient did not appear to feel responsibly aware that she was connecting the moths that had attacked her in the dream to her mother.

I asked her the next day, when she again brought up how frightening what she called the "moth dream" had been, if she thought that *moth* referred to *mother*. At first she was silent but then responded, "Of course!" and went on to talk more of her mother. Her mother had always been fond of flowing negligees and peignoirs, which made her look like "a huge white moth." This, too, reminded R of *Hamlet*, of Queen Gertrude's description of the mad and suicidal Ophelia. In the scene that begins "There is a willow grows aslant a brook" (IV.vii.166), Ophelia, singing, her arms full of flowers, falls from the willow tree:

1. The spider has been written about extensively in psychoanalytic literature from Freud onward as a symbol of the mother's genitals— with a cannibalistic (*vagina dentata*) aura. See, e.g., Abraham (1923).

When down her weedy trophies and herself
Fell in the weeping brook. Her clothes spread
   wide;
And, mermaid-like, awhile they bore her up . . .
Till that her garments, heavy with their drink,
Pull'd the poor wretch from her melodious lay
To muddy death. (IV.vii.173–78, 180–83)

My first thought about the two moths in the dream was not of the sonic similarity of *moth* and *mother* but of something I had read in *Symbol, Dream, and Psychosis* by Robert Fliess (1973) and often found useful. He declares that two categorically identical objects (here, two moths) symbolize the mother.

Moths

The moth is defined by *Webster's Dictionary* as "any of a group of four-winged, chiefly night-flying insects related to the butterflies but generally smaller, less brightly colored, and not having the antennae clubbed."[2] Butterflies and moths are the two suborders of the insect order *Lepidoptera*, a word derived from the Greek words *lepis* ("scale") and *pteron* ("wing") meaning "scale-winged insects." The two suborders are partly differentiated by their behavior:

Butterflies are diurnal in their habits, flying between sunrise and dusk, and very rarely taking the wing at night. This habit is so universal that these

2. The butterfly is defined by *Webster's* as "1. any of a group of insects having a sucking mouth part, slender body, and four broad, membranous wings covered with scales, usually bright-colored. 2. a person, especially a woman, thought of as like a butterfly in being brightly dressed, frivolous, fickle, etc."

insects are frequently called by entomologists "the
diurnal lepidoptera," or are simply spoken of as
"diurnals." It is, however, true that many species
of moths are also diurnal in their habits, though
the great majority of them are nocturnal, or cre-
puscular. . . . A more definite distinction is based
upon structure, and specifically upon the structure
of the antennae. Butterflies have long, thread-like
antennae, provided with a swelling at the extrem-
ity, giving them a somewhat club-shaped appearance. This form of antennae is very unusual
among the moths, and only occurs in a few rare
genera. . . . Moths are called *Heterocera* [derived
from the Greek words for *other* and *horn* because
of their other-than-club-shaped antennae]. [There
are] also distinctions in the veins of the wings, and
in the manner of carrying them when at rest or in
flight, which are quite characteristic of the two
groups. (Holland, 1898, pp. 61–62)[3]

For the most part, then, moths are "creatures of the
night." Although there are many moths as beautiful as butterflies, in common fantasy the moth is drab. Moths also
share some of the occult and morbid aurae that surround the
nocturnal owls and wolves and bats. But moths *are* common
enough. So is the idea, based on their photophilia, of being
compellingly drawn to something that one ought to keep
away from—a flame. The moth is portrayed as a kind of

3. I think that butterflies and moths have a psychic valence similar to that of mice and rats (who are also of the same order: rodents).
The butterfly (like the mouse) is usually thought of as benign; the
moth (like the rat) has more ominous connotations (see Shengold,
1988). Both also allude to fragility and transience.

driven victim, consumed by its desire to contact the lethally unattainable. The portrayal fits—to try to bring in what a psychoanalyst hears so often, especially from child abuse patients—a compulsive wish or need to connect with (be absorbed by, succumb to) a consuming other who is, or at least unconsciously represents, a parent whose destructiveness is disguised by the victim's conviction that contact will fulfill some sort of incandescent promise.

Many people are masochistically bound in this way; the tie is based on the psychic internalization of a relation (frequently, although not necessarily, mirroring the actual relation) with a longed-for parent who has been registered in the mind as passively resisting the child's psychic separateness, actively destructive of it, or lost. This predominantly symbiotic figure remains a powerful inner presence for the susceptible child, unconsciously retained as a needed component of the self—a component whose loss can be consciously desired but, paradoxically, is also a terrifying prospect. (To use psychoanalytic jargon, the parental destructive imago or introject acts as a kind of incubus that functions as a partitioned-off, usually unconscious or at least not responsibly acknowledged portion of the mental representation of one's self—felt as both a hindrance to be gotten rid of and as essential to one's existence.) The imago (since it stems from such an early, undifferentiated time) is, more exactly, an amalgam: part self, part other. It is genetically partly (bad) self, partly introjected primal parent—familiar in an externalized form as the cannibalistic, bisexual Theban Sphinx in the Oedipus legend (winged, like the moth). Unconsciously, this "pre-oedipal mother imago" is projected onto the initial mothering person or the real mother and, later, onto the father of early childhood.

I repeat, because it needs emphasis: an individual's personification of inner destructiveness can be, *but need not be,* based on the historical reality of bad parenting. The child's insistence on parental destructiveness is also, sometimes principally, the result of the child's projection of hostile and harmful impulses onto the parental figure—a vicissitude of our instinctual endowment. Destructiveness is also always derived from the inevitable frustration of the omnivorous developing infant's needs.[4]

So far I have been referring to the moth as a victim (most often a child-victim) subject to a desire that has gone out of control, playing with danger, and likely to give in to destructive temptation: "How, like a moth, the simple maid / Still plays about the flame!" (John Gay, *The Beggar's Opera* I.iv). The child's vulnerable seductibility is elicited by the moth metaphor here.

The moth's fragility also has a strong psychological effect. The impression of vulnerability is based not only on its relation to the flame but also on its delicate anatomy and the pathos of its short life.[5] Aileen Pippett titled her 1955 biogra-

4. None of us ever quite gives up the need for everything, and we continue long past infancy to expect and even to require it from our parents—at least in our unconscious mind. Infantile people continue in this way, but we can all become infantile intermittently, especially under stress. It follows that, to some degree and in some respect, we all can function like moths in relation to some idiosyncratic combination of beckoning instinctual libidinous and destructive flames—flames fueled by narcissistic promise.

5. Desdemona says, pleading to go to Cypress with Othello: "So that, dear lords, if I be left behind, / a moth of peace, and he go to the war, / The rites for which I love him are bereft me, / And I a heavy interim shall support / By his dear absence. Let me go with him" (I.iii.256–60). Here Desdemona (who will be destroyed) represents herself as the helpless and dependent moth wanting to stay close to the flame that "warlike" Othello aroused.

phy of the oversensitive, intermittently mad, and finally suicidal Virginia Woolf *The Moth and the Star,* calling the wise
and greatly gifted writer an "elusive and complex personality, fragile as a moth and enduring as a star" (p. viii). The
moth's fragility and easy destructibility are wont to evoke a
sadistic response that can also be elicited by projection onto or
identification with the moth's destructiveness.

In one of her last essays, "The Death of the Moth,"
published posthumously (1942), Virginia Woolf describes a
moth she sees trapped indoors. It is a day moth: "Moths that
fly by day are not properly to be called moths; they do not
excite that pleasant sense of dark autumn nights and ivy-
blossom which the commonest yellow-underwing asleep in
the shadow of the curtain never fails to rouse in us. They are
hybrid creatures, neither gay like butterflies nor sombre like
their own species" (p. 3). (One assumes that Woolf sees herself as this "hybrid creature" who doesn't quite belong in the
day or the night.)

At first the moth's dancing and zigzagging evoke the
impression of the moth as "a thread of vital light become
visible. He was little or nothing but life" (p. 4). But then the
moth begins to die and struggles heroically to continue life.
The writer describes how she vaguely tries to help the moth
right himself in his "superb . . . last protest" (p. 6).

Soon after she wrote this essay, Woolf gave in to the
suicidal impulses that had recurrently haunted her for so
long. The impending presence of death in the essay deepens
the reader's impression of a "projected identification" with
the fragile, dying, "hybrid" moth. Woolf ends her essay:

> I lifted the pencil again, useless though I knew it
> to be. But even as I did so, the unmistakable tokens
> of death showed themselves. The body relaxed,

and instantly grew stiff. The struggle was over. The insignificant little creature now knew death. As I looked at the dead moth, this minute wayside triumph of so great a force over so mean an antagonist filled me with wonder. Just as life had been strange a few minutes before, so death was now as strange. The moth having righted himself now lay most decently and uncomplainingly composed. O yes, he seemed to say, death is stronger than I am. (p. 6)

In contrast to this evocation of the moth's masochistic submissiveness, the clothes moth (a common destructive pest) especially invites hostililty and retaliatory wishes to destroy. There is a tendency to think of all moths, especially those that invade the home at night, as devourers of organic matter, household and industrial vermin that deserve to be killed.

There is some basis in reality here: "A good many moths in quite a few families [besides that of the clothes moths] are essentially scavengers, the majority feeding on miscellaneous plant and animal debris, often when it is being disintegrated by bacteria and fungi" (Klots and Klots, n.d., p. 146). This feeding on refuse and decay and its association with death can arouse disgust and fear, as do the carrion-eating hyena and vulture. But it is the clothes moth that most insistently elicits the metaphor of moths as destroyers—devouring creatures, spoilers and predators and befoulers: "Thou makest [man's] beauty to consume away, like as it were a moth fretting a garment: everyman therefore is but vanity" (Ps. 34:16). Jehovah is here depicted as a destructive god, as he is so frequently in the Old Testament—but mothlike? In relation to a primal parent imago, the moth's vulnerability is denied; this shows the child's fear of its unconscious hostility toward the moth-parent. (This quotation expresses the common fantasy that it is the moth rather than its larvae that devours cloth. In my patient's dream, the moths are seen as about to eat her.)

The New Testament also presents the moth as a spoiler: "Lay not up for yourselves treasures upon earth, where moth and rust doth corrupt, and where thieves break through and steal" (Mat. 6:19).

The larval (caterpillar) stage of the *Lepidoptera* is most often extremely destructive and has been regarded as a kind of worm in literature.[6] As such, moths have often been associated with death. The complicated metamorphosis (larva to pupa to adult) invokes transmigration of souls and immortality. (Again—as with destroyer and victim—we find contradictory connotations.)[7] The death's-head moth—accord-

6. Bolingbroke, the future Henry IV, calls the supporters of Richard II, the king against whom he is rebelling, "the caterpillars of the commonwealth, / Which I have sworn to weed and pluck away" (*Richard II* 1.iii.166–67).

7. A letter from Algernon Swinburne to his mother, apparently sent to her (as a New Year's greeting) on a sheet of paper in the shape of a butterfly, expresses an idealized meaning of *butterfly*—the self as a good and immortal winged creature symbolized as a soul. This seems especially relevant to the theme of soul murder. "Perhaps you know that the same Greek word means 'butterfly' and 'soul;' or rather the Greek word for 'soul' is 'butterfly' (or vice versa, for 'butterfly' is 'soul'). It is certainly the most beautiful and appropriate image or type of resurrection and immortality that ever was or can be thought of— and therefore very seasonable as an allegory of the new year rising from the grave of the old one" (Swinburne, 1890–1909, p. 63).

Walt Whitman was fond of butterflies, which he said he had a talent for attracting. He sat for a studio portrait with a (cardboard) butterfly apparently perched on his right forefinger, and he used butterflies (accompanied by a pointed hand) as illustrations, apparently

ing to *Webster's*, "a large hawk moth with markings on its back that resemble a human skull"—has specific lethal associations. It follows that fear, even terror, of moths is not an uncommon symptom.[8]

---

with the symbolic connotations of "soul," on the binding and in the text of the 1884 edition of *Leaves of Grass* (see Kaplan, 1980, p. 250).

8. The H. G. Wells story "The Moth" concerns two rival entomologists, Pawkins and Hapley, who spend years writing papers attacking each other's work. "It was a long struggle, vicious from the beginning, and growing at last to pitiless antagonism" ([1895?], p. 688). Pawkins, "whose health had been bad for some time, published some work upon the 'mesoblast' of the Death's Head Moth . . . but the work was far below his usual standard, and gave Hapley an opening he had coveted for years. . . . In an elaborate critique he rent Pawkins to tatters . . . and Pawkins made a reply, halting, ineffectual, with painful gaps of silence, and yet malignant. . . . Hapley had got his opponent down, and meant to finish him. He followed with a simply brutal attack upon Pawkins, in the form of a paper upon the development of moths in general, a paper showing evidence of a most extraordinary amount of mental labor. . . . It was murderous in argument, and utterly contemptuous in tone. . . . The world of entomologists waited breathlessly for the rejoinder from Pawkins. . . . But when it came it surprised them. For the rejoinder of Pawkins was to catch the influenza, to proceed to pneumonia, and to die" (pp. 688–89).

Hapley finds himself preoccupied with Pawkins. He cannot forgive him for dying; he had looked forward to "pulveriz[ing]" him, and instead he feels "a queer gap" in his mind (p. 689). He cannot work. One day he sees a new species of moth in his room and thinks of the pain the discovery would have given Pawkins. But he cannot catch the moth, and he feels it somehow resembles Pawkins. He keeps seeing the moth, even feels it brushing against his face in the darkness. He realizes with horror that others cannot see it. Trying to catch and kill the moth causes him to fall over a cliff and break his leg. His violent preoccupation with trying to kill the moth causes him to be considered insane. "Until his leg was healed Hapley was kept tied to his bed, and with the imaginary moth crawling over him . . . while he was awake

Moths, which range in appearance from the drab to the gorgeous (as well as from the tiny to the, as *Lepidoptera* go, huge), can also be seductive and beautiful. The related butterfly is usually thought of as beautiful and innocent. Both have been used to represent the "insignificant" and plain, like Virginia Woolf's moth, as well as the showy—in this case, more often the butterfly. (In this regard the pathetic and finally suicidal Cio-Cio-San, in her lovely flowing robes, can be viewed as both moth and butterfly.) It is relevant that the moth can stand for the mother (good as well as bad), that the mother can stand for the female genitals, and that the female genitals can be regarded as "nothing" (with all its meanings; see Shengold, 1991b)—as inferior, vulnerable, destructive, mutilated, castrating—and also as "everything"— good, exciting, glorious.

Like the moth, the butterfly, and the bird, the Theban Sphinx is a winged creature. Winged creatures have ambivalent aesthetic and moral connotations. There are vultures as well as peacocks, birds of prey as well as birds of paradise, the harpy as well as Athena's owl. The dove, actually a potentially ferocious creature, is also a symbol of peace. Devils as well as angels have wings, as we see in so many depictions of the Last Judgment. The winged Sphinx represents the evil

---

he longed for sleep, and from his sleep he awoke screaming. . . . Hapley is spending the remainder of his days in a padded room, worried by a moth that no one else can see. The asylum doctor calls it hallucination; but Hapley . . . says it is the ghost of Pawkins, and consequently a unique specimen and well worth the trouble of catching" (p. 693).

The murderously destructive meanings of *moth* are obvious in the story. I feel it also illustrates this chapter's thesis—the dénouement can be seen as a terrible regressive reunion with the symbiotic mother without whom the child feels he cannot live. (I am grateful to Oliver Sacks for pointing out the Wells story to me.)

side of the primal parent—the mother who eats her children. The Sphinx in the Oedipus legend can be regarded as a disguised depiction of Jocasta, who gave her child over to the shepherd to be tied up and left to die. (The stork, another winged mother symbol, although at first glance not a destructive one, does abandon the child it "brings.")

And as insects, moths—equated with vermin—are, according to Freud (1916–17), symbols of unwanted siblings. Here, as so often in life, there is a condensation of sibling rivalry and the Oedipus complex—making the brother or sister the scapegoated object of hostility basically directed against the parents, who have imposed a rival upon the child. Cannot the moth, then, be a Freudian symbol (essentially unconscious), as well as a verbal one, for the mother?

I return to the simple and not infrequent allusive use of the image of the moth as referring to the mother—partly derived from sonic similarity (at least in English and German: moth, mother; die Motte, die Mutter).[9] Might the moth indicating the mother also be an unconscious Freudian symbol that invokes a part of the child's primal psychic world (perhaps by way of the moth as one of the winged creatures or as representing a sibling in displacement for a parent)? If so, the moth, like the Sphinx, would be unconsciously equated with the primal mother or, better, primal parent—a narcissistic intrapsychic figure that promises bliss or annihilation and terror and that in the course of development becomes differentiated into the preoedipal phallic mother and then the destructive father on the way to more mature and realistic mental images of mother and father (see Shengold, 1989, 1991a).

9. The French word for moth, *la mite*, is phonically connected not with *la mère* (mother) but with *maternal* by way of the Latin *mater*.

Elizabeth Bishop

I want to go back to R's moth dream, which involved associations to *Hamlet.* While listening, I thought of a dream about moths and mother about which I had read in Brett Millier's biography of the poet Elizabeth Bishop. I will present that dream after sketching out something of the poet's childhood.

Elizabeth Bishop was born in 1911. Her father died when she was eight months old. Her mother (named Gertrude, like Hamlet's mother) almost at once suffered a mental breakdown and, says Millier, "for the next five years was in and out of mental hospitals and rest homes and moved between Boston, Worcester, and her home town of Great Village, Nova Scotia" (1993, p. 3). In the autobiographical short story "In the Village,"[10] Bishop describes her childhood reaction to this: "First, she had come home, with her child. Then she had gone away again, alone, and left the child. Then she had come home. Then she had gone away again, with her sister; and now she was home again" (1984, p. 252). "She" is the mad mother who has returned from one of a series of institutions to Nova Scotia, where her young daughter is being brought up by her maternal grandparents and aunts (the Boomer family, in real life).

The story begins with frightening sounds and sights:

> A scream, the echo of a scream, hangs over that Nova Scotian village. No one hears it: it hangs there forever, a slight stain in those pure blue skies. . . . The scream hangs like that, unheard in memory—in the past, in the present, and those

10. In a 1967 letter Bishop states: " 'In the Village' is *entirely*, not partly, autobiographical. I've just compressed the time a little and perhaps put two summers together, or put things a bit out of sequence— but it's all straight fact" (1984, p. 477).

years between. It was not even loud to begin with,
perhaps. It just came there to live, forever—not
loud, just alive forever. Its pitch would be the pitch
of my village. Flick the lightning rod on top of the
church steeple with your fingernail and you will
hear it. (1984, p. 251)

The child, then age five, is described as watching a dressmaker trying to fit the mother, who had tentatively decided
to stop wearing mourning, into a purple dress: "Unac-
customed to having her back, the child stood now in the
doorway, watching. The dressmaker was crawling around
and around on her knees eating pins as Nebuchadnezzar had
crawled eating grass." The child, watching the scene like
Polonius—at least as she is described by the forty-two-year-
old writer—shows her awareness of madness in the allusion
to the mad Nebuchadnezzar.

The mother is unsure about the implications of the new
colorful dress. Then, suddenly, "The dress was all wrong. She
screamed. The child vanishes" (1984, p. 252). A friend of
Gertrude Bishop is quoted as saying of her during this time:
"The Boomers did talk about not being able to control Gertrude and all the noise from her screaming" (Fountain and
Brazeau, 1994, p. 3). There are hints in Bishop's story that the
mad and vulnerable mother might well have evoked in the
child Elizabeth connections with moths and butterflies by
way of her clothing. It was, after all, clothing that had made
Gertrude scream. She had worn mourning for five years, and
it was her reluctance to comply with the family insistence
that she replace this dark plumage that had brought on the
never-to-be forgotten scream. And

before my older aunt had brought her back, I had
watched my grandmother and younger aunt un-

packing her clothes, her "things." In trunks and barrels and boxes they had finally come from Boston, where she and I had once lived. So many things in the village came from Boston, and even I had once come from there. But I remembered only being here, with my grandmother.

The clothes were black, or white, or black-and-white. (p. 254)

These mourning garments are then described at length. Several friends comment on Elizabeth's interest in clothes as an adult, for example: "She loved beautifully made things. . . . Elizabeth had the same sense of craftsmanship in clothes that she did in wanting her books to be beautiful" (Fountain and Brazeau, 1994, pp. 151–52). But she hated the color black and once protested against its use on the cover of one of her forthcoming books.

Among her mother's belongings there was also "sad brown perfume" (p. 255). Black, white, and brown are "moth colors" (those pertaining to the general idea of moths). There are also handkerchiefs with black hems: "In bright sunlight, over breakfast tables, they flutter" (p. 255)—again, like moths or butterflies. In a barrel of china is "a thick white teacup with a small red-and-blue butterfly on it, painfully desirable" (p. 256). Perhaps, I speculate, painfully desirable for a child whose crazy, unavailable mother is afraid of colorful dresses.

Later, the mother again tries on the purple dress. Everyone is pleased, cheerful and talkative. They address Gertrude:

"There. You see? It's so becoming."
"I've never seen you in anything more becoming."
"And it's so nice to see you in color for a change."

And the purple is real, like a flower against the gold-and-white wallpaper.

> She walks slowly up and down and looks at the
> skirt [in the mirror}. . . . But twitching the purple
> skirt with her thin white hands, she says, desper-
> ately, "I don't know what they're wearing any
> more! I have no *idea!*" It turns into a sort of
> wail. . . . She sees me in the mirror and turns on
> me: "Stop sucking your thumb!" (p. 258)

The author makes no comment about this rebuff, so intertwined with her fear of and about her mother. (Note that the
mother's reproach has to do with oral excess—doing something wrong with the mouth. Alcoholism was to be the chief
affliction of the grown-up Elizabeth Bishop.)

Then, to match the moth, comes fire:

> But one night, in the middle of the night, there
> is a fire. The church bell wakes me up. It is in the
> room with me; red flames [seem to be] burning the
> wallpaper beside the bed. I suppose I shriek.
>
> The door opens. My younger aunt comes in.
> There is a lamp lit in the hall and everyone is
> talking at once.
>
> "Don't cry!" my aunt almost shouts to me.
> "It's just a fire. Way up the road. It isn't going to
> hurt you." (pp. 268–69)

Her grandmother and aunts are worried about her grandfather, who has gone to help the neighbors put out the fire,
and especially about how Gertrude will be affected. They
leave the child's bedroom door open.

> "*She's* calling for you, Mother." My older aunt:
> "I'll go." "No, *I'll* go." My younger aunt. . . .
>
> "*She's* all right, Mother." My younger aunt
> comes back. "I don't think she's scared. You can't
> see the glare so much on that side of the house."

Then my younger aunt comes into my room and gets in bed with me. She says to go to sleep, it's way up the road. . . . I wake up and it is the same night, the night of the fire. My aunt is getting out of bed, hurrying away. It is still dark and silent now, after the fire. No, not silent; my grandmother is crying somewhere, not in her room. . . . But now I am caught in a skein of voices, my aunts' and my grandmother's, saying the same things over and over, sometimes loudly, sometimes in whispers:

"Hurry. For heaven sake, *shut the door!*"

"Sh!"

"Oh, we can't go on like this, we . . . "

"It's too dangerous. Remember that . . . "

"Sh! Don't let her . . . " (pp. 269–70)

The mother is more of a calamity for the family and the child than the fire. Or perhaps it would be better to say that the mother's presence made for a catastrophic emotional fire that threatened to consume the grandparents' household and whatever tranquillity the child had attained after the loss of both parents. ("Oh, we can't go on like this.") It must have been a heartbreaking experience for the girl, wanting so much to be loved by her mother, being rebuffed, and inevitably wishing to get rid of her mother as a disturbing invader—as it were, a destructive moth. (I wonder whether the child also had had the fantasy that the mother was responsible for having destroyed the father—was the flame to his moth.)

Fountain and Brazeau (1994) report: "Bishop told the poet Frank Bidart that her mother had once been discovered holding a knife while sleeping with her, although it was not clear to anyone that she intended her daughter any harm" (p. 3).

In 1916, after the scream, Gertrude Bishop was sent away to a mental hospital in Nova Scotia.[11] Elizabeth's favorite aunt, her mother's sister Grace, who had been a nurse, supplied a statement on a hospital form that described her sister's paranoid behavior in the months before this hospitalization: "Now she imagines she is being given electricity or is being mesmerized and hypnotized and that all medicines given her contain poisons" (p. 4). She mentions two suicide attempts— jumping out a second-story window at the start of her breakdown and an attempt to "hang herself with a sheet [in which she had] caught her mother about the throat" (p. 4). We do not know what Elizabeth witnessed of this attempt, but it is clear that there was plenty for the child to be afraid of.

In the story, the mother is sent away again after the fire: "The front room is empty. Nobody sleeps there. Clothes are hung there" (p. 271).[12]

Millier had access to Bishop's unpublished papers, and she quotes several that refer to the child's "brief time with her mother" (1993, p. 4). There is an unfinished poem called "A Drunkard," apparently "begun in 1959 or 1960 and worked on over ten years, in which she remembered being with her mother at a Bishop family summer home in Marblehead, Massachusetts, in the summer of 1914 at the time of the great Salem fire" (p. 5). This is not the same fire that is dealt with in "In the Village," which took place in Nova Scotia; the child apparently experienced two fires. The poem follows:

11. Although her mother was alive and in mental institutions until Elizabeth was in college, she never saw her again.

12. The middle-aged W. B. Yeats expresses his fear of old age, emptiness, death: "Fifteen apparitions have I seen; / the worst a coat upon a coat-hanger" (1936–39, p. 332).

> People were playing on the roofs
> of the summer cottages in Marblehead . . .
> the red sky was filled with flying moats,[13]
> cinders and coals, and bigger things, scorched
>   black
>   burnt.
> The water glowed like fire, too, but flat . . .
> In the morning across the bay
> the fire still went on, but in the sunlight
> we saw no more glare, just the clouds of smoke
> The beach was strewn with cinders, dark with
>   ash—
> strange objects seem [to] have blown across the
>   water
> lifted by the terrible heat, through the red sky?
> Blackened boards, shiny black like black
>   [feathers]—
> pieces of furniture, parts of boats, and clothes.
>   (p. 5)

Blackness, flying objects, and the contrast with the frightening light of the flames are again emphasized. The clothes, part of the debris from the fire, reinforce the connection of clothes with the mother, catastrophe, and loss in the child's mind; in Bishop's short story, the mourning clothes, the purple dress, the clothes hung in the mother's empty room after

---

13. This is a slip—*moats* for *motes*. I assume the slip is Bishop's, not Millier's. "Flying motes" is so like flying moths that I wonder if the resemblance has anything to do with the slip. A further speculation: moat—"a deep broad ditch around a fortress or castle, frequently filled with water" (*Webster's*)—might be unconsciously sought out as symbolizing the female genitals, perhaps with some cloacal connotations.

she had left. Clothes are of course the object of the moth's ravenousness;[14] the moth whose larva consumes the clothes can be consumed by the fire. Millier continues: "[The child] is alone and in trouble. She stands in her crib terribly thirsty and cannot get the attention of her mother, whom she sees out on the lawn greeting refugees, distributing coffee. In the morning, as they walk along the refuse, 'I picked up a woman's long black cotton stocking. Curios[ity]. My mother said sharply, "Put that down!"'" (p. 5). Millier comments, astutely:

> As an adult, Elizabeth remembered this event as a profound rejection of herself, her curiosity, her observant eye, and, because the forbidden object

14. Another work in which clothing and moths connect with mother-daughter conflicts of life-and-death intensity is Hugo von Hoffmannsthal's 1908 libretto (based on his play) for Richard Strauss's opera *Elektra*. Clytemnestra, Elektra's mother, has, with her lover, murdered her husband Agamemnon. (Elizabeth Bishop might well have fantasized something similar about her parents.) Elektra hates her mother, who has treated her like a slave, and wants to avenge her father. Clytemnestra suffers from bad dreams and feels that Elektra, whose misery and strangeness have made her into a kind of talismanic figure, might be able to help her. Between sleeping and waking she feels "a something crawling over me . . . and yet it is so frightening that my soul wants to be hanged; every limb in my body cries for death and yet lives. . . . Can one then wear away like a rotten carcass, fall to pieces when one isn't sick, senses alive, like a garment *eaten up by moths?*" (von Hoffmannsthal, p. 16, my translation).

Elektra goes on to try sadistically to undo her mother by telling her that only a blood sacrifice can give her peace—and after teasingly withholding the name of the requisite animal, she describes in chilling detail how the hunter will slaughter Clytemnestra herself, with Elektra watching, gleefully. Elektra is the destructive moth that orally attacks her ravaged mother.

was a piece of a woman's intimate clothing, perhaps some aspect of her sexuality as well. Com-
bined with the neglect she had felt the night
before during the fire, this rejection seemed
sweeping. She identifies it as the incipient event of
her alcoholism ("Since that day, that reprimand
. . . I have suffered from abnormal thirst"), and in
no later memory did she recall wishing for her
mother's presence. She became, in the language of
attachment theorists, an avoidant child. (1992,
pp. 5–6)

The mother's reprimand is connected with reproach ("You
are doing something wrong with your hands!") and frustration, as was the one about thumbsucking ("You are doing
something wrong with your hand and with your mouth!")
associated with the mother's scream in "In the Village"; but
here it is the writer herself who links fire, frustration, thirst,
and her own guilt-ridden alcoholism with her mother—a
mother who might well have been, or at least been seen by
the child as, being attracted to fire like a moth. ("Abnormal
thirst" could also refer to the poet's guilt-ridden lesbian longings.)

Bishop was also subject to chronic asthma. One can speculate that this expressed that oversimplified yet frequently
found psychodynamic determinant, a cry for the lost mother.
The happiest period of Bishop's restless life, much of it spent
as a transient or a traveler, was the fifteen years she lived in
Brazil with the love of her life, Lota de Soares, who took a
kind of maternal care of her. De Soares had the enthusiasm,
dynamism, and excitement that the frequently depressed and
lonely Elizabeth felt she herself lacked. (More than one
friend used the word *exuberant* to describe de Soares.) But she

was domineering and wanted things her way. When de Soares became absorbed in Brazilian politics and withdrew somewhat under the enormous pressure of work and political turmoil, Elizabeth had more bouts of drinking and severe asthmatic attacks.

The asthma also tied her for a good part of her life to a beloved physician, Anny Baumann, who looked after Elizabeth's health, sent her asthma medicine, and functioned, mostly at a distance, as a kind of mother-psychiatrist. (In her letters to Baumann, the poet confesses her alcoholic and depressive regressions and seems continually in need of absolution and reassurance—needing a mother who could accept her, faults and all. Baumann seems to have been loving but, like de Soares, somewhat magisterial toward her patients.

In 1966 the relationship with de Soares, which had started in 1951, was deteriorating. Bishop left Brazil for a while to teach at the University of Washington, partly, as she wrote to Baumann, because de Soares

> has been increasingly hard to live with. I feel like a skunk saying this much—but I felt I had to get away for a while, and I think it has been a good idea. Everyone here is so nice and *polite* to me, compared to my darling Lota, I can't get used to it, and I think I am getting a swelled head! None of them can compare with her in any way at all, naturally—but they do treat me better! I feel many of my Rio troubles are mostly my own fault. I am just not very good at handling bossy people, and Lota is bossy, of course—and I let her be for years & years, then suddenly find I can't stand it any more. Which isn't a very nice aspect of my character . . . no one can talk [to Lota], and it is

very hard to live with someone you can't talk to about things. Really, it is too much when (I'll give one example only) Lota bangs on the wall to make me go to bed, when I am entertaining an American visitor! That's the kind of thing I mean, and I know she is protecting *me*, but I hate it; the visitors misunderstand—and I can't explain to Lota, because she won't listen. I think I must still be feverish to write you this, and I am afraid it will strike you as merely childish. However, I assure you it isn't at all. I would never have taken this job if I hadn't felt I HAD to get away. (1994, p. 446, italics Bishop's)

One feels in reading this, and many other of her marvelous letters (1994), what an essentially nice and caring person Elizabeth Bishop was. The poet's situation with de Soares, who plays the role of what Margaret Mahler called the asymbiotic mother, was very complicated. De Soares was properly concerned about Elizabeth's recurrent episodes of drinking and depression, and this brought out her "bossyness."[15]

Millier cites another unpublished poem, which she describes as one of several "tentative attempts to write about [a] time when Gertrude Bishop and her daughter were together.

15. Sadly, the relationship was tragically ended by the suicide of Lota de Soares after a mental and physical breakdown. There are clothes and moths in Bishop's sad and wonderful poem "Crusoe in England," which alludes to the loss of de Soares (Bishop's Friday, who changed her life and relieved her loneliness): "The local museum's asked me to / leave everything to them: / the flute, the knife, the shriveled shoes, / my shedding goatskin trousers / (moths have got in the fur)," Later Elizabeth Bishops states: "How can anyone want such things? /—And Friday, my dear Friday, died of measles / seventeen years ago come March" (1983, p. 166).

All present a truncated mother, as she might be seen by a confused child, *represented by her clothes*" (p. 12, my italics). The poem begins:

> A mother made of dress-goods
> white with black polka-dots
> black and white "Shepherd's Plaid."
> A mother *is* a hat . . .

The last stanza—"[A mother is] / A long black glove / the swan bit / in the Public Gardens"—is based on Elizabeth's memory of seeing her mother's black (note the familiar colors in the poem) glove bitten by a swan in Boston's Public Garden. Elizabeth too can be a winged creature—swan or moth—who can bite (and ravage) "a mother made of dress goods" or a mother who is a hat.

Bishop's mother died in 1934, when the poet was in her twenties. Millier informs us that soon after this Elizabeth began to write sketches for a novel (never completed) about her childhood; in these story fragments she portrays herself as a small boy named Lucius who lives in Nova Scotia with his mentally disturbed mother (called "Easter," which connotes resurrection, in these sketches) and his aunts and grandparents. The boy is aware, as in "In the Village," of the family awaiting a catastrophe having to do with the mother. Millier says:

> In the first Lucius story, the boy and his mother arrive unannounced at her native village in Nova Scotia in the fall of 1913. Lucius's pleasure at being back in the village is tempered by his anxiety about his mother's feelings and about the reception they will get when they arrive at his grandparents' house. Other stories tell about what it is

like for Lucius to be in the house with Easter. . . .
He is aware of constant tension in the air, of implied dangers, and he feels (indeed, is made to feel)
that he is somehow responsible for it. "In the night
she began to cry very gently and complainingly
like a good child that has stood all it can. She made
little imploring noises, asking someone for something. I sat up & pulled my boots on & took the
stick from under the window & shut that, then I
sat on the edge of the bed waiting for Aunt
Grace. . . . Suddenly the door opened & Aunt
Grace, holding the little lamp, stuck her head in
and said very low: 'I guess you'll have to come,
Lucius. Maybe she wants you.' We walked along
the hall—I took the lamp. Just as we got to the
door Aunt Grace said, 'Oh—I don't know what to
do.' "

Lucius's nights are haunted by his mother's
needs; they are present in his dreams. He tells us
that his mother never appears directly; but in one,
he dreams of the large moths that inhabit Nova
Scotia in the summertime. They grow fright-
eningly, and then in a linguistic turn ("Easter
came into it somehow") become identified with
"mother." "I woke up, horrified with all the flut-
tering moths, and just as I woke, so that the feeling
was neither a sleeping one nor a waking one, I
became certain that the enemy was she." (1992,
pp. 6–7)

Of course, Lucius's (Elizabeth's) mother is victim as well
as enemy. In the dream, moths are the mother and moths are
the enemy. The mother's vulnerability makes the enmity,
the hating her, much more frightening; the terrible psychic

danger of loss of the mother is evoked in the child, and this is then compounded by the guilt over wishing the loss and then feeling that one has caused it.[16]

Bishop's last poem was "Sonnet," published by the *New Yorker* a few weeks after her death in 1979—although the magazine had kept it for more than a year before that, perhaps because it was felt to be too confessional. Ostensibly it is about a broken thermometer, an instrument of precision released from its bounds. I would like to quote it in its entirety:

> Caught—the bubble
> in the spirit-level,
> a creature divided;
> and the compass needle
> wobbling and wavering,
> undecided.
> Freed—the broken
> thermometer's mercury
> running away;
> and the rainbow-bird
> from the narrow bevel
> of the empty mirror,
> flying wherever
> it feels like, gay! (1983, p. 192)

Death can be a kind of liberation after being broken.

In a wonderful commentary on this poem, Bonnie Costello (1994) says about the poem's imagery:

---

16. The vulnerable moth is portrayed in Bishop's poem "The Man-Moth," from her 1945 book *North and South* (see Bishop, 1983, pp. 14–15). I am indebted to Dr. Harold Kudler for pointing out to me that the name Lucius is derived from the Latin *lucere*, "to shine"—as in the English *lucent*—and *lux*, "light"; the boy's name marks him as the light than can destroy the moth.

All these ways of measuring suddenly yield to
a measureless spirit, and the words themselves
seem to spring free of the sonnet's hold. Yet the
escape from measure has something eerie about
it. . . . A life and life's work is summed up as the
dialectic of captivity and freedom, of fixed form
and poetic extravagance, of social norms and personal deviance. But the ultimate freedom, she
knew, was beyond art and life. The mirror must be
empty to release the rainbow-bird; the thermometer must be broken for the liquid to escape. (p. 356)

There is no indication that the poet, although chronically
ill with asthma and alcoholism, expected to die. (Just before
her last hospitalization she posted notes to the college classes
she was teaching, saying that she was going to be back on
what turned out to be the morning after she died.) In 1979,
gay and *liberation* ("Freed") certainly went together easily,
but it is doubtful that this was ever true personally (in private
or in public) for Elizabeth Bishop. Her gifts, her genius,
inhibited as they were by neurotic conflict, still enabled her
to liberate herself in poetic creativity. One hopes that when
the restless, homeless poet, then sixty-eight, wrote "Sonnet,"
she had come to some sort of terms with her unhappiness and
her homosexuality and had achieved some sort of liberation—like that achieved (after a break, one must note) by the
iridescent mercury of the thermometer in this poem.

"Sonnet" seems to have been the beginning of Bishop's
public acknowledgment of being, sexually, "a creature divided" (compare Woolf's "hybrid creature"). In her perceptive remarks on "Sonnet," Millier (1993) writes, "Its
mischievously disguised confessions of alcoholism and homosexuality are nonetheless terribly serious" (p. 546). I have

characterized the mercury as iridescent because this quality irradiates "Sonnet" (the bubble, the rainbow-bird, the mirror, the broken glass); it is also implicit in the imagery of many of Bishop's poems. Iridescence is allied to luminosity, the light that fatally attracts the moth, the compulsion that prevents it from "flying wherever it feels like." Millier says that "Sonnet" echoes many of the early poems: " 'The broken / thermometer's mercury' recalls the moonlight in 'The Man-Moth' which shines at a 'temperature impossible to record in thermometers' " (p. 546). It is the moon's luminosity that causes the Man-Moth, one of the first of Bishop's "creatures divided," to climb skyscrapers to try to reach it.

The death of her father and the madness of her mother in infancy were losses that destroyed much of Elizabeth Bishop's sense of individuation and security. And, partly in identification and partly in relation to people she attempted to love, sexually and nonsexually, she remained fundamentally tied to her mother until her own death. And yet, what an achievement—in art and in life—to have fought with so much success against that strangling, sticky, emotional matrix of longing and hatred, to have been capable of such warm friendship and devotion, and to have created such prose and such poetry.

The sense of identity Bishop finally forged, no matter how marred by self-deprecation and masochism, was magnificent. As an illustration, I want to quote from her last letter (her letters are, in their own way, as wonderful as her poems), written on the day she died, to an editor who wished to quote from Bishop's work in a textbook for college students. The letter shows how high her standards were, how deeply she felt about them, how much she cared about people and, above all, how concerned she was about precision and dedication, about her art.

I'm going to take issue with you—rather violently—about the idea of footnotes. With one or
two exceptions . . . I don't think there should be
ANY footnotes. You say the book is for college
students, and I think anyone who gets as far as
college should be able to use a dictionary. I know
. . . most of them don't—but they should be made
to, somehow. [She refers to a footnote the editor
had added to her poem "The Moose":] "Mac-
adam" is in the dictionary. And—a lot of the
poem is about "childhood recollections"—I almost say it in so many words. If they can't figure
that out, they shouldn't be in college—THERE!
You can see what a nasty teacher I must be—but I
do think students get lazier and lazier & expect to
have everything done *for* them. . . . My best example of this sort is what one rather bright Harvard honors student told me. She told her room-
mate or a friend—who had obviously taken my
verse-writing course—that she was doing her paper with me, and the friend said, "Oh don't work
with her! It's awful! She wants you to look words
up in the dictionary! It isn't creative at all!" In
other words, it is better *not* to know what you're
writing or reading. Perhaps [some of my classes
have] embittered me . . . although there have
been good students and a few wonderful ones from
time to time. But they mostly seem to think that
poetry—to read or to write—is a snap—one just
has to *feel*—and not for very long either. Well, I
could go on and on—but I won't. . . . . I do hope I
haven't offended you now—but I think the teaching of literature now is deplorable—and if you can

get the student to *reading*, you have done a noble work. Affectionately . . . (1994, pp. 638–39)

The editor of her collected letters, Robert Giroux (1994), comments: "Her closing word, 'affectionately,' is proof that her goodwill and good manners persisted to the end" (p. 639).

In her much-anthologized poem "In the Waiting Room," she describes herself at age seven, waiting for her aunt (a paternal aunt, not one of the beloved maternal ones),[17] who is in another room with the dentist. The little girl is surrounded by adult strangers in a dark room and feels alone and afraid. Once more darkness and blackness—with all their connotations of death and nothingness and the female genitals—are emphasized:

> And while I waited I read
> the *National Geographic*
> (I could read)

[The child's identity as an intellectual is already established at seven.]

>   and carefully
> studied the photographs:
> the inside of a volcano,
> black, and full of ashes;
> then it was spilling over
> in rivulets of fire.

[The child's curiosity is linked with a black hole and fire, and other awful, even cannibalistic, sights.]

---

17. Bishop felt that she had been kidnapped by her father's family when, as an older child, she was taken away from Nova Scotia and her maternal grandparents' nurturing home to the cold, dark house of the well-to-do Bishops in Worcester, Massachusetts.

A dead man slung on a pole
—"Long Pig," the caption said.
Babies with pointed heads
wound round and round with string;
black naked women with necks
wound round and round with wire
like the necks of light bulbs.
Their breasts were horrifying.

[The dangers of the body, of disfigurement, of (especially female) anatomy assault the child. The black women evoke the mother in mourning clothes.]

Suddenly, from inside,
came an *oh!* of pain
—Aunt Consuelo's voice—
not very loud or long.[18]
I wasn't at all surprised;
even then I knew she was
a foolish, timid woman.
I might have been embarrassed,

18. It has been suggested that this cry can be connected to the maternal scream that resounds through "In the Village": "The aunt's cry is a squeak of pain at the dentist's, but it is also a woman's cry. David Kalstone's suggestion that it is akin to the scream of Elizabeth's mother in 'In the Village' finds support in the poem's nervous contention that it 'could have / got loud and worse but hadn't.' Elizabeth's identification here is with womanly pain, her view of the impossibly conflicted life a self-aware woman must lead, the prospect of a startling and inexplicable acquisition of 'awful hanging breasts.' Elizabeth's ambivalence about the value of femininity affected her thinking about herself and her eventual sexual orientation and her complex handling of questions of gender in her poems as well" (Millier, 1993, p. 27).

but wasn't. What took me
completely by surprise
was that this was *me:*
my voice, in my mouth.
Without thinking at all
I was my foolish aunt,
I—we—were falling, falling,
our eyes glued to the cover
of the *National Geographic,*
February, 1918.

[Here the girl has lost her identity, merging with a devalued mother figure. But this is followed by a heroic and successful struggle for insight and individuation:]

I said to myself: three days
And you'll be seven years old.
I was saying it to stop
the sensation of falling off
the round, turning world
Into cold, blue-black space.[19]
But I felt: you are an I
you are an *Elizabeth,*[20]

19. According to Robert Fliess (1973, p. 101), a rotating object symbolizes ego dissolution. Rotating symbols are recurrent in this poem (note "round and round").

20. Compare this statement, made by a classmate about Elizabeth as a teenager: "Elizabeth was very modest, although keenly aware of her own . . . I wouldn't use the word 'power.' There was no question in her mind of her own rightness, or of her being at the center of her own world and being able to find her way through it. She was absolutely sure of that in a way which at that age not many people are" (Fountain and Brazeau, 1994, p. 28).

[A wonderful declaration of identity—but marred for the girl by her identification with her mother and with the unknown adults who surround her in the dark, cold waiting room]

> you are one of *them*.
> *Why* should you be one, too?
> I scarcely dared to look
> to see what it was I was.
> I gave a sidelong glance.
> —I couldn't look any higher—
> at shadowy gray knees,
> trousers and skirts and boots

[Here, again, people are reduced to clothing.]

> and different pairs of hands
> lying under the lamps.
> I knew that nothing stranger
> had ever happened, that nothing
> stranger could ever happen.
> Why should I be my aunt,
> or me, or anyone?
> What similarities—
> boots, hands, the family voice
> I felt in my throat, or even
> the *National Geographic*
> and those awful hanging breasts—
> held us all together
> or made us all just one?
> How—I didn't know any
> word for it—how "unlikely"—
> How had I come to be here,
> like them, and overhear

> a cry of pain that could have
> got loud and worse but hadn't?[21]

[Now, a crisis, overstimulation; darkness turns to light.]

> The waiting room was bright
> and too hot. It was sliding
> beneath a big black wave,
> another, and another.

[And, after the crisis, a recovery.]

> Then I was back in it.
> The War was on. Outside,
> in Worcester, Massachusetts,
> were night and slush and cold,
> and it was still the fifth
> of February, 1918. (1983, pp. 159–61)

The poem shows terror of the body, of pain, of being female, of loss as experienced with a bodily intensity, of a destructive (sadomasochistic) view of sex and of life—and something of how will and creative thought can help one transcend the dangers attendant on such terrible feelings. The last few lines also show the need for obsessive-compulsive sticking to orientation and to the facts, looking around and knowing what is there to be observed—the restorative need for the thermometer from "Sonnet," whose breaking paradoxically makes freedom possible.

Elizabeth Bishop had a wonderful sense of identity and purpose. Her friend the poet and critic Randall Jarrell paid her a great tribute in a recorded recitation of some of her

---

21. The scream that began "In the Village" is also described as "not loud" (1984, p. 251).

poems: "Occasionally you meet someone and you feel an astonished joy. You feel 'this is what people OUGHT to be' " (1964). But this wonderful persona existed alongside uncertainty, anxiety, depression, alcoholism, asthma, and masochism. She had to struggle with her hostility (most of it turned on herself), but she could care for others. None of us escapes the ravages of the moths of time and fate, of our heredity and surroundings—but Elizabeth Bishop shows how someone whose early childhood made for a ravaged life can still, both in life and in art, enrich those we live with and those who come after us.

One of her poems, written during World War II and published in 1946, begins:

> Lullaby.
> Adult and child
> sink to their rest.
> At sea the big ship sinks and dies,
> lead in its breast.
>
> Lullaby.
> let nations rage,
> let nations fall.
> The shadow of the crib makes an enormous cage
> upon the wall. (1979, p. 49)

And the crib-cage certainly cast its shadow on Bishop's life and art. It may have made for soul murder, but it does not account for the miracle of her creativity.

IV

"Did It Really Happen?"

11

Narcissistic Pathology
Stemming from Parental Weakness

*To breed an animal with the right to make promises—is not
this the paradoxical problem nature has set herself with
regard to man?*
—*Friedrich Nietzsche*

In recent years, often as a consequence of having read some of
my writings on soul murder, a number of people who had
memories of child abuse and seduction have consulted me. I
have also seen a few who had no such memories but appeared
to be in search of them. I have now studied three of these
would-be victims as analytic patients. They had developed
passionate intellectual interests that seemed also to serve
them as defensive isolation posts guarding against and distancing their varied sexual impulses and their rage. They did
indeed, in their character structure, defenses, and symptomatology, resemble some of the soul murder cases about
which I had written (and they had read). In spite of their
strong need to accuse their parents of something grievous,
however, the analytic explorations turned up very little that
was unusual in the way of parental evil or criminality. Much

as they desired to charge their fathers and mothers with
cruelty and sexual abuse, the accusations were not convincingly substantiated—neither to the analyst-observer nor,
more important, to the analysand—although that did not
take away the need for the accusation. Memories of dramatic
or chronic mistreatment were not forthcoming, nor was either construction by the analyst or the more desirable mutual
reconstruction of traumata (which, when done optimally, is
arrived at mostly through work by the patient) deemed appropriate.[1]

Despite some striking similarities, these patients, two
men and a woman, were three very different people with six
very different parents. The parents, as described and evoked,
varied in their capacity to love and their ability to empathize,
but none of them, despite many failings, came through as
psychopathic, psychotic, indifferent, or uncaring. What all
the parents did have in common was weakness of character
and relative inability, for various reasons, including long
absences and illness, to be forceful and to firmly say "No!" All
appeared to their children to have not completely grown up,
and the analyses revealed them to have been (and still be)
chronically anxious and afraid of anger. In various ways, they
denied both anger and evil or transferred them onto groups
outside the family. They subtly or crudely insisted on what I
have called narcissistic delusions (Shengold, 1995): for the
family members, they promised, there would be no tragedies
or failures, only happy endings, and no death. For the child,
the loss of this narcissistic promise was terrifying. The threat

1. I feel I would have done these patients a great disservice if I
had adopted the advice of Davies and Frawley (see the appendix) and,
on the basis of the presence of "dissociation," initially and confidently
"confirmed" the wished-for actuality of the assumed abuse in childhood.

of that loss, brought out by the frustrating but inevitable awareness of the limitations and inadequacies of self, parents, and parental substitutes, as well as the inexorable limits imposed by external reality, enhanced the child's inevitable rage—thus increasing the anxiety in a vicious cycle. This, then, amounted to a kind of chronic trauma that accompanied maturation. The parental promise made for a Garden of Eden to which they felt entitled and from which they were continually being evicted. To restore it, denial and delusion were required.

All three of these patients were precociously bright as children. This enhanced the aura of promise. (Greatness was expected and, in one case, demanded by the parents.) Past the period of infancy, the children seemed to have felt and been treated more like little adults than like children—or, rather, like a combination of adult and infant. Their wills and whims emerged as stronger than those of the parents, who characteristically, seemingly out of fear of the rage of the child (but, of course, concomitantly out of fear of their own anger), were unable to refuse their child's demands and to impose consistent and dependable discipline. In a sense, the generations had been reversed, the parents turning to these children (who may have been brighter than their parents) for advice and sometimes even for control. ("At five, I was my mother's chief adviser," the female patient said.)

The children grew up alternately too infantile and too grown-up, too willful and demanding and too controlled—given to helpless rage and temper tantrums and yet full of claims to omniscience and omnipotence, impossibly conflicting claims that lead to delusions of privilege and to terror.[2]

____

2. The delusions of narcissism, when accompanied by rage, threaten to annihilate the parents or the self. The feeling of omnipo-

The parents made inadequate or ineffectual efforts to modify the grandiose pretensions of the children they apparently needed to idealize, probably in the service of maintaining their own need for narcissistic promise; there was apparently a symbiotic requirement for their child's greatness. The children, whose demands could override parental opposition, would nonetheless feel completely dependent on the parents as fulfillers of their needs. Simultaneously the children could feel that they were in danger of losing the parents they could not survive without—the danger of loss kept at a frightening pitch by the children's intermittent conviction that their rage could destroy the parents. The parental vulnerability in the mind of the children made any separation intolerable and any actual parental failure or display of weakness or illness terrifying.

The children, despite periods of (sometimes blissful) delusional invulnerability, were haunted by the potentiality of an unbearable pitch of bad feeling. They could not tolerate the intensity of their mixed anxiety and rage; all three had developed a basic fear of emotional involvement and commitment. Deadening defenses became mandatory. In my view, this represents a pathological exaggeration of what happens to some extent to every child; we must all moderate our earliest perceptions, sensitivities, and feelings in order to defend against the overwhelmingly intense primal affects derived from instinctual drives aiming at murder, cannibalism, and fusion. In the prepubertal years that Freud called the period of latency, the child loses some of the ardent intensity of the mind's early development. Some sort of bio-

---

tent rage can be unbearable to a child who expects that the intense feeling itself can kill and that he or she will therefore be killed in retaliatory punishment.

logically determined dampening repressive force operates to inhibit both the marvelous intellectual giftedness and the instinctual perfervidness of later infancy and toddlerhood. Also, in the course of maturation and development, good or good enough parenting—featuring a balance of permissiveness and firm and realistic refusal—usually helps to modulate both affects and defenses.

For my patients, the parental attitudes of apology and indulgence had seemingly made it difficult or impossible for the children to internalize no's. The resulting lack of self-discipline weakened both the child's sense of self and its conscience (ego and superego) while augmenting the power of aggressive and sexual wishes of all kinds directed toward the parents. (Weak parents who can't say no, frequently—there are exceptions—make for weak psychic structure in the child.)[3] The children despised the parents for their irresolution, further intensifying the cycle of rage, guilt, and fear of loss in the children. The increasingly exigent sexual wishes of all kinds are directed at the parents with inordinate expectations of their fulfillment—again, promise. The children feel entitled to seduction and tend to be seductive. I have seen patients with similarly weak parents who remembered them as either overtly seductive or easily seduced. But

3. I may be exaggerating the parental contribution to my patients' pathology. Individual development is very complex, and (as I have repeatedly written) we know too little about constitutional givens and inherited powers. Children overindulged by weak parents both identify with and, adaptively, react against these internalized weaknesses in an interpsychic struggle whose outcome (always a mixture of weaknesses and strengths) cannot be predicted. In addition to the mystery of constitutional givens, the preservation or adaptive attainment of relative psychic health also depends on the presence or absence of good parental substitutes, especially in the child's earliest years.

it appeared that my three analysands reacted to ordinary contact as if it were overt seduction; the result was over-stimulation. (It must be remembered that mutual seductiveness of some intensity is always present between parent and child. The child often needs sexualization to try to undo what is experienced or anticipated as rejection or loss as well as to neutralize frightening destructive rage.)

These patients had also, as children, felt devastated by the rage generated in reaction to frustration by these parents, who were so afraid of anger. The children's relative inability to modify and therefore tolerate rage had become chronic. The children could all too easily feel like incipient murderers whose very wishes (felt as full of omnipotence) could kill. All three patients had a distinct paranoid tendency and needed to project their own rage onto their parents and subsequent parent substitutes such as the analyst. This projection took place, of course, alongside the masochistic and depressive direction of their rage toward the self. (The three people each had qualitatively and proportionately different combinations of these two directions and their emotional concomitants.) For all three, there were (nonpsychotic) guilt-ridden feelings of persecution manifested mainly by chronic complaining. Each had his or her own idiosyncratic style of complaining, but all three could be called "righteous." All three displayed a versatile range of sadistic as well as masochistic phenomena. The feeling of being persecuted was at least in part a reversal of the child's relatively unchecked bent for persecuting the parents with provocative behavior and verbal abuse. Such expression was both suppressed and too freely allowed, in individually different combinations. Not the least damaging aspect of the recurrent accesses of rage was that they tended to dissolve the caring love for their parents that the children needed for the feeling of well-being. These patients, like so many actual soul murder victims (each in his or her individual way), could not really sustain love for another human being.

In analysis it became apparent that the children had felt that their parents had violated the narcissistic promise they had enhanced with their frightened overindulgence. (A child needs to internalize the power to renounce some gratification in order to feel safe.) The dimming of the promise was inevitable once the children ventured beyond the nursery and realized, at first vaguely, that the inexorable conditions of life would not always permit the fulfillment of wishes. The rage at the unfulfilled promise of "everything" was displaced onto various exaggerated charges of mistreatment and misunderstanding directed toward the parents (alongside alternative defensive idealizations of them). None of the three patients had the conviction that they had been abused, but reading my book had induced the expectation—preconscious and conscious—that I (viewed as full of idealized promise) would lead them to that belief. In the course of their analyses, the initial imperative need for parental promises, indulgences, and reassurances was alleviated for these patients, but it could return in regressive response to stress.

For them, psychoanalysis meant chiefly a struggle to feel and become responsible for their own anxiety-ridden conflicts over narcissistic, libidinal, and especially murderous wishes, feelings, and impulses. This meant examining their defenses, especially projection and denial. I found all this to be much like working with adult victims of child abuse. Some insight was attained, but all three left analysis with some dissatisfaction. I felt that there had been no true termination, at least for two of them, and am not informed as to how much was accomplished and consolidated after the analyses—a crucial ignorance. Their ability to care for others seemed somewhat enhanced, considerably so for one of them. There were enough differences in the three people and their reactions to treatment to render of doubtful value generalizations about analyzability in similar cases. I do feel that all three made considerable progress and were better off at the end of the treatment.

It is not possible for an analyst of adults either to establish or to rule out conclusively that an individual was born with an inherited endowment that included stronger-than-ordinary drives. This seemed to me likely for at least one of my three patients, a woman whose intense, passionate nature was initially disguised and largely canceled out by her massive inhibitions. Certainly in these (as in all) people, one should think of the constitutional variations in intensity of sexual and murderous drives when assessing forces that contribute to psychic pathology—alongside the parental inadequacies and the faulty internalizations I have mentioned. For these three patients, the result (resembling what would be found in cases of actual abuse) appears to have been that as children their motivating fantasies were full of unmodified sexual and murderous impulses that were still present in the adult. These adults also presented the massive defensive characterologic armor—largely anal narcissistic defenses and character— masking and deadening the terrifyingly intense sadomasochistic affective disposition found in soul murder victims.

For these patients parental weakness supplied the main environmental psychopathological factor. One can obviously view parental "spoiling" as a kind of abuse; it certainly stems in large part from parental pathology.[4] (Overindulgent parenting usually goes along with a need to inhibit the separa-

4. There are of course many different ways of spoiling children and no uniform results, but all would, I believe, eventuate in the child's having trouble with curbing desires.

tion and maturation of the child—frequently repeating the childhood of the parent, I would speculate.) Yet there is a great contrast between the history of the three people I am writing about and that of those who bring, or discover, memories of predominant parental criminal monstrousness, overt hatred, or uncaring indifference. I am sure there are many childhoods that feature both kinds of parental pathology.

Both actual soul murder victims and these false ones defend their parents as well as attack them, but the emphases seem to be different. The parents appear to be largely spared by those more directly abused (much of the hostility is turned inward, on the self, or outward, on others), but they were predominantly, indeed extravagantly, blamed by the three people I am describing.[5] What makes a separate category for such narcissistic pathology worth considering is the clamorous but ultimately unsubstantiated claim of overt parental abuse—where, after analytic investigation, both analyst and patient feel that the parents have been brought up on false or greatly exaggerated charges (charges whose modification has, in the course of treatment, been strongly resisted by the patient). If the treatment works, the patient will have learned not only to have a new perspective involving less blame toward his or her parents but, more important, to bear the responsibility for his or her own past and present feelings, experiences, impulses, and deficiencies.

I alluded to but did not feature or name this (mainly narcissistic) syndrome in my 1989 book on soul murder. I feel that the seemingly specific environmental psychopathologi-

---

5. I am sure that with more experience I would find that here too there are all sorts of individual variations, since the internal registration of parents is so variable—as is the relation of their psychic images in the child's mind and fantasy life to the real parents from whom those images are derived.

cal factor of parental overindulgence and inadequacy makes it worth differentiating from soul murder and child abuse as a kind of "pseudo–soul murder"—a descriptive, not a diagnostic, term. There are many kinds of psychopathology besides the one I have described that can produce similar effects, and the many ways in which parents spoil their children do not always produce similar or predictable results. More observations and communications about different kinds of pseudo–soul murder are needed in these times of controversy about charges of child abuse. We can profit from clinical evidence rather than passionate prejudice.

In psychoanalysis we explore, clarify, and seek to understand our patients' charges and claims against their parents on an individual basis; this depends on establishing a working analytic process. That is not easy, since it requires both parties to the analysis to be or become able to tolerate the terrible burden of murderous rage transferred onto the analyst. Child victims of abuse as well as those overindulged by weak and frightened parents can experience rage so intense that it terrifies the child simply to feel fully and consciously what is there to be felt. The imminence of murder makes the child's dependency and incestuous fixation on the parents an unbearable nightmare. In later life these destructive emotions are partly defended against and partly expressed in sadomasochistic impulses and actions. The resultant variable mixture is usually manifested in analysis as resistance to intense feelings about the analyst—both loving and hostile feelings—and by negative therapeutic reactions.[6] But the patient's burden of intense feelings must be modified, and

6. This means that every time the patient feels better, he or she is threatened by the change (change has the unconscious meaning of the prelude to trauma and loss) and is motivated to take a regressive step toward undoing what made for the good feeling.

sometimes only a treatment as intense as analysis can accomplish this. It follows that the mutual work on transference is, to quote from Brian Bird's (1972) classic paper, the "hardest part of analysis" (p. 267) for victims of either soul murder or pseudo–soul murder.

What became clear to me from the patients discussed in this chapter is that their similarity to patients who were convinced and convincing about having been criminally traumatized or neglected was based on an issue that is larger than the question "Did it really happen?" Optimally, children must acquire some balanced internalization of the power to say both yes and no to their impulses. Both self and conscience, ego and superego, need a flexible power to control with a renunciation or modification of gratification. The overstimulation associated with trauma creates a compulsion toward discharge into action in the abused child. This makes for defective internalization of parental controls, defenses, rules:[7] some unfortunate combination of too little and too

7. Vann Spruiell, in a masterly paper, shows how necessary it is, if one tries to induce real modification of the structure and functioning of the mind of the patient, to keep to (with some flexibility based on common sense) what he calls "the rules and the frames" of psychoanalytic technique.

Ambivalence toward rules and controls can sometimes produce denial of their necessity. Rousseau's social contract has frequently been regarded as simply an expression of the need for freedom, for the breaking of chains. But it is also an expression of the need for government. "Man was born free, and he is everywhere in chains," is always remembered, but what follows is frequently forgotten: "How did this transformation come about? I do not know. *How can it be made legitimate?* That question I believe I can answer" (1762, p. 49, my italics). Chains can be loosened, can and should be modified into laws, but they are still needed.

much no and too little and too much yes. Similar combinations can result from different causes, and in this chapter I have emphasized the unfortunate influence of parents who have been unable to provide models for the child's acquisition of the means to limit narcissistic gratifications. The results are similar. Compulsive defensive narcissistic retreat makes separation from the early parents difficult or impossible. The children are left with a hole in the self and, to use the title of Richard Rhodes's (1990) moving account of his own soul murder, a hole in the world.

12

Murder, Violence, and Soul Murder
"Did It Really Happen?" and a Note on Therapy

Satan (near Eden): *For never can true reconcilement grow*
  Where wounds of deadly hate have pierced so deep:
  Which would but lead me to a worse relapse . . .
  All hope excluded thus, behold in stead
  Of us outcast, exil'd, his new delight,
  Mankind created, and for him this World.
  So farwel Hope, and with Hope farwel Fear,
  Farwel Remorse: all Good to me is lost;
  Evil be thou my Good.
—*John Milton,* Paradise Lost

Why is there violence in the world? What is the origin of evil? How can benevolent and omnipotent deities permit the triumph, or even the existence, of evil and violence? These philosophic and religious questions have preoccupied human beings since the beginning of recorded history, and even earlier, according to archeological evidence. Homer, the great Greek dramatists, and the ancient Hebrew writings dealt directly with these enigmas. The Greeks, in myth and in literature, portrayed the gods as immortal and powerful versions of human beings, with all the human faults and passions. The God of the Hebrews, as he evolved from a tribal deity of fearsome and destructive "jealous" mien into an omnipotent creator, presented more problems. How can evil stem from benevolent omnipotence? If there is an evil God as powerful as the good God, then there is at least a logical explanation. Belief in the devil is an approach to this position, made much of by the Manicheans. Milton has his rebellious Satan motivated to evil by malignant envy of God's favoritism in granting Eden to Adam and Eve.

Satan does not appear at first in the Bible, although in Genesis the sinful rebellion of Adam and Eve is inspired by the evil serpent. The devil makes his first appearance as the adversary (*Satan* is the Hebrew term for "adversary") in Chronicles and the book of Job. In that fascinating and gripping philosophical drama, Satan challenges God to test the faith of his good and prosperous servant Job. Both supernatural beings, who play the role of a bad set of parent figures, carry out this test by torturing that innocent man with the utmost cruelty in what sounds like a parable of child abuse. The book of Job attempts to address the origin and meaning of the evil in the universe and the justification for it. The answer Jehovah gives poor Job to the question of why the good suffer and the wicked thrive may be true enough, but it is far from satisfying: "Don't ask! It's beyond your understanding." At least we can insist on asking, but wisdom dictates keeping hope humble for a really satisfactory answer (philosophic, religious, or scientific).

Is our nature inherently violent? Are we imbued with some inherent equivalent of a death instinct, as Freud pessimistically intuited? Must we hope for some external, miraculous intervention by some extraterrestrial or supernatural being or count on some biologically based evolutionary change in our inner natures? If aggression and evil are an inextricable part of human nature, can proper nurturance modify these forces so that we will not be condemned to destroy one another?

Hannah Arendt has made the term "the banality of evil" familiar to us, a familiarity confirmed and extended by subsequent decades of exposure to the reality of its everyday presence in the world from headlines and especially television news. The waxing and waning of individual and mass violence, viewed over the centuries of human history, may not necessarily have changed enough to justify our impression of a crescendo in the present. (Modern advances in weapons of mass destruction and in communication have certainly furnished an increased awareness of violence.) I was very much impressed as a boy by the reactions of my mother, generally a rational and rather atheistic person, who would cry out at the news of a murder, "God! Let the killer not be Jewish!" She had experienced pogroms as a child before World War I, and their shadow had left the expectation of repetition. I thought of her after the 1993 massacre of many Arabs by a Jew at Hebron. He may have been crazy, but the reaction of so many righteous justifiers again showed the banality of violence—what we all can regress to under stress. Here is what the American poet E. E. Cummings (who had been analyzed but was not writing as an advocate for Freudian drive theory) wrote about what was going on in the world as World War II approached in the late 1930s:

> red-rag and pink-flag
> blackshirt and brown
> strut-mince and stink-brag
> have all come to town

some like it shot
and some like it hung
and some like it in the twot
nine months young. (1940, p. 497)

Violence is the loss of control of aggressive impulse leading to action. Psychoanalysts rarely have direct contact with violence in their offices; they deal mainly with fantasies of violence. Like Hamlet, analysands usually present what Shakespeare called "the show of violence" (I.i.144) to the analyst, who represents a ghost of their parent; that is, analysts get a direct or disguised emotional revelation, usually expressed in words and tone of voice, rarely in attenuated or token actions.[1] Violent action is of course sometimes resorted to by psychotic and psychopathic patients, but even then it usually occurs in the world outside the consulting room.

I won't attempt a review of the history of the place of aggression as it developed in psychoanalytic theory (see the excellent review by Perelberg, 1995). I will start with current controversy. No serious psychoanalytic scholar doubts the existence of aggression as an internal force central to understanding psychic conflict, defense, and motivation of violence as a seemingly uncontrollable and ineradicable human characteristic. The origin of aggression has been hotly disputed, however—especially since instinct theory has come under attack. No one questions the *experiential* evocation of aggression—aggression as a response to frustration, deprivation, pain, overstimulation. What we don't know is whether it starts from within as an innate drive or is only a reaction to

---

1. Anna Freud was wont to remind us ot Freud's quotation from "an unknown English writer" (perhaps Hughlings Jackson): "The man who first flung a word of abuse at his enemy instead of a spear was the founder of civilization" (1893, 36).

something without. Are we born good and corrupted by civilization, as Rousseau urges, or is life in the state of nature poor, nasty, brutish, and short (Hobbes) because we are born full of sin and evil, would-be incestuous murderers and cannibals, and attain civilization by renunciation, as Freud thought? He quotes Diderot on children: "If the little savage were left to himself, preserving all his imbecility and adding to the modicum of reason of a child in the cradle the violent passions of a man of thirty, he would strangle his father and go to bed with his mother" (Freud, 1916–17, 338).

In order to illustrate preoedipal violence—cannibalism and murder—that merges into oedipal violence I will quote a passage from the Circe chapter of James Joyce's *Ulysses* (1914). Leopold Bloom begins to feel that he "must eat" as he is walking through Dublin. His thoughts turn from hunger to sex: "Perfumed bodies, warm, full. All kissed; yielded: in deep summer fields, tangled pressed grass, in trickling hallways of tenements, along sofas, creaking beds." He then goes into a restaurant:

> Stink gripped his trembling breath: pungent meatjuice, slop of greens. See the animals feed. . . . Smells of men. His gorge rises. Spaton sawdust, sweetish warmish cigarette smoke, reek of plug, spilt beer, men's beery piss, the stale of ferment.
>
> Couldn't eat a morsel here. Fellow sharpening knife and fork, to eat all before him, old chap picking his tooties. Slight spasm, full, chewing the cud. Before and after. Grace after meals. Look on this picture and on that. Scoffing up stewgravy with sopping sippets of bread. . . . A man spitting back on his plate: halfmasticated gristle: no teeth

to chewchewchew it . . . . Bolting to get it
over. . . . Bitten off more than he can chew. Am I
like that? See ourselves as others see us. Hungry
man is an angry man. Working *tooth and jaw*. . . .
That fellow ramming a knifeful of cabbage down
as if his life depended on it. Good stroke. Gives me
the fidgets to look. . . . Tear it limb from limb.
Second nature to him. . . . Out. I hate dirty eaters.

He backed towards the door. Get a light snack
in Davy Byrne's. . . . Every fellow for his own,
tooth and nail. Gulp grub gulp.

He came out into clearer air and tuned back
towards Grafton Street. Eat or be eaten. Kill! Kill!
(pp. 166–68, my italics)[2]

And as he approaches Davy Byrne's, Bloom (Ulysses as Everyman) thinks: "Hot fresh blood they prescribe for decline.
Blood always needed. Insidious. Lick it up, smoking hot,
thick sugary. Famished ghosts. Ah, I'm hungry" (p. 169).[3]
(Genitality—the allusion to Hamlet brings in the oedipal—
yields to orality: nature "red in tooth and claw." Bloom's
disgust pervades the scene; the anal references ["reek,"
"stink," "dirty"] mark an anality that can both express rage
and violence and raise powerful forces against their expres-

2. "Look on this picture and on that" is a quotation from *Hamlet:*
the prince is forcing Gertrude to look at pictures of his father and of
Claudius in the closet scene. Joyce is blending the preoedipal with the
oedipal: cannibalism, murder (fratricide and patricide), and incest.

3. Freud (1900), speaking of the indestructibility of unconscious
wishes, states: "They are only capable of annihilation in the same
sense as the ghosts in the underworld of the *Odyssey*—ghosts which
awoke to new life as soon as they tasted blood" (p. 553). Joyce's great
novel is of course based on the *Odyssey,* a work in which cannibalism
is featured (the Cyclops and Laestrygones).

sion.) Rage and potential violence are present at every libidinal level.

In their writings Abraham and Klein have emphasized
and expanded Freud's ideas about innate preoedipal (early
infantile) violent aggression that makes for a developmental
progression of murderousness—an urge to kill that optimally is increasingly transformed and attenuated by defensive psychic structure but never relinquished, with early intensities expressed in fixations and returned to in regression.
We need to know more about the earliest development of
object relations in order to be sure of the interplay between it
and the aggressive drive. Even if we accept the aggressive
drive, we don't know if it is first directed toward the self and
projected, or directed toward the other and introjected, or
both. Does it matter? Does aggression have an inborn pattern
of relatively fixed timed waves of intensification and reces-
sion, as appears to be true in other animals? Observers of
infants note great differences in the activity and aggressivity
of individual newborns, but the facts of psychic life in the
first months of existence are going to remain a mystery. This
is the time of the unrememberable (Frank, 1969). There need
be no either-or here—nature as well as nurture is involved.
Studies of identical twins (I am thinking of the work, mostly
unpublished but presented and widely discussed, of Peter
Neubauer and Samuel Abrams) have increased most analysts'
humility with respect to the amount of psychic endowment
we are born with. (People in general and psychoanalysts in
particular are more comfortable with the potentially more
reversible environmental determination.) But what is experienced—trauma and deprivation that range from the avoid-
able to the inevitable, from the tolerable to the unbearable—
undeniably also leads to *reactive* aggression and violence.

I do not intend to present more than my own way of

regarding the onset and power of violent impulses. I base my conviction mainly on my clinical observations; these have been strongly influenced by drive theory and have in turn supported my theoretical bent. (I realize that this can be called circular reasoning.) Drive theory is our mythology, Freud tells us, and in this moot area mythology may turn out to be as useful as "scientific" observation. I find drive theory to be perfectly consistent with other explanations, such as Joseph Sandler's idea of the central concern for safety (1987). This compatibility is especially obvious in Freud's range of psychic danger situations, which seem to me clinically verifiable—constantly revealed as "clinical facts." Most of us do not remember our murderous impulses from these early (and especially earliest) times. What have observation and clinical practice to offer? I realize that my prejudices and convictions are also influenced greatly by the adults, traumatized as children, whom I have seen in my practice, especially since I started presenting my work on soul murder.

I am convinced that murder, the aggressive drive to violence—central to both the preoedipal and the oedipal in Freudian and Kleinian theory—has been consistently underplayed as a motivational force because it gives rise to so much anxiety and so much resistance in clinical work, on the part of analysts as well as patients. When, in teaching psychic development, I have asked students what the Oedipus complex is, I have repeatedly had answers featuring incest but leaving out the negative Oedipus complex and, most frequently, omitting parenticide—the murder of both parents. One patient (not, in my judgment, a soul murder victim), whose father died when he was five, had a nonpsychotic delusion that his father was still alive. He could give lip service to its irrationality but believed it all the same. He had dreams of intercourse with his mother that, at the start of his analysis, bothered him relatively little. In contrast, he never dreamt about the death, much less the killing, of his father. (Of course, one cannot necessarily generalize from this neat illustration of my thesis.)

I want to emphasize that soul murder is attenuated murder. In Chapter 8, on Freud's paper on beating fantasies, I express the opinion that such universal fantasies are not only degraded and disguised wishes to fulfill incestuous sexual desires but also attenuations of destructive wishes to kill and be killed. Whatever the validity of Freud's theory, I have no doubt of the existence and the importance of murderous and cannibalistic wishes that I set forth at the beginning of this chapter.[4] These primal wishes become transformed as the child matures and develops more complicated defenses against them along with a stronger grasp on reality. This occurs especially during the oedipal period of development. But the aggression-laden primal drives continue to exist in the child's unconscious mind with great motivational power beside and beneath their transformed and moderated later versions.

Instinctual wishes, derived ultimately from the body, evolve and exist in differing combinations and intensities for every individual. These variations always include the terribly powerful initial instinctual surges that, if the balance between defenses and drives changes, still retain the potential to be transformed into impulse and even action. We all have

4. Freud was fond of quoting something Charcot said: "Theory is good, but it doesn't prevent things from existing" (1916–17, p. 145). (This was, Freud wrote in a letter, Charcot's response to a remark that Freud, then a young student in Paris studying under Charcot, had addressed to the famous neurologist. Freud demonstrates the unforgettable impact of the great man's reply by quoting it in his writings at least six times.)

to deal with this onslaught of cannibalism, murder, destructive sexuality, and incest; and the partial or massive regression to, or failure to advance beyond, very early instinct-ridden and ego-deficient functioning underlies much of our psychic conflict and psychopathology. Soul murder is just one path to and from this psychopathological cauldron and should be placed in this larger perspective.

I feel that, like other animals but to a lesser extent, we have inherited patterns of instinctual and ego development that are greatly, sometimes overwhelmingly, influenced by the environment. The most important influence we know for good and bad is maternal care. But there is still so much mystery—disturbed and violent children whose parents seem to be adequate or better; relatively healthy and non-violent children who somehow emerge from an environment dominated by disturbed and even violent parents—that we tend to fall back on what the genes have contributed. We psychoanalysts have mapped out separate lines of development, most useful for our purposes, oversimplifying the kaleidoscopic complexity of each individual's slightly differing fate. Karl Abraham's sequence of libidinal and erogeneic development, schematized and oversimple as it may be, still has considerable clinical validity as well as heuristic usefulness. It has to be coordinated with the development of object relationships (a coordination started by Abraham himself) as well as with ego and superego development.

No part of psychoanalytic thought can exist in isolation, and if I have so far emphasized drives and object relations, it is important now to bring in the ego defenses. (For example, Sally Weintrobe [1995] has reminded us of the *adaptive* potential of violence.) An essential part of the mystery of violence, if one accepts the drive to, or at least the ubiquity of, violence and murder, has to do with the development of adequate defenses against them. (*Optimal* defenses might be a better way of putting it; enough aggression but not too much should be allowed expression.) How and why does an inadequacy of defense against the discharge of violent impulses arise? We see this deficiency as a characteristic of many psychopaths or psychotics. We see it in people who regress in traumatic or catastrophic circumstances. We all tend toward regression (ego and superego) in the carnival-traumatic atmosphere of war and catastrophe. (Macaulay says that the essence of war is violence.) Inadequacy of defense is a developmentally primitive psychic trait, and in order to try to mask our comparative ignorance and helplessness, we ascribe its continuance into later childhood, adolescence, and adult life to true but not very useful generalizations such as deficiencies in psychic structure or imbalances in instinctual endowment—with consequences for the establishment of object relationships.[5]

In all this we fall back on the mystery of inborn strengths and deficiencies—and on the assumption of a basis for psychic health that is familiar, obviously true, and yet too general and too subject to exception to be fully satisfying: the presence in psychic development of a consistent nurturing-and-restraining parental presence that has been internalized. Since we can say more about pathology than about health, we are more certain that the existence of a violent (destructive, murderous, sadistic) parent or, perhaps even more damaging, a profoundly negligent one (one who is either incapable of caring about the child or forced to neglect or desert it) can cause harm in a way that frequently brings on violence di-

5. I am convinced of the central importance of generally successful passage through the vicissitudes of anal erogeneity and libido in relation to control of aggression and violence; see Shengold, 1988.

rected against the self or others. These violent tendencies
arise by way of identification with the aggressor as well as
with the aggressive reaction to frustration and torment; curi-
ously enough, parents who are frightened, weak, and overindulgent can also evoke violent inclinations in children who
have consequent deficiencies in internalizing the necessary
"no" in relation to their impulses. Civilization depends on
our neurotic renunciations and compromises. Yet violent
(what I have called soul-murdering) or absent or spoiling or
even nonloving parental presences do not invariably figure in
the histories of children and adults who show violent tendencies.

"Did It Really Happen?" And Does It Matter?

The conviction that something traumatic has happened,
right or wrong, should originate with the patient, not with
the therapist. Patients who have been tortured and seduced
as children, especially if this was done by parents or parent
figures, have usually had their ability to register what was
done to them impaired; sometimes this has amounted to
brainwashing—self-imposed, demanded by the parent, or
both. Therefore, even if the trauma has been unmistakably
registered—remembered, observed, confessed to by the per-
petrator, performed on others—there is still a kind of pathological doubting in the victim who does not want to hate a
parent who is felt to be vital for support and even for survival.
So there is always doubt—sometimes existing alongside conviction in a kind of Orwellian "doublethink." There are also
false convictions. It is sometimes very difficult for the patient
and—therefore for the therapist—to know what actually
happened. And even if this is not so, if the trauma is clearly
remembered, the need to work out the accompanying and

obfuscating denial and distortion is a large part of the work of
the therapy.

I have written a clinical paper titled "Did It Really Happen?" in order to demonstrate how difficult it can be for the
therapist or analyst to help a patient differentiate fantasy
from reality. I am unable to publish the paper because important details might jeopardize confidentiality. The patient, W,
felt that she had been seduced as a child by her father. I will
say only that the fairly long treatment was interrupted when
the patient's work required a move to another part of the
country before a satisfactory termination was achieved; both
the analyst and the patient concluded that no definitive decision as to whether she had actually been seduced was yet
possible. It was clear, and finally became undeniable by the
patient, that keeping herself in a limbo of indecision about
what her father may or may not have done to her sexually
meant holding onto him as the center of her life with the
fantasy that he owed her a future. W was not yet willing to
give up that promise. Although married and a mother, her
relationship to her new family had an as-if quality compared
to the intensity of her feelings about her parents. She tormented herself and others with her obsession about whether
she had been sexually assaulted by her father. In contrast, her
father's generally cruel, dominating, and frightening treatment of her and her brother was remembered clearly and was
corroborated by her brother. It ultimately became apparent
that for her (and for every patient I have seen in a similar
quandary) it was crucially important to be able to deal with
and become responsible for how the past is registered in the
mind rather than with whether it "really" happened.[6] "I

6. Lawrence Friedman writes that "to be worthy of the name,
psychoanalysis had to give up hunting for traumas and examine the
way a person pictures his world" (1996, vii).

may never be able to know for sure," W stated when she was leaving analysis with me, "but at least I feel partly free now. I can ask the questions; and I can know that it might have happened, and that I am not sure and perhaps never will be sure. I know now that I have been held back by obsessing rather than really being able to think about it. Now at least I can think about it and put it in some perspective. I can see that my father is not a complete monster; and I know that the bad things he did to me that I am sure of are worse than seduction—whether or not I was literally seduced."

For my part, I felt, from the variety and specificity of peripheral details that she seemed to remember clearly and from her father's reactions to her attempts to talk to him about her childhood, that sexual contact may have taken place—but I could not be sure. I stressed our mutual uncertainty and the necessity for her to become responsible for where she was and how much she had gained (especially in the direction she had stressed: her freedom to think) in her search for certainty. I counseled that she also try to remain aware of the tie that bound her to her father through her obsessional uncertainty, and I recommended that she continue her analysis in her new location. W called on me several years later when on vacation in New York City. She had not sought further sustained treatment but seemed to have consolidated her work with me. The relationship with her husband had become authentic, loving, and satisfying; that with her children (already an achievement in caring when she started) was even better than before. She tearfully and convincingly expressed her gratitude and pleasure at the change. Here is part of what she said:

> I've had no sustained therapy, but there has been real improvement. I am working again. I can be a

good wife and mother. My spirits are now generally good. There has been a dimming of sexual
compulsions. The hatred and self-hatred are still
there, but so much less. Finally, I can have sex
playfully. There has been a great change. Crying
has stopped, and so has the continuous sense of
guilt. I can care for my husband and appreciate
that he is helping me. I have had a lot of support
from my brother; he hasn't taken father's side, and
that has helped. I have confronted my father gently; he angrily changes the subject. I'm no longer
the innocent who is taken by surprise. It gets
clearer and clearer that in my symptoms and sexual actions I'm repeating some fundamental experience from the past. But I am not sure exactly
what did happen to me. Your presence is always
there in my mind, but I have gained conviction
about the traumatic past on my own now, it
doesn't come from you. [She starts to cry.] I am so
grateful. You have helped me own my life!

I was moved by the emotional liberation W was describing. I was gratified that W, who had not read any of my
writings, used the word *own* in the sense that I have often
given it: the need to be responsible for how the past and
present are currently registered in the mind. (It is of course
possible that I had used the word in this sense in the course of
the treatment.) She seemed to have become able to acknowledge her father's bad character (whether or not he was a
sexual abuser)—instead of using her seemingly unresolvable
obsessions to avoid responsibility. For example, her father's
exhibitionism and sadistic teasing, although clearly remembered and corroborated by her brother, had not been fully

emotionally integrated ("owned") until what she called the "consolidation" that occurred after the analysis had been interrupted and she was "on her own."

W vowed to go into analysis in her new location, feeling (correctly, I judged) that she had not worked out the emotions that had arisen in her relationship with me—she had not fully faced the dangers attendant on trusting me, although the trust had helped her distance and own her past. I felt that her primary motivation for this was her awareness of the incomplete work on her hostile feelings toward me rather than her looking for the answer to "Did it really happen?" I do not know if she has fulfilled her vow.

Therapy

For the therapist-analyst, working with patients who have been or may have been abused takes skill, tact, patience (this is true with all patients who have to bear the terrible intensities and anxieties of violence-laden impulses), and—above all—knowledge of the need to be neutral, to suspend belief and disbelief in the possibility that abuse and neglect have occurred.

There is, one sees from clinical work, always a formidable inner resistance that contributes to one of the contradictory current trends—that toward denying the abuse of children. And yet, one also sees from work with patients that, important as it can be to an individual's sense of identity to establish some conviction of the reality of the past, what is crucial for psychological change is not chiefly being able to answer the question "Did it really happen?" but being able to acknowledge and to own the inner registrations of the past that continue to motivate the mind in the present. The ability to explore the relation between the past and the present with more freedom and flexibility is a major force for psychic change and increased mastery in psychoanalytic work and in life. This cannot be accomplished without considerable responsibility for what one feels, what one knows, and what one does not know. (This of course is true for all people, but especially for soul murder victims.) A perceptive patient once said to me, "Now I understand. You want me to be responsible for what is going on in my mind." This understanding was his first giant step toward realizing his deficiency and acquiring that responsibility. The attainment of owning gives perspective; the patient can distance compulsion and reduce overwhelming emotions as well as overwhelming defenses against the flow of passions.

Caritas

In psychotherapeutic treatment, we know *what* to do; the mystery lies in *how* to do it. We cure through love. Love for the analyst-therapist makes it possible for the patient to accept as his or her own the insight the analyst provides and evokes. If—it is a big, sometimes, alas, an impossible, if—the therapist or analyst can get the person prone to violence (too full of sadomasochism, conscious and unconscious) to care about him or her as a separate person, and to tolerate that caring, control over violence can be at least partially achieved or restored. I have repeatedly stated in this book that the acquisition and toleration of love for another person are needed to temper the overload of murderous hatred and its associated terrors in those abused as children. This love is the *caritas* referred to in Chapter 6—a different kind of love from the narcissistic variety described by Proust and Freud that I outlined in Chapter 7. It is not primarily felt as sexual but is composed of loving kindness, sympathy, empathy, and trying to help others. Soul murder victims are only some of the many who are unable to care passionately about other people, about causes, about ideas, even about themselves—and who are condemned to regard others mainly as fulfillers of needs. (In order to care about oneself with more than transitory satisfaction, with joy, one must be able to care lovingly about others.) Freud says that it is necessary to be able to love (here he means *caritas*) and to work to attain psychic health, and perhaps the most reliable index of that health is an individual's ability to care. (The most dependable estimate of who will make a good psychoanalyst, or a good psychoanalytic patient, is the intuitive grasp one gets in initial interviews of, to put it in dehumanized analytic jargon, the person's "capacity for object relations.")[7]

If it is possible (with some degree of safety) to estab-

7. In interviews, the intuitive guess is, I feel, best based on the individual's ability to evoke in more than one dimension the people he or she is talking about. Do the important others come alive, are they imbued with emotion, can the individual speak of love and hate convincingly? With many people this is not always easy to determine at first. Emotional evocation involves talents that some people lack, although the emotions may turn out to be present. Some people have a dramatic ability to portray emotions that can turn out to be hollow. It can take time and patience and a trial of therapy or analysis to get to know an individual's capacity to love and to care. (I have repeatedly stressed individual differences because soul murder—chronic traumatization—destroys individuality.) Sometimes being able to "really" care for causes, even for things, indicates the potential for going on to care for people—and sometimes it turns out to be a defensive bastion that cannot be overcome. One must be modest about one's estimates and willing to be patient. Of course, one never knows beforehand with any certainty what the potentials are for unblocking inhibited emotions. This is the art, not the science, of psychoanalytic therapy.

lish in relation to the analyst the sense of the dearness of
another person that has been crushed because it made the
child feel vulnerable, the caring can become in the patient's mind a capacity for mutual dearness that can be extended to others. This allows for an interweaving of the
newly acquired feelings toward the analyst with feelings
for the important people in the patient's present as well as
those from the past—even those who have been the
abusers. Hatred as well as love must be able to flow and to
be contained in the mind at the same time. If the external
relationships with others are allowed to change, so can the
mental pictures of the parents that have become part of
the self. This can modify the primitive either-or dimension
that so often characterizes the emotions of the abused
child, as well as the zombielike emptiness that can serve as
a defense against the too-intense extremes. The inner pictures of the much-hated and much-idealized parent figures
from childhood can, with the achievement of enough emotional moderation, be integrated sufficiently to provide
some perspective and toleration, to enhance the capacity
for self-reflection; this means becoming able to attenuate
identifications with abusers and to relax the compulsion to
repeat the abuse, to become able to love-and-hate (that
mixture is compatible with the conditions of life) rather
than feel the unbearable intensity from earliest childhood
of either hating or loving that cannot be tolerated for long.
If one feels that all must be perfect or nothing, one ends
with nothing.

With my patients I have found that the ability to care
for another comes most often (and most easily, although it
is never easy) in relation to children—if the patient is a
parent. (This was true of my patient W, described above.)
If not, they sometimes become able to tolerate the idea of

or the wish to have children. This goes along with an increasing ability to care about oneself as a child. This is one path toward caring that begins with the kind of narcissism that is optimally invested in a child by a parent—a healthy transition between primitive narcissism and true object love. This of course can be seen in relation to a spouse or a lover too.

It may be instructive to document a failure of healing, here from literature rather than from clinical practice. This is how Orwell evokes the result of the soul murder (accomplished by torture and brainwashing culminating for Winston in his scream, "Do it to Julia!") of the former lovers Winston and Julia in *1984*—it is their last meeting:

> "I betrayed you," [Julia] said baldly.
> "I betrayed you," he said.
> She gave him another quick look of dislike.
> "Sometimes," she said, "they threaten you with something—something you can't stand up to, can't even think about. And then you say, 'Don't do it to me, do it to somebody else, do it to so-and-so.' And perhaps you might pretend, afterward, that it was only a trick and that you just said it to make them stop and didn't really mean it. But that isn't true. At the time when it happens you do mean it. You think there's no other way of saving yourself, and you're quite ready to save yourself that way. *You want it to happen to the other person. You don't give a damn what they suffer. All you care about is yourself.*"
> "*All you care about is yourself,*" he echoed.
> (1948, pp. 294–95, my italics).

In Orwell's parable, love has led to soul murder, which has destroyed the capacity for real love; only primal narcissism is left. But, for survival, there is a clinging to the shadow of love, to the delusion of love—loving the one who has done the torture—in the novel, loving Big Brother. The renunciation of the caring for and about others is done partly in order to hold onto the parent who has become a necessary part of the self. For Winston and Julia, to betray one another is to identify with the soul-murdering parental figure, to carry out the orders of the internalized soul murdering parent, to direct rage onto and reject love for anyone (including aspects of one's self) who might interfere with the primal tie to that parent (the moral of Chapter 2—Medea's "Love will not triumph!"). The essence of therapy for soul murder victims is to diminish the power of this link to the internalized primal destructive parent. This can be accomplished if the therapist or analyst can enable the patient to form an emotional tie with him or her, and perhaps with others, that is *meaningful as a relationship with a separate person,* an other who can be cared about and even loved.

For patients in psychoanalysis and psychoanalytic psychotherapy, gaining access to loving feelings toward these others depends on the patient's gradual acquisition of the ability to tolerate caring about the analyst and accepting (and psychically registering) the analyst as a separate and predominantly benevolent person different from the internalized traumatizing parent. That means the acquisition of a considerable feeling of trust that in relation to the analyst, caring will not lead to abuse and abandonment. James McLaughlin (1996), with his characteristic bravery and honesty, furnishes a rare and moving documentation of an analytic patient's transition from distrust of to caring about the analyst.

McLaughlin shows his patient, Q, traumatized and deprived as a child, fighting to own (I am using my word for it) his feelings—the good as well as the bad. It seems clear that good feelings—especially loving himself and loving others—have been most difficult for this characteristically distrustful man. He is depicted as having been seesawing through a search for a separate identity while also struggling to hold onto the internalized images of his bad parents in the context of a long period of confrontational repetitions of themes full of emotion and conflict between patient and analyst. (Freud calls this the working-through process in the transference.) This material from the last year of the long analysis comes after a period in which the patient was expressing (and fighting off in the working through) the feeling that the analyst was trying to rob him of his identity. Q voiced

> his increasing grasp of "my basic self, my gutsy kid-self that would never give in, even if it meant I had to hide all of my life. I *love* him! He's real, and he's mine: He's me!" His voice dropped in vigour and insistence. "Even as I say this I'm fading, losing hold."
>
> [Analyst]: "Such strength and conviction in your voice as you held him, and now [you] sound sad and meek giving him up?" (my italics)

The patient apparently then reacted regressively to what appears to me to have been an empathic intervention by feeling that the analyst (like his parents as he had registered them in his mind) was threatening his shaky hold on his identity:

Mr. Q. (Half sits up as he replies): "Are you putting me on? You know we've just again been talking about how saying anything I really mean means I give it up. It's not mine. It's yours. It's nothing!" (Sinks back into the couch) "But I know that's not really so. I could hear your voice. No teasing in it. I *will* hold onto this [basic] self, regardless. . . . This is harder to say, to stick with. When I feel this me that seems real, I'm also feeling something about you that feels real. I'd like to say it feels good. But that would mean giving you something. And I can't give anything that is real, that's worthwhile. Something goes wrong."

The patient is threatened by loving feelings and impulses toward McLaughlin, but the owning is being worked through in the transference. He continues: "[Once] when I was talking about how good it felt between little Ben [the patient's lovable young nephew] and me, you said something about the generosity of loving back. I didn't get it. I know it's time to go now. I'm going to hold on to this basic feeling. *That* I feel I'm getting" (p. 221).

In the next session the patient goes on to express his hatred toward the analyst, but now it has not taken away his feeling about his "basic self"—"I've held onto me all this time" (p. 222)—and the hatred ("I'm hating you right now!" p. 222) does not keep him from also feeling love: "I can feel you've had a lot of caring for me, respect for me. And say! I think I've got it, about that generosity of loving back. I have felt it with Ben. I'm feeling it now with you. That my loving you for your loving me makes me feel I do have something good to give back! It feels safe here. Will it be safe out there?

I've been slow to get there, but I'm going to give it my best try" (p. 222).

McLaughlin comments: "And, as his own words say clearly enough, when he could trust me enough to feel I loved and believed him, he found in himself capacities to trust and claim his own positive as well as negative feelings toward himself and others" (p. 223). I usually find it difficult to tell whether the ability to own loving and hating the self or loving and hating the other comes first for any given patient. This can be as moot and as inconsequential as discovering the primal priority of the chicken or the egg. In our work, the hatching and separation are all.

Toleration of caring about and loving an other (necessary also in order to be able to care for and love one's self optimally) is not easy for victims of violence and soul murder. For those who have been seduced or beaten as children, for example, it was usually the love for, or at least the need for, the parents that led the children toward the overstimulation and torment that ensued. The children learned to keep themselves emotionally closed, especially to positive feelings. It can be safer to stay on the level of regarding others primarily as fulfillers of need (while concomitantly keeping the parents as part of the self, consciously or unconsciously). In Chapter 6 I stressed the important implications for successful therapy of soul murder victims in the anecdote about reviving the young girl, exceptionally regarded as a real human individual, who had survived exposure to poison gas.

I repeat: in relation to treatment, it is how to help the patient to allow loving feeling (alongside the hatred) that is the mystery. We have to find individual and sometimes idiosyncratic ways to evoke and sustain caring in each patient.[8]

8. August Aichhorn (1925) wrote a book about his special methods of creating an emotional bond with violent and delinquent juveniles

This is the intuitive art of psychoanalytic therapy, guided by empathic understanding: tact, patience, reliability, the honesty to admit one's mistakes and failures, and some flexibility in relation to a grasp of the patient's individual needs. Above all one must be able to tolerate the onslaught of hatred that has to emerge. The soul-murdered (or those who are similarly burdened by violent and murderous impulses) expect that either they or those they feel too close to will be killed. The therapist's comparative lack of alarm in the face of the patient's murderous wishes and, above all, feelings, helps; but perhaps it is most reassuring that the feeling and expression of rage don't result in death or catastrophe. People who have been traumatically abused are saddled with the worst expectations—terrifying anxiety, loss of control, feeling like killing and being killed, being alone and unable to survive in a murderous universe. (One has to recall Primo Levi's pointing out that once one has been helpless and tortured one never really gets over it.) In many cases the former victims of God's concentration camps can, if caring for the analyst is allowed as a result of the comparative stability provided by a long (and, realistically speaking, predominantly benevolent) relationship with the analyst, attain the kind of emotional insight that grants strength and perspective. These achievements can ultimately reduce the overwhelming intensities involved in the malign and violent expectations that have been forced on them by a traumatic past (in cases of attempted soul murder); this is true even for patients whose pathology stems mainly from having been born with initially inadequate psychic structure. New and more flexible

---

and adolescents based on his empathic grasp of the disturbed young people.

defenses and strategies can be developed. The ability to use the conscious will to fight for health and love can be increased.

"Did it really happen?" Important as the question can be to an increased feeling of identity if it can be answered definitively or at least settled on as unanswerable, it is less relevant to healing than being able to tolerate and own one's deficiencies sufficiently to allow love to triumph, predominantly or occasionally. There is a kind of psychic economic determinism here that may become more malleable when and if we get to know more about the sources of psychic health and strength and how to tap them. We cannot change the basic conditions for human life, but for some unfortunates, soul murder victims or not, it is possible, with therapy that can restore some authenticity of feeling for others and for oneself, to help release the capacity for joy and distance the need for sadomasochistic holding onto the past.

The gifted psychoanalytic essayist Adam Phillips, in his 1988 book *Winnicott*, points to the evolution of psychoanalytic technique away from "an analytic setting in which the patient does not undergo authoritative translation—having his unconscious fed back to him, as it were—but is enabled by the analyst, as Winnicott wrote, 'to reveal himself to himself'" (p. 11). Psychoanalysis could never have been exclusively based on interpretation, but early practitioners undoubtedly caricatured Freud's early and imperfect technique by something like magisterially "translating" the patient's associations into "You have an Oedipus complex!" Interpretations of this kind are still made—more tactfully worded, one hopes, and at the appropriate time. They frequently have to be followed up by a working-through that would or could enable the patient to accept emotionally, to "own," the interpretation.[9] Phillips quotes Winnicott's description of psychoanalysis as "not just a matter of interpreting the repressed unconscious [but] . . . the provision of a professional setting for trust in which such work may take place" (Phillips, 1988, p. 11). Winnicott is not favoring eliminating interpretations but rather pointing out the effectiveness of the patient's discovering with full emotional involvement what will lead to a responsible grasp of his own mental functioning and content. Winnicott sees the analyst as a kind of host whose job is "first and foremost the provision of a congenial milieu, a 'holding environment' analogous to maternal care" (Phillips, 1988, p. 11). He views premature interpretation as a risk "that interpretation in analysis would be formative in a way that actually pre-empted the patient's own half-formed thoughts and feelings. Interpretation could be merely a way of hurrying—on the analyst's behalf—and analysis, like development, was, for Winnicott, about people taking their own time" (Phillips, 1988, p. 12). It follows that it is optimal for the victim of child abuse to be allowed to "discover" what has or has not happened to him or her as far as possible and not be deterred (directed or misdirected) by premature (and especially not by authoritative) interpretations from the analyst. A process of mutual discovery, with as much as possible coming from the patient, is best. Such analytic work on the part of the patient minimizes the repetition from the past that passive reception always involves, and it enhances the owning of frightening feelings and ideas.

9. One patient, a very rich and successful woman in an intellectual field, unconsciously expressed the turning point in becoming able to own what was threateningly too important to her by finding herself able to resist the compulsion always to borrow her books from a public library and became not only able to buy her own but to enjoy buying and keeping them.

Does It Matter If It Really Happened?

The answer is yes and no.[10] In any individual case it really matters. It can shore up the sense of identity so regularly threatened in soul murder victims to know with conviction that abuse occurred, that parents were predominantly or repeatedly brutal, indifferent, crazy, psychopathic, absent, or deficient psychologically and empathically.[11] One can put the question in its complicated perspective by asking, "Does it matter to its victims or the children of its victims if the Holocaust really occurred?" It matters greatly for each individual who feels traumatized or neglected and asks, "Did it really happen?" to be able to be or become reasonably certain about the subsequent interplay between the offending or indifferent parent and the child: what he did, what I did; what she was like; what I was and am like. These questions need to be settled in relation to the past (very difficult to impossible to do with certainty) and in relation to how they are registered and active in the mind in the present (still difficult but possible). As I have said, establishing what is there in the mind about and between the parent and the self

10. Once, when I had said something like this to a group of analytic candidates, one brave person said, "Dr. Shengold, you talked to us about George Orwell's *doublethink*, but here you seem to be talking out of both sides of your mouth." I could see his confusion but reminded him that contradictions and complexities are essentially denied in those who use the kind of mind-splitting involved in doublethink. Part of its definition is that impossibly contradictory opinions can be maintained without any need to recognize or reconcile them or any awareness that something is wrong. Containing and owning (being responsible about) contradictions is an adaptive strength rather than an inhibiting denial.

11. Walt Whitman wrote: "I am the man, I suffered, I was there" (1851, p. 102).

(usually patterned in contradictory and complicated ways) can furnish perspective as well as a kind of mastery that can modify emotional intensities and help reverse pathology.

But with respect to individuals with established pathology, one must be aware that it often cannot be ascertained how that pathology came into being. It can look to the observer as if it doesn't make much difference how the propensities for evil or the devastations of the capacity for loving and for joy came about. Ralph Greenson is reported to have said, "Parents who lie create children who deny," and he also could have reversed it—"Parents who deny create children who lie." These can be truths, but it doesn't always happen that way. We must also account for the children who lie and who deny, who are violent and evil, who cannot love, whose malignant and pathological qualities do not seem to stem simply or primarily from the depredations and deficiencies of their parents. There are also those whose strength and good character, even the crucial ability to care for others, seem not to have been derived from criminal or defective parents. And sometimes the child who says with Milton's devil, "Evil, be thou my good!" has not necessarily been criminally treated and can be the bad seed of good fruit. These are the mysteries of powers and handicaps that we are born with, for good and for bad.

But acknowledging mystery does not mean abandoning what we can and do know. (Simone Weil wrote that evil is to love what mystery is to intelligence [quoted in Auden, 1970, p. 344].) We must not forget, painful as it is to know it as a child and as a parent, that the helpless dependency and the overwhelming emotional needs of the infant and child make brutalizing them all too easy. Soul murder exists, and it does matter.

Therapeutic Moral of This Book

The therapist of the victim of soul murder (and of others not significantly traumatized or deprived as children but similarly pschologically burdened) requires the utmost in empathic tact and patience to guide the patient toward becoming able to tolerate the need for love (caring, *caritas*). (Loving and caring have been avoided since they have made the former victim so vulnerable.) Love must be felt in order to acknowledge and attentuate the terrible legacy of murderous hatred that has become too much to bear without destructive or self-destructive action accompanied by crippling inhibitions and defenses. Restoring the capacity to care about oneself and others is the therapeutic challenge.

APPENDIX

A Discussion of "Dissociative Processes and
Transference/Countertransference Paradigms in
the Psychoanalytically Oriented Treatment of Adult
Survivors of Childhood Sexual Abuse,"
by Jody Messler Davies and Mary Gail Frawley

The map appears to us more real than the land.
—D. H. Lawrence

There is much I have to find fault with in Davies and
Frawley's essay, but I want to begin with praise. Theirs is a
serious study of a most important subject. We see, in their
clinical material if not in their theoretical and technical formulations, that they are aware of the tragic, painful, contradictory, conflict-ridden burdens the victims of child abuse
have to bear. They appreciate how much is demanded of the
therapist who undertakes the challenge of helping people
whose bodies and souls have been violated—whose experience makes them intensely distrustful and even terrified of
change and of help. They can empathize with and are trying
to understand their patients; they know that therapists of the
soul-murdered have to be tough-minded and not sentimental
purveyors of compensatory "love." These attitudes will go a
long way in therapy.

But, but—I found myself sputtering with *but*s as I encountered many of the authors' opinions, generalizations, and
ideas. Above all, I feel alienated by their tone of (sometimes

This is an extended and revised version of an article published in
Psychoanalytic Dialogues 2:49–59 (1992).

militantly righteous) certainty. For more than thirty years I have been treating adult patients who were abused and neglected as children, and I find that in every new case, alongside some previously observed characteristics, I am surprised by the unexpected, full of doubts, and left with a sense of how much remains to be discovered about the effects of what I have called soul murder. I have also learned a great deal and have some limited islands of certainty achieved in relation to specific individuals. But I am not ashamed of hesitations and modesty in drawing general conclusions. The mysteries inherent in human nature in general and in pathogenesis in particular are vast; one must be prepared for surprises, contradictions, uncertainties. I have become very wary of facile generalizations and formulae, my own as well as others'.

Davies and Frawley suggest that is easy to differentiate between fantasies and memories; that the finding of what they define as "dissociation" makes this possible; and that a treatment plan can be outlined that would be applicable to most victims—a plan that seems to me so simplified and specific that it would not be useful to many former victims and could easily lead to misunderstanding that would interfere with the conduct of a psychoanalytic treatment and the acquisition of the insight needed to transmute pathology significantly. Implicit or explicit certainty in the therapist can lead to transformations of symptomatology in some sick people, who develop a (usually transient) faith in the powerful parental person. But these are transference "cures," akin to what can be achieved by hypnosis; they are dependent on an external source, effected by a borrowed certainty, and reversible. Achieving an enhanced sense of identity requires true insight based on self-awareness. For abused children now grown up, this means being able to bear and integrate the hitherto unbearable, about themselves and about needed others.

Soul murder patients are individuals who have suffered complicated, overwhelming traumata—experiences that have evoked damaging defenses, destructive compulsions to repeat their traumatic past, and crippling (but sometimes also constructive) reparative adaptive efforts to absorb and transcend what life has thrust upon them. People who have suffered so in the concentration camps of childhood do seem to have certain burdens in common: murderous rage; the terrible double bind of (on one hand) feeling absolutely dependent for rescue on parental figures who may have been the abusers or at least are held responsible for it and (on the other) wanting to kill off these people, who are felt to be indispensable; massive and multiple defenses that can bring about denial and achieve brainwashing. But, but (and these are enormous *buts*), despite these common features the individuals are also very (and often surprisingly) different, and many other circumstances besides childhood abuse can bring about similar effects.

Pathological effect cannot be reduced to a single simple cause. We are not just the mechanical products of what has been done to us. Freud (1905, pp. 239–40) designated the interrelated pathogenic elements of constitutional dispositions and traumatic and environmental influences (what we are born with and what happens to us) as "complementary series." Both parts of the series are always present in varying proportions in the determination of psychic structure, functioning, and pathology. Once the mind begins to mature and develop, all kinds of modifications, transformations, and regressions are possible. The child acquires the power to integrate what comes from outside the mind and body with what comes from within the mind and body. One of the driving forces becomes the unconscious motivating fantasies of the individual; these, like everything else, arise in relation to the complementary series. Davies and Frawley's paper criticizes what they call the "classic" Freudian position for emphasizing fantasies while disregarding reality. Jeffrey Masson made this accusation in his (in more ways than one) *Assault on Truth* (1984).

There can be no neat differentiation between fantasy and reality; they are inextricably intertwined. What is clinically relevant is how real events affect the dynamic fantasies (unconscious and conscious) that bear on psychic conflict and the motivation of our mental life. Freud was the discoverer of our unconscious primal fantasies, but he repeatedly acknowledged the actuality of childhood seduction and traumata (see Hanly, 1987). Masson's extreme view (which reduces the impact of fantasy while he accuses "Freudians" of reducing the impact of reality) amounts to equating neurosis to the effects of traumatic seduction.

Davies and Frawley espouse a Massonian view of what they call "classic" psychoanalysis. Their history of the seduction hypothesis is deficient. It is true that Freud probably reacted against his initial assumption that neurosis results from seductions by the father by subsequently underestimating the frequency of childhood sexual abuse. So did almost everyone until recently. Ferenczi's view—that the frequency of occurrence was greater than had been assumed—was probably closer to the actuality than Freud's. But one should not infer (as Masson and these authors do) that it was because of his ideas on pathogenesis that Ferenczi was banished from Freud's favor. It was more probably his views and practices involving compensatory gratification and physical contact by the therapist that caused Freud to feel concern for the welfare of Ferenczi's patients, for his friend, for his friend's reputation, and for the reputation of psychoanalysis. The Freud-Ferenczi correspondence shows how complex the disagreements between the two men were.

Masson derives his views from a man who certainly considered himself a true follower of Freud, Robert Fliess. Fliess stated in 1956 that "one recognizes that the patient in need of a long and thorough analysis would appear to be, by and large, someone who has been damaged by and has identified with a psychotic parent" (p. xvii). In his 1973 book, Fliess repeated this quotation and elaborated as follows: "1. The neurotic seriously in need of analysis is apt to have at least one psychotic parent. 2. He has been victimized by the bizarre sexuality of this parent. 3. He has suffered the (largely defused) aggression of which the parent has made him the object" (p. 206).[1]

Fliess's view, especially as interpreted by Masson, comes very close to a statement that all neurotics have been abused as children.[2] This position is much too all-inclusive. The frequency of both child abuse and what Fliess calls "ambulatory" (that is, nondiagnosed and nonhospitalized) psychotic parents and of their sexual abuse of children has been underestimated—and not only by Freud and psychoanalysts (aside

1. Davies and Frawley quote from Fliess's 1953 article on hypnotic states but do not list his three relevant books (nor Masson's, for that matter) in their bibliography. The authors would appear not to know about Fliess's work on abused children. They quote Dickes as the first to link autohypnosis with childhood abuse in a 1965 paper that Dickes acknowledges to be based on Fliess's prior work.

2. But Fliess adds a qualification that shows that he is aware of the importance of constitutional factors: "Such is, I am convinced, the environmental etiology of the neurosis when a sufficiently susceptible 'constitution' (in the sense of Freud's 'complementary series' [1905, pp. 239–40] between environment and constitution) is present" (1973, p. 206).

from Ferenczi). But one cannot assume that all neurotics (which to me means, putting aside psychotics, all of us) have been seduced, severely beaten, or badly neglected as children. And one cannot assume that all abusers are psychotic parents (although in what appear to be universally held fantasies seduction is ascribed to the parent).[3]

I cannot help wondering, on the basis of the inadequacy of the authors' quotations from the psychoanalytic literature and their inaccurate conclusions, about the depth of their knowledge of psychoanalytic theory and psychoanalytic practice. Their remarks about oedipal fantasy make me question how much analytic experience they have had with patients who do not fit within their definition of sexually abused children. They seem to lack a clinical feel for the enormous power of unconscious fantasies. They present a simple dichotomy between people who suffer from "the reality of early childhood sexual abuse" and those suffering from "wishful oedipal fantasy" (p. 33). This is followed by the confident statement, "The presentation of these *two clinical phenomena* is so vastly different that they can be recognized as such and treated each in the appropriate way" (pp. 33–34, my italics). I find the reduction of so many different individuals to "two clinical phenomena" mind-boggling.

Psychic development is a continuity. The oedipal phase of development comes after and is molded by preoedipal development. Preoedipal psychic development involves not only the drives (in which the authors seem to have no interest) but also development of the ego and the superego, of the self and of object relations, and more. Psychic development is

---

3. For example, some abusers of children are not psychotic but have identified with psychotic parents and are operating under a compulsion to repeat their past.

an infinitely complicated business; despite similarities, it is as different for individuals as are their personalities. One's sexual and aggressive fantasies are products of both preoedipal and oedipal development—the latter molded by the former. These fantasies are dynamic, reflecting all sorts of transformations that occur as the mind develops, and there is a constant alternation of maturation and regression to earlier stages.

What then do the authors make of patients with predominantly preoedipal (for example, cannibalistic, destructive) fantasies? Are they all based on childhood sexual abuse? Has everyone been abused? Even if one arbitrarily isolates oedipal fantasies, one needs to be aware that these are full of murderous impulses; the authors also need to be reminded that the incestuous are not directed only toward the parent of the opposite sex. There is inevitably a negative Oedipus complex. (If Davies and Frawley do not accept these theories, what do they do with the clinical facts of bisexuality and parricidal impulse on which they are founded?) Our metaphor of theory has to be based on what people feel and think and do. I will indulge in some certainty of my own derived from my clinical experience and will restate categorically, in contradiction of the authors, that in many people it is not easy but difficult and sometimes impossible to differentiate fantasy from reality in their stories of abuse in childhood.

There is no room for simple-mindedness in the study of psychic events, and specifically not in relation to the power of fantasy. How complex the phenomena are and how sophisticated one's thinking ought to be are demonstrated by Grossman's 1991 hypothesis that the effects of trauma in both child and adult are best understood "in connection with the development and functioning of the capacity to fantasize." He continues: "I suggest that to the extent that fantasy formation is possible, some transformation and mastery of traumatic experience is possible. Severe trauma impairs the capacity for fantasy, . . . leading to a failure to transform the traumatic experience through activity. . . . Repetitions in fantasy may contribute to the mastery of trauma" (p. 26).[4] Trauma increases sadomasochism and inhibits thinking about threatening experience and working it over in fantasy; the effect of trauma on fantasy is all-important and not always completely predictable. It is the effect of trauma on the motivational power of a child's fantasies that can make having actually gone through an overwhelming experience significantly and powerfully different for a given individual—different in relation to psychic economics. One must always deal with constitutional deficiencies that can make even slight neglect and abuse overwhelming to some. This can make establishing what has happened difficult or impossible; but, as I have noted, once having been in a concentration camp, some part of one's mind remains in the concentration camp.

Davies and Frawley state that "adults who have been sexually abused as children are only too willing to believe that the nightmarish memories which begin to flood their

4. This is a complex business. I have seen adult patients traumatized as children who have reacted defensively by retreating into excessive and obsessional daydreaming and fantasizing. Their quantitative increase in fantasy can amount to a deficiency of ability to live in the present and seems to be not in the service of mastery but narrowly fixed by the compulsion to repeat the past. Others appear to have globally inhibited their power of fantasy and banished daydreaming, with marked effects on their ability to think. There is probably a whole range of defective functioning of fantasy. None of this contradicts Grossman's statement about the pathologic effects of trauma on the (under optimal conditions) predominantly healthy—transforming, ameliorating, healing—power of fantasy.

waking thoughts are not real" (p. 32). This is true. But the opposite can also be true: most people, whether or not they have been sexually abused, are only too willing to explain away their own terrifying sexual and murderous (sado-masochistic) fantasies and impulses and project them onto others, especially their parents. Both kinds of disavowal can be present in adults abused as children (frequently employed alternatively so that responsibility for either is canceled out). Over the course of many years, I have seen patients who have consulted me because of my soul murder publications who were eager to enlist themselves as victims of seductive parents. In a few of these patients studied in analysis, the initial accusations of abuse were not substantiated, and eventually both the patients and I accounted for the accusations as arising from conditions other than overt abuse and neglect in childhood. This was in spite of the fact that these patients presented with the familiar facade of severe and massive defensive processes (including some that Davies and Frawley would probably characterize as "dissociation"). This is the subject of Chapter 11 (also see Shengold, 1991a).

I want to repeat that the key effect of traumatic experience (not all sexual and not all soul murder) is on the child's power of fantasy and subsequent life of fantasy. The primarily defensive "dissociation" is evoked mainly by the intensity of sadomasochistic feeling and fantasy. There is an urgent need to discharge the exciting, destructive feelings, and this threatens the internal images of both self and parents and leads to potentially paralyzing compromises.

The authors are mistaken, in my opinion, when they focus on their concept of dissociation as the hallmark of child abuse (as "pathognomonic of it," p. 7) in the adult. Our defense mechanisms are arbitrarily defined. The definitions can be very useful; some are more specifically descriptive of clinical events than others, and our metaphorical and descriptive classifications should not be reified. Dissociation is an especially broad mechanism, as is denial; both involve isolation of feeling and of idea. Both denial and dissociation refer to ways of warding off the traumatic past and unbearable affect, found not only in soul murder victims but also in some form in people suffering from many other conditions—organic defects and illnesses, psychoses, traumatic losses and catastrophes in childhood. Further, there is some dissociation and some denial in all of us (as there is some part of everyone's functioning that resembles the psychotic's and the pervert's). It must also be borne in mind that each individual exhibits an idiosyncratic combination of our arbitrarily and loosely defined defense mechanisms. The human phenomena are much more complex than our terms can encompass. (For a more clinically useful view of dissociation, see I. Brenner, 1996.)

There is no neat line of division between defensive functioning and expressive or revelatory functioning; this is another complicating feature that the authors seem to question. All phenomena are compromise formations (C. Brenner, 1982). Therefore I do not find controversial the authors' wish to view dissociation as not "merely a defense against drive" (p. 8) but also something expressive of impulse, affect, and past events. But (another *but*) they go on to make statements about "entering into" the dissociated states "with the patient" that I do not understand. They compare dissociated states to dreams, referring to Freud's description of dreams as the royal road to the unconscious,[5] and the dynamic contents

5. Freud says, "The interpretation of dreams is the royal road to a knowledge of the *unconscious activities of the mind*" (1900, p. 608, my italics). He is talking of the road to *understanding* psychic structure and functioning. This is not a technical precept. It certainly has techni-

of dissociated states can certainly be likened to those of dreams since both involve pronounced shifts in consciousness: "Only by entering, rather than interpreting, the dissociated world of the abused child can the analyst 'know,' through his own countertransferences, the overwhelming episodes of betrayal and distortion that first led to the fragmentation of experience" (p. 30).

Do the authors imply more here than empathizing with the patient—trying to sample the patient's experience, past and present, including the shift in consciousness—in order to analyze him or her? Of course, one must first understand what is there before one can interpret it. But one would not want to "enter into" the patient's dream state, in the sense of sharing it in order to analyze it, any more than one would want to become psychotic in order to empathize with the psychotic patient. Technically, the shift in consciousness involved in dissociation has to be regarded eventually as a resistance. The authors recognize this when they state the obvious fact that the dissociated state must be given up in order for its contents to be integrated. In order to own what is dissociated, the patient must experience and take seriously the defensive power of dissociation, and this usually cannot be done without interpretive help from the therapist. Either I do not understand what the authors mean by "entering into," or they are setting up a false controversy by implying that the "classical" analyst simply supplies passionless "verbal interpretations" and ignores what the patient is feeling and resist-

cal relevance, and dream interpretation can lead to understanding of the patient's unconscious functioning. But Freud also said that a dream is an association like any other. Whether one statement is of greater technical use than another depends on who, and where in the analysis, the patient is.

ing feeling. Psychoanalysis means working with transference (which includes countertransference) *and resistance* (defense) as phenomena that take place between two human beings; this involves emotions—even passions.

My penultimate *but* has to do with what I consider dangerous oversimplification on the part of the authors in their advice to use favorite metaphoric ways of picturing intrapsychic forces, as if these have obvious priority and general value. I am referring to their hypothetical personae: the child self, the adult self, and the adolescent self. In some cases this might be a useful way of approaching what is wrong within the patient's mind; I think this would be so, for example, in cases of multiple personality disorders where the metaphors might well fit the phenomena. But the authors seem to have reified their metaphors:

> We view dissociation . . . as a process which preserves and protects, in split off form, *the entire internal object world* of the abused child. . . .
>
> [The therapist is] undertaking the treatment of two people: an adult who struggles . . . ultimately to forget, and a child who, as the treatment progresses, strives to remember. . . . The dissociated child self has a different ego structure, a more primitive and brittle system of defenses. (pp. 8, 16–17, my italics)

These metaphors seem here to be equated with actuality: "We stress that this child is a fully developed, dissociated, rather primitively organized alternative self. We speak, in this regard, *concretely*, not metaphorically" (p. 16, my italics). I don't think this is wise. One certainly can talk meaningfully, if loosely, to most patients about the child within the adult. This can be a useful way of making interpretations and promoting understanding. But it is not to be taken literally. And it is certainly neither a paradigm of psychic structure nor clinically useful for every patient. Quite specifically, soul murder patients are overcharged with conflicts about sadomasochistic impulses directed against both the self and parental mental representations in a dynamic, confused, and confusing mixture. It is essential to try to "locate" and isolate the parental imago within the child and the adult self-representations in order for the patient to separate from, to undo the identifications with, the abusive parent. (This too is a loose and metaphoric statement—but it represents a useful and necessary therapeutic aim.) I feel concerned that the authors' series of "selfs" leaves out the parents. I trust that they do not do so in their actual treatment, but inexperienced therapists could be dangerously misled by the authors' prescriptions. One should use the therapeutic metaphors deemed most appropriate to one's knowledge of the individual patient and try to adapt them to that patient's idioms.

I am also made uneasy by the authors' repetitions of "she" and "her" to characterize child victims and the "child self." (Male soul murder casualties have no sexist advantage here.) There seems to me to be too great a search for a set of dynamics that will cover all cases, dynamics that may be based on limited experience with some (female) victims. When I read that "once the participation of all the psychic players [adult self, child self, adolescent self] has been assured, the goal and direction of the analytic treatment is relatively straightforward" (p. 23),[6] I feel that I live in a

6. The authors state later that "specifically, the internal object world of this child-patient is organized about the representations of *only* three major players: a victim, an abuser; and an idealized omnipotent rescuer" (p. 26, my italics). I am concerned by the oversimplifica-

different therapeutic world from that of the authors. I agree with them that integration is necessary, but I have found nothing "straightforward" in the task of trying to help the soul murder victims I have treated to achieve it. Frawley and Davies's confidence seems unwarranted. Indeed, they belie it themselves in their empathic description of their patients' "mourning"—the terrible and complicated (in their text they happily use the word *kaleidoscopic*) struggle to give up the idealized false promise of childhood and the idealized sexual parent.

Finally, I am somewhat confused about the extent to which the authors share Ferenczi's views on gratifying the patient's needs. There certainly are people who were abused as children who are not suited to analysis and who may require parameters and reassurances and even concessions to their "often-necessary demands for extra-analytic contacts" (p. 27) in order to be able to bear the therapy. (The authors show that they are aware of the dangers of such contacts.) I have treated patients who needed no modifications of ordinary analytic technique. And there are patients who fall between these extremes.

I would like to end this discussion, as I began, with praise. Davies and Frawley are aware of the need for a proper balance of distance and empathic closeness in treating people who feel endangered by the intimate and loving feelings they so long for but which have led them to torment, and the authors describe very well the transference/countertransference work that is so difficult for patient and therapist alike. In this struggle they insist on the need to set boundaries

---

tion implicit in the "only." I think that these metaphors, describing the contents of the "child self," would be of much more general use than the "child self" and the "adult self."

and limitations for the patient. The patient must be able to
bear wanting to kill the therapist in order to learn that both
patient and therapist can survive. Not all abused children can
bear that burden; many can. Despite my *but*s, I feel that the
authors' views (especially if taken more lightly and speculatively than as presented) will help enlighten the dark
mysteries of the effects of massive trauma and will help
ameliorate the tragic plight of those who were abused as
children and come to us for therapeutic rescue.[7]

7. In 1998 I heard a clinical description by Dr. Davies of the therapy of a patient who seemed clearly to be a soul murder victim. It was
a moving account of a skillfully conducted empathic psychoanalytic
treatment that evoked both my admiration and the high tribute to a
colleague with whose work I have not had a direct acquaintance of
wanting to send her a patient who came to me for consultation.

References

Abraham, K. 1923. The spider as symbol. In *Selected essays of Karl Abraham.* Edited by E. Jones. London: Hogarth, 1947.

Aichhorn, A. 1925. *Wayward youth.* New York: Viking, 1935.

Anissimov, M. 1997. *Primo Levi ou la tragédie d'un optimiste.* Paris: Lattes.

Auden, W. H. 1970. *A certain world: A commonplace book.* New York: Viking.

Auden, W. H., and L. Kronenberger, eds. 1962. *The Viking book of aphorisms.* New York: Viking, 1966.

Bird, B. 1972. Notes on transference: Universal phenomenon and hardest part of analysis. *J. Amer. Psychoanal. Assn.* 20:267–301.

Bishop, E. 1983. *Complete poems, 1927–1979.* New York: Farrar, Straus and Giroux.

———. 1984. *Collected prose.* New York: Farrar, Straus, and Giroux.

———. 1994. *One art: Letters selected and edited by Robert Giroux.* New York: Farrar, Straus, and Giroux.

Blake, W. 1789. Infant joy. In *The Norton anthology of English literature.* Vol 2. Edited by M. H. Abrams. New York: W. W. Norton, 1979.

———. 1794 Infant sorrow. In *The Norton anthology of English literature.* Vol. 2. Edited by M. H. Abrams. New York: W. W. Norton, 1979.

———. 1803. Auguries of innocence. In *Master poems of the English language.* Edited by O. Williams. New York: Trident, 1966.

Bloom, H. 1973. *The anxiety of influence.* New York: Oxford University Press.

———. 1994. *The Western canon: The books and school of the ages.* New York: Harcourt, Brace.

Blum, H. 1996. Seduction trauma: Representation, deferred action, and pathogenic development. *J. Amer. Psychoanal. Assn.* 44:1147–64.

Brenner, C. 1982. *The mind in conflict.* New York: International Universities Press.

Brenner, I. 1996. Trauma, perversion, and "multiple personality." *J. Amer. Psychoanal. Assn.* 44:785–814.

Burton, R. 1886. Terminal essay. In *The book of a thousand nights and a night.* Vol. 10. London: Burton Club, n.d.

Butler, S. 1903. *The way of all flesh.* New York: Macmillan, 1925.

Chasseguet-Smirgel, J. 1978. Reflections on the connexions between perversion and sadism. *Inter. J. Psycho-Anal.* 59:37–48.

———. 1983. Perversion and the universal loss. *Inter. R. Psycho-Anal.* 10:293–302.

———. 1984. *Creativity and perversion.* London: Free Association.

Cohn, F. 1957. Time and the ego. *Psychoanal. Q.* 26:168–89.

Costain, T. 1958. *The three Edwards.* Garden City: Doubleday.

Costello, B. 1994. Afterword. In *Remembering Elizabeth Bishop: An oral biography.* Edited by G. Fountain and P. Brazeau. Amherst: University of Massachusetts Press.

Crews, F., et al. 1996. *The memory wars.* New York: New York Review of Books.

Cummings, E. E. 1940. Red-rag and pink-flag. In *Collected poems.* New York: Harcourt Brace Jovanovich, 1972.

Davies, J. M., and M. G. Frawley. 1992. Dissociative processes and transference / countertransference paradigms in the psychoanalytically oriented treatment of adult survivors of childhood sexual abuse. *Psychoanal. Dialogues* 2:5–36.

Euripides. 431 B.C. *Medea.* Translated by G. Murray. In *Fifteen Greek plays.* Edited by L. Cooper. New York: Oxford University Press, 1943.

———. 431 B.C. *Medea.* Translated by F. Prokosch. In *Greek plays in modern translation.* Edited by D. Fitts. New York: Dial, 1947.

Ferenczi, S. 1924. Thalassa: A theory of genitality. *Psycho. Q.,* 1934.

Fliess, R. 1956. *Erogeneity and libido.* New York: International Universities Press.

———. 1973. *Symbol, dream, and psychosis.* New York: International Universities Press.

Fountain, G., and P. Brazeau, eds. 1994. *Remembering Elizabeth Bishop: An oral biography.* Amherst: University of Massachusetts Press.

Frank, A. 1969. The unrememberable and the unforgettable. *Psychoanal. Study Child* 24:48–77.

Frazer, G. 1890. *The new golden bough.* Edited by T. Gaster. New York: Centurion, 1959.

Freud, A. 1922. Beating fantasies in daydreams. C.W. 1.

———. 1942. Notes toward the essay "About losing and being lost." In

Anna Freud in her own words. Edited by R. Rosen. *Bull. Anna Freud Ctr.* 18:293–305, 1995.

———. 1965. *Normality and pathology in children.* New York: International Universities Press.

Freud, S. 1893. On the psychological mechanisms of hysterical phenomena. S.E. 3.

———. 1900. The interpretation of dreams. S.E. 4, 5.

———. 1905. Three essays on the theory of sexuality. S.E. 7.

———. 1909. Notes upon a case of obsessional neurosis. S.E. 10.

———. 1910. A special type of choice of object made by men. S.E. 11.

———. 1914. On narcissism: An introduction. S.E. 14.

———. 1916–17. Introductory lectures on psycho-analysis. S.E. 15, 16.

———. 1918. The taboo of virginity. S.E. 11.

———. 1919. "A child is being beaten": A contribution to the study of the origin of sexual perversions. S.E. 17.

———. 1923. The ego and the id. S.E. 19.

———. 1926 The problem of anxiety. S.E. 20.

———. 1930. Civilization and its discontents. S.E. 21.

———. 1940. An outline of psychoanalysis. S.E. 23.

———. 1941. Findings, ideas, problems. S.E. 23.

Friedman, L. 1996. Introduction. In *The place of reality in psychoanalytic theory and technique.* Edited by S. Abend, J. Arlow, D. Boesky, and O. Renik. Northvale, N.J.: Jason Aronson.

Fuller, J. 1968. *Swinburne: A critical biography.* London: Chatto and Windus.

Gay, J. [1722?]. *The beggar's opera.*

Glover, E. 1938. A note on idealization. In *On the early development of mind.* London: Imago, 1956.

Gorki, M. (Maksim Gor'kij). 1904. Memoir. In *Collected works (Sobranie sochinenni).* Vol. 18. Moscow: Government Printing House of Artistic Literature, 1963 (English translation of the text by David Shengold).

Gosse, E. 1917 *The life of Algernon Charles Swinburne.* New York: Macmillan.

———. [1920?]. An essay (with two notes) on Swinburne based on the manuscripts in the British Museum hitherto unpublished. In appendix to *The Swinburne letters.* Vol. 6. Edited by C. Lang. New Haven: Yale University Press, 1962.

Graves, R. 1955. *The Greek myths.* Vol. 2. Baltimore: Penguin.

Grinberg, L. 1991. Letter to Sigmund Freud. In *Freud's "On narcissism: An introduction."* Edited by J. Sandler, E. Person, and P. Fonagy. New Haven: Yale University Press.

Grossman, W. 1991. Pain, aggression, fantasy, and concepts of sado-masochism. *Psychoan. Q.* 60:22–52.

Hamilton, E. 1940. *Mythology.* New York: Penguin.

Hanly, C. 1987. Review of *The assault on truth: Freud's suppression of the seduction theory* by J. Masson. *Internat. J. Psychoanal.* 67:517–21.

von Hoffmannsthal, H. 1908. Libretto for *Elektra,* opera by Richard Strauss. London Records OSA 1269. London: n.d.

Holland, W. 1898. *The butterfly book.* New York: Doubleday, Page, 1902.

Holroyd, M. 1994. *Lytton Strachey: The new biography.* New York: Farrar, Straus, and Giroux.

Hyde, H. M. 1975. *Oscar Wilde: A biography.* New York: Farrar, Straus, and Giroux.

Ibsen, H. 1896. John Gabriel Borkman. In *Works of Henrik Ibsen.* Translated by William Archer. New York: Charles Scribner's Sons, 1911.

Jarrell, R. 1962. On preparing to read Kipling. In *Kipling and the critics.* Edited by E. Gilbert. New York: New York University Press.

———. 1964. Randall Jarrell reads Elizabeth Bishop's poetry, 10/27/64. New York: The Academy of American Poets (audiotape).

Jones, E. 1953–55. *The life and work of Sigmund Freud.* New York: Basic Books.

Joyce, J. 1914. *Ulysses.* New York: Random House, 1934.

Kaplan, J. 1980. *Walt Whitman: A life.* New York: Simon and Schuster.

Kernberg, O. 1991. A Contemporary reading of "On narcissism." In *Freud's "On narcissism: An introduction."* Edited by J. Sandler, E. Person, and P. Fonagy. New Haven: Yale University Press.

Kipling, R. 1899. Stalky & Co. In *The collected works of Rudyard Kipling.* Vol. 14. New York: Doubleday, Doran, 1941.

———. 1937. Something of myself. In *The collected works of Rudyard Kipling.* Vol. 24. New York: Doubleday, Doran, 1941.

Kitto, H. 1957. *Greek tragedy.* New York: Dutton.

Klots, A., and Klots, E. n.d. *Living insects of the world.* New York: Doubleday.

Kohut, H. 1971. *The analysis of the self.* New York: International Universities Press.

Kris, E. 1956. On some vicissitudes of insight in psychoanalysis. In *The selected papers of Ernst Kris.* New Haven: Yale University Press, 1975.

Lang, C. 1959. Introduction. In *The Swinburne letters.* Vol. 1. New Haven: Yale University Press, 1959.

Levi, P. 1987. *The drowned and the saved.* London: Abacus, 1990.

Mahony, P. 1987. *Freud as a writer.* Expanded ed. New Haven: Yale University Press.

Mann, T. 1964. *The biochemistry of semen and of the male sexual tract.* London: Methuen.

Masson, J. 1984. *The assault on truth: Freud's suppression of the seduction theory.* New York: Farrar, Straus, and Giroux.

McLaughlin, J. 1996. Through the patient's looking-glass: Reflections upon the analyst's self-inquiry. *Canadian J. Psychoanal.* 4:205–24.

Millier, B. 1993. *Elizabeth Bishop: Life and the memory of it.* Berkeley: University of California Press, 1993.

Milton, J. 1667. Paradise lost. In *The student's Milton.* Edited by F. Patterson. New York: F. S. Crofts, 1946.

The new shorter Oxford English dictionary. Vol. 1. Edited by L. Browne. Oxford: Clarendon, 1993.

Novick, J., and K. K. Novick. 1995. *Fearful symmetry: The development and treatment of sadomasochism.* Northvale. N.J.: Jason Aronson.

Orgel, S. 1965. On time and timelessness. *J. Amer. Psychoanal. Assn.* 13:102–21.

Orwell, G. 1948. *Nineteen eighty-four.* New York: Harcourt, Brace.

Painter, G. 1956. *Marcel Proust: Letters to his mother.* London: Rider.

———. 1965. *Marcel Proust: A biography.* Vol. 2. London: Chatto and Windus.

Panter-Downes, M. 1971. *At the pines: Swinburne, Watts-Dunton, and Putney.* Boston: Gambit.

Perelberg, R. 1995. Violence in young children and adults: A review of the literature and some new formulations. *Bull. Anna Freud Ctr.* 18:89–122.

Person, E. S., ed. 1997. *On Freud's "A child is being beaten."* New Haven: Yale University Press.

Phillips, A. 1988. *Winnicott.* Cambridge: Harvard University Press.

Pippett, A. 1955. *The moth and the star.* Boston: Little, Brown.

Proust, M. 1913–1927. *Remembrance of things past.* Translated by C. K. Scott-Montcrieff. New York: Random House, 1934.

Rhodes, R. 1990. *A hole in the world: An American boyhood.* New York: Simon and Schuster.

Rhodes, R., and G. Rhodes. 1996. *Trying to get some dignity.* New York: William Morrow.

Romano, J. 1993. The life and death of Primo Levi, part II. In *Bull. Rochester Psychiatric Clinic Medical Staff* 2, no. 2:15–19.

Rose, H. 1959. *A handbook of Greek mythology.* New York: Dutton.

———. 1960. *A handbook of Greek literature.* New York: Dutton.

Rousseau, J. J. 1762. *The social contract.* Translated by M. Cranston. New York: Viking Penguin, 1968.

———. 1781. *The confessions of Jean-Jacques Rousseau.* New York: Modern Library, 1945.

Sacks, O. 1996. *An anthropologist on Mars.* New York: Knopf.

———. 1997. *The island of the color-blind.* New York: Knopf.

Sandler, J. 1987. *From safety to superego.* New York: Guilford.

Shakespeare, W. 1595. *A midsummer-night's dream.* In *The complete plays and poems of William Shakespeare.* Edited by W. Neilson and C. Hill. Boston: Houghton Mifflin, 1942.

———. 1598. *The merchant of Venice.* In *Shakespeare: Twenty-three plays and the sonnets.* Edited by T. Parrott. New York: Scribner's, 1938.

———. 1605. *King Lear.* In *Shakespeare: Twenty-three plays and the sonnets.* Edited by T. Parrott. New York: Scribner's, 1938.

———. 1613. *The tempest.* In *Shakespeare: Twenty-three plays and the sonnets.* Edited by T. Parrott. New York: Scribner's, 1938.

Shengold, L. 1963. The parent as sphinx. *J. Amer. Psychoanal. Assn.* 11:725–51.

———. 1985. Defensive anality and anal narcissism. *Inter. J. Psychoanal.* 66:47–73.

———. 1988. *Halo in the sky: Observations on anality and defense.* New Haven: Yale University Press, 1992.

———. 1989. *Soul murder: The effect of childhood abuse and deprivation.* New Haven: Yale University Press.

———. 1991a. A variety of narcissistic pathology stemming from parental weakness. *Psychoanal. Q.* 60:86–92.

———. 1991b. *"Father, don't you see I'm burning?" Reflections on sex, narcissism, symbolism, and murder: From everything to nothing.* New Haven: Yale University Press.

————. 1995. *Delusions of everyday life.* New Haven: Yale University Press.

Spruiell, V. 1983. Rules and frames of the psychoanalytic situation. *Psychoanal. Q.* 52:1–33.

————. 1993. The word "just": An essay on resistance, words, and multiple meanings. *Psychoanal. Q.* 62:437–53.

Spurgeon, C. 1935. *Shakespeare's imagery.* Boston: Beacon, 1958.

Stendhal, M. [Marie-Henri Beyle]. 1822. *On love.* Garden City: Doubleday Anchor, 1957.

Stern, E. 1948. The Medea complex: The mother's homicidal wishes to her child. *J. Mental Sci.* 94:321–31.

Swinburne, A. 1861. Reginald Harewood (Kirklowes Fragment). In *The novels of A. C. Swinburne.* New York: Farrar, Straus, and Cudahy, 1962.

————. 1862. The triumph of time. In *The works of Algernon Charles Swinburne.* Edited by E. Wilson. Ware, Hertfordshire: Wordsworth Editions, 1995.

————. 1863. *Love's cross currents.* In *The novels of A. C. Swinburne.* New York: Farrar, Straus, and Cudahy.

————. 1864. *Lesbia Brandon.* In *The novels of A. C. Swinburne.* New York: Farrar, Straus, and Cudahy, 1962.

————. 1865. Dolores. In *The works of Algernon Charles Swinburne.* Ware, Hertfordshire: Wordsworth Editions, 1995.

————. 1866. Anoractia. In *The complete works of Algernon Charles Swinburne.* Vol. 3. Edited by E. Gosse and T. J. Wise. London: Heinemann, 1926.

————. 1871. To Walt Whitman in America. In *English poets, Romantic, Victorian, and later.* Edited by J. Stephens, E. Beck, and R. Snow. New York: American Book, 1934.

————. 1854–69. *The Swinburne letters.* Vol. 1. Edited by C. Y. Lang. New Haven: Yale University Press, 1959.

————. 1869–75. *The Swinburne letters.* Vol. 2. Edited by C. Y. Lang. New Haven: Yale University Press, 1959.

————. 1875–77. *The Swinburne letters.* Vol. 3. Edited by C. Y. Lang. New Haven: Yale University Press, 1960.

————. 1877–82. *The Swinburne letters.* Vol. 4. Edited by C. Y. Lang. New Haven: Yale University Press, 1960.

————. 1883–90. *The Swinburne letters.* Vol. 5. Edited by C. Y. Lang. New Haven: Yale University Press, 1962.

————. 1890–1909. *The Swinburne letters.* Vol. 6. Edited by C. Y. Lang. New Haven: Yale University Press, 1962.

————. 1892. *The sisters: A tragedy.* In *The complete works of Algernon Charles Swinburne.* Vol 10. Edited by E. Gosse and T. Wise. London: Heinemann, 1926.

————. 1896. The Garden of Cymodyce. In *The complete works of Algernon Charles Swinburne.* Vol 3. Edited by E. Gosse and T. Wise. London: Heinemann, 1925.

Tarachow, S. 1966. Coprophagia and allied phenomena. *J. Amer. Psychoanal. Assn.* 14:685–99.

Thomas, D. 1979. *Swinburne: The poet in his world.* New York: Oxford University Press.

The Torah: The five books of Moses. Philadelphia: The Jewish Publication Society of America, 1962.

Treurniet, N. 1991. Introduction to "On narcissism." In *Freud's "On narcissism: An introduction."* Edited by J. Sandler, E. Person, and P. Fonagy. New Haven: Yale University Press.

Trilling, L. 1955. Freud: Within and beyond culture. In *Beyond culture.* New York: Viking, 1965.

Valenstein, A. 1973. On attachment to painful feelings and the negative therapeutic reaction. *Psychoanal. Study Child* 28:365–92.

Webster's New World dictionary of the American language. College ed. New York: World, 1953.

Weintrobe, S. 1995. Violence and mental space. *Bull. Anna Freud Ctr.* 18:149–65.

Wells, H. G. [1895?]. The moth. In *Works of H. G. Wells.* Edited by G. Gesner. New York: Avenel, 1982.

Whitman, W. 1855. *Leaves of grass.* New York: Modern Library, 1921.

————. 1859. Out of the cradle endlessly rocking. In *Leaves of grass.* New York: Modern Library, 1921.

Wilson, E. 1962. Introduction. In *The novels of A. C. Swinburne.* Edited by R. Hughes. New York: Farrar, Straus, and Cudahy, 1962.

Wilton, A., and R. Upstone, eds. 1997. *Catalogue for the exhibit: The age of Rossetti, Burne-Jones, and Watts: Symbolism in Britain, 1860–1910.* London: Tate Gallery Publishing.

Wittels, F. 1933. Psychoanalysis and literature. In *Psychoanalysis today.* Edited by S. Lorand. New York: Covici-Friede.

Woolf, V. 1942. The death of the moth. In *The death of the moth and other essays*. New York: Harcourt, Brace.

Yeats, W. B. 1936–39. The apparitions. In *The collected poems of W. B. Yeats*. New York: Macmillan, 1950.

Yorke, C. 1991. Freud's "On narcissism": A teaching text. In *Freud's "On narcissism: An introduction."* Edited by J. Sandler, E. Person, and P. Fonagy. New Haven: Yale University Press.

Young-Bruehl, E. 1988. *Anna Freud: A biography*. New York: Summit.

Acknowledgments

I want to thank Gladys Topkis for her dependably wonderful overall care for the welfare of this book, for her invariably fine suggestions, and for her compulsive but invaluable copyediting. For the latter I also am most indebted to my wife, and above all to Jane Zanichkowsky, my manuscript editor. Margaret Otzel overlooked the finishing touches and the final transformation of the manuscript into the book with great care, kindness, and good humor.

Permissions

INDEX

Abraham, K., 209*n*1, 263, 266

Abrams, S., 263

Abuse. *See* Child physical/sexual abuse; Soul murder

Adam and Eve, 258

Aggression, 132–33, 140–42, 160–61, 203, 260–68. *See also* Sadism; Sadomasochism; Violence

Aichhorn, A., 280–81*n*8

Alcoholism, 183–84, 183*n*14, 199–200, 223, 229, 234, 242

Améry, J., 98, 98*n*2, 106

Anaclitic object choice, 29*n*8, 126–27, 129–30

Anal odors, 48, 49–50, 56

Anal sphincteric ring, 78–80, 93, 94–95

Anality and anal erogeneity, 66–67, 153–56, 155*n*12, 171*n*4, 203, 267*n*5

Analysis. *See* Therapeutic situation

Anger. *See* Aggression; Rage

Anissimov, M., 104*n*3

Anxiety, 70–71, 139, 248, 251, 264, 281. *See also* Castration anxiety

Aphrodite, 23

Apple symbolism, 33, 33*n*14

Arendt, H., 259

Asthma, 228, 229, 234, 242

Asymbiotic mother, 31, 230

Auden, W. H., 1, 116*n*2, 285

Autism, 114

Auto-fellatio, 88

Autohypnosis, 105

Baumann, A., 229

Beating. *See* Child physical/sexual abuse

Beating fantasies, 137–63, 143*n*3, 167–205, 265

Bergman, I., 55, 208

Bergmann, M., 134*n*14

Bible, 97, 123*n*6, 141*n*1, 215, 216, 257–58

Bidart, F., 224

Biography writing, 196–97, 204–05

Bird, B., 255

Birds, 218, 219

Bisexuality, 53, 71*n*2, 128, 131–32

Bishop, Elizabeth: and alcoholism, 223, 229, 234, 242; and asthma, 228, 229, 234, 242; and Baumann, 229; and De Soares, 228–30, 230*n*15; homes during childhood, 237*n*17; and homosexuality, 234–35; identity of, 235–42, 239*n*20; last poem of, 233–35; moth imagery in works of, 207, 220–42; mother of, 13, 220–28, 225*n*11, 230–31, 235; as soul murder victim, 16, 220–42

—works: "Crusoe in England," 230*n*15; "Drunkard," 225–26; "In the Village," 220–24, 220*n*10, 225, 226–28, 238*n*18,